ACES AND AIRMEN
OF WORLD WAR I

85 Squadron, commanded by Major Mick Mannock VC, at St. Omer.

ACES AND AIRMEN
OF WORLD WAR I

Alan C. Wood

BRASSEY'S

To James Francis

First published in 2002 by Brassey's

A member of **Chrysalis** Books plc

Brassey's
64 Brewery Road, London N7 9NT

Alan C. Wood has asserted his moral right
to be identified as the author of this work.

Library of Congress Cataloging in Publication Data available

British Library cataloguing in Publication Data
A catalogue record for this book is available
from the British Library

ISBN 1 85753 380 1

Printed in Great Britain by the Bath Press, Bath.

CONTENTS

INTRODUCTION

World War One – 1914 to 1919 – was truly a global conflict, with 57 nations involved. However, the main fighting powers were Britain, France and Russia, known as the Allies or the Triple Entente, who were opposed by the Central Powers: Germany and Austria-Hungary. Non-European countries, members of various Empires, were also brought into the conflict.

As the war progressed, other nations joined the main power blocs. Italy and Belgium joined the Allies, to be followed in 1917 by the United States of America; Turkey aligned itself with the Central Powers.

World War One was the first air war, and at the beginning of the conflict, aerial warfare was an unknown factor. Aviation being in its infancy, only eight nations had an air arm to their fighting services: Britain, America, Italy, Belgium, France, and Russia amongst the Allies, and Germany and Austria-Hungary of the Central Powers. When the first crude aircraft were equipped with bombs and machine-guns, the air arm came into its own and had a decisive effect on the battlefield. Troop concentrations could be attacked and decimated from the air – a new concept in war. Vital artillery spotting balloons were shot down, with the result that artillery had to rely on map references alone, and became much less accurate.

At first, the generals placed little value on aerial warfare, then changed their minds when the new aerial dimension began to take effect. With their worth recognised, the air services needed bigger, better and faster aircraft, and, as always, war gave impetus to development.

Outstanding airmen began to appear, who were, in general, chivalrous during and after combat. Their behaviour provided an echo of feudal times when knights were expected to be honourable to both friend and adversary, as well as brave. This concept of chivalry distinguishes the First World War from World War Two and explains why air aces such as Manfred von Richthofen are so well remembered.

As always, partly due to the heat of battle, the number of total kills claimed and given can vary widely. Many victories were shared, and many were unconfirmed. A classic example comes from the Battle of Britain during World War Two: 175 German aircraft were reported shot down on one day when in fact the figure was under 100.

This book covers a selection of the outstanding airmen of the major power blocs. It would be impracticable to include biographies of all those who scored over five aerial victories and therefore qualified as an 'ace'; there are far too many for one volume. Although this book does deal only with aces, it is not mainly concerned with individual victory totals – an airman may shoot down but one aircraft and be hailed as a national hero.

GREAT BRITAIN

British military aviation dates back to 1863 when a Mr Henry Coxwell was commissioned by the Army to make a series of balloon ascents at Aldershot. One ascent was made by two officers from the Royal Engineers, who made a favourable report. By 1879 the Royal Engineers had five balloons at Woolwich Arsenal. Meeting with success, the Balloon Section was enlarged and moved to the open spaces of Aldershot during 1881.

In 1884 the Bechuanaland Expedition included a detachment of three balloons and sixteen personnel under the command of Major Elsdale of the Royal Engineers; later campaigns would also see the use of balloons. During 1890 a Balloon Section was officially established as a unit of the Royal Engineers. During the winter of 1905–6 the Balloon Section R.E. moved to Farnborough, Hampshire, where the Royal Engineers Balloon Factory was established.

On 1 April 1911 the aviation element of the Royal Engineers was expanded to battalion strength with its headquarters at South Farnborough. No.1 (Airship) Company was also at Farnborough, and No.2 (Aeroplane) Company was at Larkhill. The latter was the first British military unit equipped with heavier-than-air craft. The commander of the Air Battalion was Major Sir Alexander Bannerman; Captain E. M. Maitland commanded the Airship Company and Captain J. D. B. Fulton the Aeroplane Company.

One of the leading supporters of an air force in the early 1900s was a Royal Field Artillery officer, Captain Bertram Dickson. In a memorandum submitted to a sub-committee of the Imperial Defence Committee, Dickson emphasised Britain's need for an air force as 'The fight for supremacy of the air in future wars will be of the first and

The first Central Flying School course 1913, Major H. M. Trenchard is third from left, back row.

greatest importance.' Dickson was no stranger to upsetting the status quo: he had learned to fly at his own expense at Châlons-sur-Marne in 1909 and had been reprimanded the following year for flying over British Army manoeuvres in a Bristol aircraft and 'unnecessarily frightening the cavalry's horses'.

The Imperial Defence Committee had been tasked with creating efficient military and naval air services, and evaluating the need for aerial navigation. In Germany – the likely war opponent – development of rigid airships was progressing rapidly, with nearly all such aircraft capable of carrying out reconnaissance and bombing flights over the North Sea and English Channel. The German aircraft could carry a small bomb load, whilst British aircraft had virtually nothing.

The Imperial Defence Sub-Committee – far-sightedly – decided that a mere Air Battalion was insufficient for military needs, and decreed it be replaced with a 'Flying Corps' – separate from the Army. Accordingly, on 13 April 1912 the Royal Flying Corps (RFC) was constituted by Royal Warrant and on 13 May it absorbed the Royal Engineers Air Battalion. The intention was that the Corps could serve both Army and Navy requirements – an obvious cost-cutting plan. Accordingly, the original Royal Flying Corps consisted of three wings: a Military Wing at Larkhill in Wiltshire, a Naval Wing at Eastchurch in Kent, and a Central Flying School (CFS) at Upavon in Wiltshire for training all pilots. To administer the new corps, the Air Ministry was formed and a Royal Aircraft Factory created at Farnborough to carry out research into aeronautics.

The Aeroplane Company of the Air Battalion became No.3 Squadron RFC and No.2 Squadron RFC was formed from pilots from the Air Battalion Depot at Farnborough. No.1 Squadron RFC was formed from the Air Battalion's Airship Company and remained as the RFC Airship Detachment until 1 May 1914. On the same day a cadre No.1 Squadron was formed at Brooklands with heavier-than-air craft. It is therefore open to question whether No.1 Squadron was the first RFC squadron.

All airships became the responsibility of the Royal Navy on 1 January 1914 and the RFC had transferred its airships to the Navy by the end of 1913.

This unwieldy state of affairs continued until 23 June 1914 when the Admiralty insisted that the Naval Wing become a service in its own right – the Naval Wing had in any case maintained from the beginning an independent autonomy. The Royal Naval Air Service came into being on 1 July that year, leaving the Royal Flying Corps consisting of the Military Wing and Central Flying School at Upavon, Wiltshire.

By the beginning of 1912 the Royal Flying Corps had eighteen aircraft on charge, fourteen of them monoplanes. However, a number of aircraft accidents led to the RFC being prohibited from flying its monoplanes. which were now deemed to be unsafe. The Corps was now left with the four biplanes of 3 Squadron.

In time, with the formation of more squadrons, the fledgling Corps slowly built up its aircraft strength. B.E.2s, Maurice Farmans, Bréguets and Avros were obtained and a pool of aircraft built up. This progress was reflected when 4 Squadron was able to detach two complete flights – consisting of eight aircraft – to the new Royal Naval Air Service.

In June 1914 the entire might of the RFC Military Wing was assembled at a 'concentration camp' (a Boer War term, as distinct from its evil overtones in World War Two) at Netheravon on Salisbury Plain. Nos. 2, 3, 4, 5 and 6 Squadrons were present, with 1

Squadron being converted from airships and 7 Squadron being formed at Farnborough. The 700 officers and men of the RFC assembled there were put through a month's intensive programme – they finished in time for the imminent war with Germany.

On 4 August 1914 Britain went to war with Germany. At that point the RFC had Nos. 2 and 4 Squadrons equipped with B.E.2 biplanes; No.3 Squadron with Blériots and Henri Farmans; and No.5 Squadron with Henri Farmans, Avro 504s and B.E.8s. No.6 Squadron's personnel and aeroplanes had been dispersed among the other squadrons to bring them up to strength, but the squadron later acquired R.E.5s, B.E.s and Blériots.

The RNAS assumed a Home Defence role, with the RFC ordered to support the British Army in France. Lieutenant-Colonel H. M. Trenchard – one of the first instructors at CFS Upavon – was appointed to command all that was left of the RFC in Britain. Trenchard would take command of the RFC in France on 19 August 1915, and later become known as the 'Father of the Royal Air Force'.

On 11 August the first RFC ground staff embarked at Southampton for France, and on 13 August the first RFC squadrons began to fly to France; the first aircraft to land – at Amiens at 08.20 hours – was B.E.2a No.347 of 3 Squadron, flown by Lieutenant H. D. Harvey-Kelly. The first RFC casualties of World War One were Lieutenant R. R. Skene and Air Mechanic Barlow, killed in their Blériot aircraft while flying to Dover en route for France.

Initially, Nos. 2, 3, 4 and 5 Squadrons were sent to France, making the strength of the RFC there 63 aeroplanes, 95 vehicles, 105 officers and 755 other ranks, commanded by Brigadier-General Sir David Henderson, Argyll and Sutherland Highlanders. In November 1914 two wings of two squadrons each were formed, 1st Wing to serve with First Army, 2nd Wing with Second Army.

The Royal Flying Corps went to war in small numbers – 'an aerial cavalry reconnaissance unit' was how one senior officer described their role. But by the end of hostilities the RFC (which by then had become the RAF) had become the largest air force in the world, and had fought not just on the Western Front, but also in East Africa, Italy, Mesopotamia, Palestine and Russia. Some cavalry unit.

Opposing the RFC in France would be the Imperial German Air Service with approximately 1,000 aircraft, which had the advantage of mainly fighting over German-held territory. On 19 August 1914 the RFC lost its first aircraft in action, when an Avro 504 of 5 Squadron, flown by Lieutenant V. Waterfall, was shot down by ground fire in Belgium.

By early March 1915 the RFC's Order of Battle showed seven squadrons in the field in France with a total complement of 85 aircraft of twelve different types. Six months later there were twelve squadrons totalling 161 aircraft with some fourteen different types.

The first RFC Victoria Cross was awarded – posthumously – to Lieutenant W. B. Rhodes Moorhouse of 2 Squadron, flying a B.E.2 on a low-level bombing raid on Courtrai railway station on 26 April 1915.

2nd Lieutenant William Barnard Rhodes Moorhouse, VC of No. 2 Squadron RFC. Died of wounds received whilst bombing Courtrai rail junction in a BE2 aircraft from 300 feet, winning the VC for aerial combat.

In July 1915, 11 Squadron RFC became the first single-purpose squadron to be equipped with a single type of fighter aircraft, the Vickers F.B.5. One year later, most RFC squadrons were single-purpose squadrons, each equipped with but one type of aircraft.

On 1 July 1916 the Battle of the Somme began, with the RFC strength some 421 aircraft in 27 squadrons at home and in France. The squadrons in France were as follows:

Squadron	Aircraft Type(s)	Squadron	Aircraft Type(s)
1	Nieuport 12 and Morane Parasol	23	F.E.2b
		24	D.H.2
3	Morane Parasol	25	F.E.2b
11	F.E.2b	27	Martinsyde G.100
15	Bristol Scout	29	D.H.2
18	F.E.2b	32	D.H.2
20	F.E.2d	60	Morane Parasol
22	F.E.2b	70	Sopwith 1½ Strutter

The ferocious land battle sucked in seven more RFC squadrons and seven RNAS squadrons in a struggle of attrition. By the end of November 1916 the RFC and RNAS had established air superiority over the opposing German Air Service.

Shortly to emerge were the Bristol Fighter, the S.E.5, Sopwith Pup and Sopwith Triplane. Later came the superb Sopwith F.1 Camel, whose pilots shot down more enemy aircraft than did any other single British type used in the war.

By April 1917 and the Battle of Arras, the strength of the RFC had increased to over 900 aircraft, organised into five brigades of ten squadrons each. The R.E.8 biplane with a 150hp engine was coming into service and proved a stable flying and gun platform. April 1917, however, proved to be the lowest point of the RFC's fortunes, with a third of its aircrews falling to German aircraft such as the Albatros D III, which outclassed the RFC's aircraft. The Third Battle of Ypres (July-November 1917) saw the RFC regain its spurs in air combat with types such as the S.E.5, the SPAD, the Sopwith Pup and Camel, the Nieuport Scout and the D.H.5.

The Royal Flying Corps started life with nothing but a few flimsy aircraft and a couple of balloons. When war was declared, the fighter aircraft itself had been developed to a degree, but the art of fighting in the air was an unknown quantity. It was those who were able to grasp and understand the rudiments of this new form of warfare who stood the greatest chance of survival – these men were to become the 'aces'.

The first recorded incident involving a British and German aircraft was on 25 August 1914. Lieutenant Harvey-Kelly, and two other members of No.2 Squadron, intercepted an unarmed German Rumpler observation aircraft whilst on a reconnaissance flight. The three British aircraft, also unarmed, dived repeatedly at the Rumpler and flew circles around it until the pilot was forced to land in a field. Upon doing so, the German pilot and his observer ran away, whilst Lieutenant Harvey-Kelly landed his aircraft alongside and set fire to the German aircraft. This was the first German aircraft to be brought down in the war, albeit without a shot being fired.

As the war progressed and the number of losses increased daily, taking its toll on the general morale of those back in England, a new word came into being 'ace'. French journalists created the word for the French pilot Roland Garros, after he had shot down his third enemy aircraft. It was picked up by an unknown American war correspondent, who stated that a pilot who shot down five enemy aircraft was an ace. The British did not like the word and would not use it, but the Germans revelled in the term and saw the use of it in propaganda, setting out the requirement that ten victories were needed for a pilot to become a 'Kanone' (ace).

One of the first Allied 'aces' was a shy young man, Captain Albert Ball, VC, DSO, MC. He flew a variety of aircraft in his short but illustrious career, among these the Nieuport Scout, R.E.8 and S.E.5. He received his pilot's wings in January 1916 and died – just twenty years old – on 7 May 1917, during which time he had shot down 44 German aircraft.

There were over 200 'aces' in the RFC during World War One, if one were to use the 'five kills' requirement as a measure, though only a relatively small number scored over twenty. Among them were those who became household names like Major Lanoe George Hawker, VC, DSO, who although only scoring seven 'kills' was regarded as Britain's first 'ace'. He was to be shot down and killed by Manfred von Richthofen, the 'Red Baron'. Then there was William Avery Bishop, VC, DSO, MC, a Canadian who joined the RFC in July 1915 as an observer, but soon progressed to become a pilot: his score at the end of the war was the highest in the RFC at 72; Major George William Barker, VC, DSO, MC, who gained 50 victories, flying Sopwith Camels and Snipes; Captain Anthony Frederick Weatherby Beauchamp-Proctor, VC, DSO, MC, with a total of 54 victories flying S.E.5s; Major James Thomas Byford McCudden, VC, DSO, MC, who scored 57 kills flying a D.H.2; and one of the most famous of all the RFC's pilots, Major Edward 'Micky' Mannock, VC, DSO, MC, who in just eighteen months destroyed 61 enemy aircraft, before he himself was brought down and killed by ground fire.

Then there were the others who never became household names, but contributed just as much and, in some cases, even more. Men like Captain Alfred Clayburn Atkey, MC, who claimed 38 victories, flying D.H.4s and Bristol F.2bs; Lieutenant Leonard Monteagle Barlow, MC, who gained twenty victories flying an S.E.5; Captain Douglas John Bell, MC, a South African who joined the RFC in June 1916 and was shot down less than a year later, but accounted for twenty enemy aircraft in that short period of time; Major Geoffrey Hilton Bowman, DSO, DFC, who shot down 32 enemy aircraft; Captain William Gordon Claxton, DSO, DFC, a Canadian, who shot down 37 enemy aircraft; Captain Philip Fletcher Fullard, DSO, MC, flying the Nieuport and whose score reached 40 in just six months; Major Tom Falcon Hazell, DSO, DFC, from southern Ireland, who flew Nieuports and S.E.5s and accounted for 43 enemy aircraft; and Major Donald Roderick Maclaren, DSO, DFC, MC, a Canadian who in one year accounted for 54 enemy aircraft and balloons.

One member of the Empire who joined the RFC at the outbreak of war was 2nd Lieutenant Indra Lal Roy from Calcutta, India. He was at school in England when the war broke out and immediately joined up. On graduating as a pilot, he joined 40 Squadron and in July 1918 accounted for ten German aircraft, before he himself was shot down and killed. He was the first Indian ace.

40 Squadron early in 1918. From left: Lieutenant C. Usher (three victories), Major R. S. Dallas (commanding officer), Captain I. P. R. Napier MC, C de G, Lt. C.D. Rusden, (three victories).

Between them, the S.E.5a, the F.E.2b, the French-built Nieuport and the Sopwith Camel were responsible for the majority of German losses. The Camel was one of the most respected, but also most unforgiving, aircraft in the RFC. Tough, fast and reliable, it was a pilot's aircraft and could be devastating in the right hands. The F.E.2b, on the other hand, although looking fragile, was one of the most durable of aircraft and more than capable of holding its own in battle. The S.E.5a was the aircraft most feared by the Germans, with its agility, speed and firepower.

AIRCRAFT FLOWN BY THE RFC AND RAF DURING WORLD WAR ONE

Sopwith Camel	SPAD VII and XIII	Nieuport Scout	De Havilland
Sopwith Dolphin	S.E.5 and 5a	Bristol Scout	(D.H.) 5
Sopwith 2-seater	R.E.8	Bristol F.2b	De Havilland
Sopwith Pup	B.E.2	Bristol M.1c	(D.H.) 9
Sopwith Snipe	F.E.2b	De Havilland	Vickers F.B.5
Sopwith 1½	F.E.2d	(D.H.) 2	Morane-Saulnier
Strutter	F.E.8	De Havilland	Parasol
Sopwith Triplane	Nieuport 17	(D.H.) 4	

Both the RFC and the RNAS had grown in strength to such an extent that they became unwieldy to manage as a global fighting force. In 1917, recognising this situation, Lloyd George appointed a special committee – The Committee on Air Organisation and Home Defence Against Air Raids – chaired by the South African General Smuts, to enquire into and make recommendations as to the future of the two air services.

In mid-August 1917 the Smuts Committee made its report. It recommended that the RFC and the RNAS be amalgamated into a single air service and that an Air Ministry be established to control the new service.

On 29 November 1917 King George V gave Royal Assent to The Air Force Bill and on 2 January 1918 the Air Ministry came into being. Hugh Trenchard, now Major-General Sir Hugh Trenchard, KCB, DSO, was appointed Chief of the Air Staff. Later he rose to the rank of Marshal of the Royal Air Force, The Viscount Trenchard.

On 1 April 1918 the Royal Air Force and the Women's Royal Air Force were formed by the amalgamation of the RFC and the RNAS. (Women had been employed in the

RFC from early in 1917.) The new service was the first independent air force in the world; 22 years later it would become the most famous air force in the world when it defeated the German Luftwaffe in the Battle of Britain.

Captain Albert Ball, VC, DSO and 2 Bars, MC, DFC and Bar, MM, LdH, Russian Order of St George (1896–1917) 44 victories

Albert Ball was born in Nottingham on 14 August 1896. He enlisted in the army as a private on 21 September 1914, but by 29 October was a 2nd lieutenant.

In June 1915 he paid for private tuition and trained as a pilot at Hendon with the Baumann Flying School. On 15 October 1915 he obtained Royal Aero Club Certificate No.1898 and requested transfer to the RFC. The transfer granted, he further trained at Norwich and Upavon, being awarded his pilot's brevet on 22 January 1916.

On 18 February 1916 he was posted to 13 Squadron at Maneux, France, flying B.E.2cs. Ball saw much action in these slow reconnaissance aircraft, but wanted to fly fighters. His wish was granted on 7 May 1916 when he was posted to 11 Squadron, flying Nieuport Scouts. Now in his chosen element, Albert Ball began to display the hallmark of the finest fighting men: the urge to be at the enemy. He built a small wooden hut next to his aircraft hangar, in which he lived, ate and slept 'over the shop' so that he could be airborne almost immediately and into combat. On 16 May 1916 – flying Bristol Scout 5512 – he opened his score, shooting down an Albatros C-type over Beaumont at 08.45 hours. On 29 May 1916 he shot down two LVG C-types, whilst flying his Nieuport No.5173.

Albert Ball's desire to be at the enemy's throat was shown when he took off in Nieuport 5173 on 1 June 1916 and deliberately circled over the German airfield at Douai, challenging and inviting combat. Two German pilots took up the challenge but were driven down by Ball who claimed one – a Fokker E-type – as his fourth victory.

Albert Ball.

On 26 June Ball attacked and destroyed with phosphor bombs an observation balloon; next day he was gazetted to receive the Military Cross and cited for his continuous determination to be at the enemy. His next victories were over a Roland C.II and an Aviatik C on 2 July 1916, both shot down within the space of half an hour. On 29 July, Ball was posted to 8 Squadron, once again flying lumbering B.E.2cs. This reconnaissance and artillery spotting role did not suit his desire to be in combat, and on 14 August 1916 (his twentieth birthday) he was posted back to 11 Squadron, flying Nieuports.

Ball was allocated a brand-new Nieuport, A201, and during the last two weeks of August he gained ten victories, all but one being Roland C.IIs. On 22 August he scored a hat-trick – the first in the RFC – when he downed three Roland C.IIs within threequarters of an hour. His total now stood at seventeen. The next day – 23 August – Ball was moved to A Flight of 60 Squadron with a 'roving seek and destroy the enemy' role. This pleased him, as he preferred to fight alone.

On 1 September 1916 Ball went on leave for two weeks, and honours began to be heaped on him. He received the Distinguished Service Order, promotion to flight commander and the Russian award of the Order of St. George, 4th Class.

Returning from leave, Ball was immediately in combat. Between 15–30 September he scored fourteen victories, including three hat-tricks! The first of these was on 21 September when three Rolands went down in the space of two hours. The next trio – three Albatros C-types – went down within the space of an hour and threequarters on 28 September. The final three – an Albatros C-type and two Rolands – went down at 10.55 hours, 18.30 hours and 18.45 hours on 30 September 1916: Ball's score was now 31.

Ball was sent back to Britain for rest and recuperation and was fêted as a national hero. On 18 November 1916 he went to Buckingham Palace to be invested with the DSO and Bar, and MC. A week later he was gazetted with another Bar to his DSO, making him the first triple DSO.

Ball chafed at his lack of combat and managed to get a posting to 56 Squadron; on 7 April 1917 he was back in France at Vert Galand. On 23 April he was back in aerial combat, flying Nieuport B1522 as flight commander, and shot down an Albatros C-type at 06.45 hours. Four more victories followed during April, when Ball was flying S.E.5 No.A4850, and then he had three 'pairs', on 1, 2 and 5 May, making his total 43. He had his final combat victory on 6 May 1917 when – flying Nieuport B1522 over Sancourt – he destroyed an Albatros D III at 19.30 hours, taking his total to 44 victories.

Captain Albert Ball made his final flight on 7 May 1917 when he flew S.E.5 A4850 as part of an eleven-strong hunting patrol into action against JG11, led by Lothar von Richthofen (brother of Manfred von Richthofen). A large-scale dogfight erupted over a large area and Ball was last seen attacking Lothar von Richthofen's red Albatros, causing it to crash-land. Ball was seen to crash by several German officers on the ground near Seclin, and died soon afterwards of his injuries. He was given a full military funeral by the German Air Service at Annoeullin Cemetery, France, on 9 May.

Captain Ball was awarded the Victoria Cross on 8 June 1917 and France admitted him as a Chevalier de la Légion d'honneur. His father and mother received his Victoria Cross from King George V on 22 July 1917.

Major William George Barker, VC, DSO and Bar, MC and 2 Bars, LdH, CdeG, VM (1894–1930) 53 victories

Barker was born in Canada on 3 November 1894. He enlisted in the Canadian Army during December 1914 and was sent to France in September 1915, serving with a machine-gun unit.

In March 1916 he transferred to the RFC, becoming an observer with 9 Squadron and then 4 and 15 Squadrons, all of which flew B.E.s. He claimed two enemy aircraft, one on 21 July 1916 and another on 15 August. He was commissioned in April 1916 and decorated with the Military Cross (gazetted 10 January 1917) for excellent duty as an observer.

He was sent for pilot training on 16 November 1916, then posted to 15 Squadron on 24 February 1917. On 25 March he forced down an enemy scout and on 18 July he was awarded a Bar to his Military Cross. In April he began flying R.E.8 aircraft, being wounded by ground fire on 7 August 1917.

He was posted to England as an instructor, but chafed at the lack of action and was posted to command A Flight of 28 Squadron, flying Sopwith Camels. The Squadron was posted to France, arriving on 8 October 1917. The same day Barker was airborne in Camel B6313 and shot down an Albatros D V, which he did not claim as a victory. Most of his following victories were in B6313, which became the most successful individual fighter in the RFC/RAF, accounting for no fewer than 46 of the enemy in Barker's hands.

His first confirmed victory was on 20 October 1917 when he shot down an Albatros D III over Roulers, followed by two Albatros D Vs shot down in flames on

Major William George Barker, VC, DSO and Bar, MC and two Bars, C de G.

26 October. On 7 November 1917, 28 Squadron – commanded by Major H. Glanville – was sent to the Italian Front to aid the Italian fight against Austro-Hungarian and German forces. Barker scored the first three RFC victories over the enemy and by 29 December his score was at seven, including two balloons, and he had been awarded the Distinguished Service Order. On 12 February 1918 he shot down (with others) five balloons over Fossomerlo, bringing his total to nineteen. By 19 March he had downed another three, bringing him up to 22.

In spite of his outstanding record, Barker was passed over for command of 28 Squadron when Major Glanville was posted off squadron. Aggrieved, Barker applied for an exchange posting and was sent to 66 Squadron, flying Camels on the Italian front.

With 66 Squadron he scored another sixteen victories, making his total 43 by the end of July 1918. He was promoted to major and given command of the newly formed 139 Squadron at Villaverla in northern Italy. He was also awarded a Bar to his DSO. Unusually, Barker took Camel B6313 with him to 139 Squadron, which was equipped with Bristol F.2b fighters.

On 12 September 1918 Barker was awarded the Italian *Medaglio d'Argento Valore Militare* (Silver Medal for Military Valour) for a clandestine exploit, when he flew an Italian Savoia-Polilo SP4 behind enemy lines, landed, dropped a spy, then took off back to Italy. His last combat flight and victory in B6313 was on 18 September when he downed a D-type over Queroe.

Barker was sent to England to command an aerial fighting training unit, but managed to return for a ten-day combat mission in France, nominally attached to 201 Squadron but free to fly where he thought he could find his enemies in Sopwith Snipe E8102, based at La Targette airfield. On 27 October he found fifteen Fokker D VIIs, and took them on single-handed. Some contemporary ground-based reports state that 60 enemy fighters were ranged against him.

Barker shot down a Rumpler two-seater, but then had to fight for his life. A Fokker's bullet wounded him in the left thigh causing him to faint momentarily; recovering, he gave battle with his Snipe's two .303 Vickers machine-guns. He was wounded in his other thigh and then a bullet went through his left elbow, yet in spite of his wounds he shot down three D VIIs and drove off the others: an incredible feat. Barker managed to crash-land his badly shot-up Snipe on British lines and was taken to No.8 General Hospital, Rouen, where he remained unconscious for three days.

Major William George Barker was awarded the Victoria Cross for his epic fight and received the supreme honour from King George V on 1 March 1919.

Barker left the RAF and returned to Canada. He went into business with Fairchild Aviation Corporation of Canada, and was killed on 12 March 1930 while testing a Fairchild two-seater. He was buried at Mount Pleasant Cemetery, Toronto.

Captain Anthony Weatherby Beauchamp-Proctor, VC, DSO, MC and Bar, DFC (1894–1921) 54 victories

South African ace Captain Anthony Wetherby Beauchamp-Proctor VC of 84 Squadron.

Beauchamp-Proctor was born on 4 September 1894 at Mossel Bay, Cape Province, South Africa. After university he joined the Army and saw service in German South-West Africa. On 12 March 1917 he enlisted in the RFC and sailed for England.

After ground and flying training at Farnborough, Oxford, Castle Bromwich, Netheravon and Upavon, he was awarded his RFC pilot's wings on 29 July 1917. Of small stature – 5 foot 2 inches tall – 2nd Lieutenant Beauchamp-Proctor had some difficulty in adapting to the controls of his aircraft, but he overcame this and proved a brilliant pilot.

His first squadron was No.84 at Beaulieu, Hampshire, then commanded by Major Sholto Douglas. On 21 September 1917, equipped with the S.E.5a, 84 Squadron moved to Flez, France, and began working up for battle.

On 22 November 1917 Beauchamp-Proctor shared in the destruction of a German balloon, then another balloon, followed by forcing down two German observation planes. None of these were confirmed and it was not until 3 January 1918 that Beauchamp-Proctor – flying S.E.5a B.539 – 'officially' shot down a C-type two-seater over St. Quentin. By 28 February 1918, his score stood at five. On 17 March 1918 he downed two Albatros D Vs and one Pfalz D III in one day, bringing his tally to nine. May 1918 proved prolific for Beauchamp-Proctor: on 31 May his official record showed 21 enemy aircraft downed – his actual total was greater, albeit unconfirmed.

1 April 1918 had seen the birth of the Royal Air Force, and Beauchamp-Proctor was promoted to lieutenant (the RAF still used army ranks at this time). Seven days later he

was promoted to captain and placed in command of C Flight 84 Squadron. He was awarded the Military Cross on 28 May 1918.

During the first fortnight of June he downed seven more enemy aircraft, including four balloons. August resulted in fifteen more enemy going down – five of them balloons. During September he concentrated on balloons, downing four, and was awarded the DSO. On 8 October he had reached what would be his final tally of 54 confirmed victories, but on that day he was wounded in combat with eight of the enemy. He was sent to hospital in England. On 30 November 1918 he was awarded the Victoria Cross for valour in his aerial battles with the enemy.

Beauchamp-Proctor remained in the RAF with a permanent commission, but was killed flying Sopwith Snipe E8220 on 21 June 1921 whilst practising for an air display at Upavon. His body was returned to his native South Africa on 8 August 1921 and given a state funeral before being laid to rest at Mafeking.

Lieutenant-Colonel William Avery Bishop, VC, DSO and Bar, MC, DFC, LdH, CdeG (1894–1956) 72 victories

William Avery Bishop was born at Owen Sound, Ontario, Canada, on 8 February 1894. In August 1911 he entered the Royal Military College (Canada) and three years later was commissioned into the Canadian Army.

At the end of June 1915 Bishop arrived in England. He did not like the idea of trench warfare and in July applied for transfer to the RFC as an observer: he was posted to 21 (Training) Squadron at Netheravon, Wiltshire, for training. Passing out as an observer, he was posted to 21 Squadron, which was due to be moved to France.

On 1 January 1916, 21 Squadron was stationed at Boisdinghem, St. Omer, flying R.E.7 two-seater observation and reconnaissance aircraft. Bishop remained on reconnaissance duties – coming under enemy fire on occasion – until 2 May 1916 when, due to an injured knee, he was taken off flying.

The Canadian Lieutenant-Colonel William Avery Bishop in the cockpit of his Nieuport.

Bishop then trained as a pilot at the Central Flying School at Upavon on Salisbury Plain and applied for transfer to front-line duties in France. On 9 March 1917 he was posted as a pilot to 60 Squadron at Filescamp, flying the small Nieuport Scout, armed with a single Lewis machine-gun mounted to fire over the top wing.

Bishop had difficulty in landing the Nieuport and after several heavy landings crashed on 24 March 1917. Authority ordered him back to England for further flying training, but fate intervened. On 25 March 1917 Bishop was in formation with three other Nieuports of 60 Squadron when they clashed with three German Albatros D III scouts over St Leger. Bishop closed with one Albatros and poured bullets into the pilot's cockpit, causing it to spiral out of control into the ground. This was his first victory, and it caused his posting to England to be cancelled.

Bishop's marksmanship and his new-found flying skills earned him five more victories – four Albatros and one balloon – by 8 April 1917. On 25 April he was promoted to captain and had his Nieuport's engine cowling and wing V-struts painted bright blue. By 30 April 1917 he had fourteen victories to his credit – including another balloon, at Artois – and he was awarded the Military Cross.

By 31 May 1917 Bishop had downed 22 German aircraft, mostly Albatros D IIIs. On 2 June 1917 he made a lone dawn attack in Nieuport B1566 on the German airfield at Estmourmel, destroying three D IIIs in a half-hour action. On 11 June 1917 he was gazetted to be decorated with the Victoria Cross for this action.

By 16 August 1917 Bishop's victory score had reached an incredible 47. He was now flying S.E.5a A8936. During September 1917 Bishop was decorated with the Victoria Cross and Distinguished Service Order to add to his Military Cross; a Bar to his DSO followed. He was promoted to major on 13 March 1918 and took command of the new 85 Squadron, which moved to Petite Synthe, near Dunkirk, on 22 May 1918.

Bishop was back in the air at once, he scored his 48th victory on 27 May, shooting down a two-seater C-type over Passchendaele. A day later he shot down two Albatros D Vs over Cortemarek. His victory total now stood at 50. By the end of May it was 55, and by 19 June 1918 had reached 72 enemy aircraft.

Bishop survived the war and died in Florida on 11 September 1956.

Captain William Gordon Claxton, DSO, DFC and Bar (1899–1967) 39 (37) victories

Yet another great colonial fighter pilot – born in Gladstone, Manitoba, Canada, on 1 June 1899 – Claxton was a natural marksman and superb pilot: in three months he shot down 37 enemy aircraft and two balloons.

He enlisted in the RFC in Canada on his eighteenth birthday and trained for his pilot's brevet at Camp Borden. Qualifying as a pilot, Claxton was posted to 41 Squadron, flying S.E.5as, and began an incredible period of victories.

On 27 May 1918 he opened his score by shooting down a Fokker Dr I over East Estaires while flying S.E.5a B38, and the next day he shot down two Pfalz D IIIs. From 12–30 June he shot down no fewer than seventeen aircraft and one balloon; on 30 June 1918 he downed six enemy aircraft on that one day, an amazing feat. Six more victories followed during July, making his total by the end of that month 27 victories.

On 3 August he was awarded the Distinguished Flying Cross, and between 1–13 August 1918 he shot down a further nine aircraft and one balloon. On 17 August 1918, Claxton took off with another Canadian, Frederick Robert McCall, of 41 Squadron and clashed with a 40-strong enemy force, believed to be from Jasta 20. Outnumbered twenty to one, the two Canadians fought hard, each shooting down three Germans. Claxton was wounded in the head by a machine-gun bullet fired by Leutnant Hans Gildmeister of Jasta 20. He managed to crash-land his S.E.5a behind the German lines without suffering any further injuries; surgery to his skull by a German surgeon saved his life.

Claxton was awarded the Distinguished Service Order on 2 November 1918, having been awarded a Bar to his DFC on 21 September. Captain Claxton died on 28 September 1967 in Canada.

Lieutenant-Colonel Raymond Collishaw, DSO and Bar, DSC, DFC, CdeG (1893–1976) 60 victories

Raymond Collishaw was born in British Columbia, Canada, on 22 November 1893. He served in the Canadian Merchant Marine and went on Scott's 1911 Antarctic Expedition.

In January 1916 Collishaw joined the Royal Naval Air Service (RNAS), joining No.3 Wing RNAS, flying Sopwith 1½ Strutter aircraft on long-range bombing missions to the Saarland. On 25 October 1916 he opened his score in air-to-air combat by shooting down two Fokker D IIs over Luneville.

On 1 February 1917 he transferred to No.3 Naval Squadron. On 15 February he shot down a Halberstadt D II, followed by another on 4 March. In April he joined No.10 Naval Squadron at Fumes as commander of B Flight, flying Sopwith Triplanes. On 28 April, flying Triplane N5490, he shot down an Albatros D II over Ostend. Two days later he repeated the feat over Courtemarek, bringing his total to six.

Ray Collishaw, DSO, DSC, 13 (N) Naval Squadron, January 1918, with the famous F.1 Camel 'Black Maria'.

Collishaw chose four other pilots to form his flight – all Canadians: Flight Sub-Lieutenants Reid, Sharman, Nash and Alexander. These five pilots formed the 'Black Flight': their Triplanes were painted black on the engine cowling, wheel discs and forward fuselage, with names in white lettering on the fuselages: Black Maria (Collishaw's 5492), Black Death (Sharman), Black Sheep (Nash), Black Roger (Reid) and Black Prince (Alexander).

Collishaw scored at an amazing rate: on 9 May 1917 his score stood at seven, yet by 27 July 1917 he had downed 38 enemy aircraft. On 6 June he shot down three Albatros D IIIs; on 15 June he destroyed four more enemy aircraft. Incredibly, on 6 July he accounted for no fewer than six Albatros D Vs on the same day. The 'Black Flight' was decimating the German Air Service: Jasta 11 was ordered to stop them – they failed.

Squadron Commander Raymond Collishaw, 60 victories, in a Sopwith Camel of 203 Squadron RAF, July 1918.

On 10 December Collishaw scored his 39th victory when he shot down an Albatros C-type over Dunkirk; on 19 December he reached 40 when he downed an Albatros D V over Ostend. On 29 December 1917 he was placed in command of No.13 Naval Squadron, equipped with new Sopwith Camels.

1 April 1918 saw the creation of the Royal Air Force; Collishaw was promoted to major and placed in command of 203

Squadron RAF, which had been formed that day from No.3 Squadron RNAS. From 11 June to 26 September Collishaw downed another nineteen enemy aircraft, bringing his score to 59. On 1 October, just 25 years old, he was promoted to lieutenant-colonel.

In July 1919 Collishaw went to Southern Russia in command of 47 Squadron, in aid of the White Russians. He scored his 60th and last victory on 9 October 1919, bringing down an Albatros D V over Tsaritsyn (now Volgograd). However, it is thought he scored at least another fifteen unconfirmed victories.

Raymond Collishaw remained in the RAF post-war and retired in the rank of Air Vice-Marshal. He died in 1976.

Major Arthur Coningham DSO, MC (1895–1948) 14 victories

Arthur Coningham was born on 19 January 1895 and was serving in the New Zealand Army in Egypt and Somaliland when World War One broke out.

He was discharged as medically unfit through typhoid in 1916 and – somehow – managed to get back into combat, enlisting in the RFC in 1917. After flying training he was posted to 32 Squadron, flying D.H.2s and D.H.5s, and scored his first victory, flying a D.H.2, when he sent a C-type down in flames over Ervillers.

Between 11–30 July, flying a D.H.5, he scored nine victories: seven Albatros D Vs and two C-types. He was awarded the Distinguished Service Order and the Military Cross, and was made a flight commander. In early 1918 he was promoted to command 92 Squadron and scored another four victories: a C-type and three Fokker D VIIs. He always led his flight or squadron and was twice wounded in air combat, once with 32 Squadron and once with 92 Squadron.

Being a New Zealander, Arthur Coningham was nicknamed 'Maori', which was corrupted to 'Mary' – a strange nickname for a brave officer. He was granted a permanent commission in the RAF after the Armistice and during World War Two became AOC Desert Air Force in 1941–3. He then took command of 2nd Tactical Air Force until 1945. He was made Air Marshal and knighted as Sir Arthur Coningham, but

92 Squadron, 14 November 1918, at Bertry. Seated from left: Lt. T. S. Horry, Captain J. M. Robb, Major A. Coningham, Captain W. E. Reed, Capt. O. J. Rose.

died on 30 January 1948 en route to Bermuda in an Avro Tudor of British South American Airways.

Major Roderic Stanley Dallas, DSO, DSC and Bar, CdeG (?–1918) 32 (39) victories

Roderic Dallas was born at Mount Stanley, Queensland, Australia, and joined the Australian Army in 1913. He applied for transfer to the RFC in 1914 but was turned down. Undaunted and eager to get into the air and combat, he applied and was accepted by the Royal Naval Air Service and began pilot training in June 1915.

Qualifying and gaining his pilot's certificate on 5 August 1915, he joined No.1 Wing RNAS at Dunkirk on 3 December 1915.

His first victory came on 22 April 1916 when flying a Nieuport Scout near Dunkirk. He was awarded the Distinguished Service Cross (DSC) on 6 September 1916, and the French Croix de Guerre. By February 1917 his score had risen to seven victories, several of them gained when flying Sopwith Triplane prototype N500.

On 14 June 1917 he took command of No.1 Naval Squadron – renamed from No.1 Wing RNAS – equipped with Sopwith Triplanes. The same month he was awarded a Bar to his DSC. In April 1917 1(N) Squadron was put under RFC control and sent to the Somme, where Dallas gained eight more victories.

On 1 April 1918 the Royal Air Force was formed from the RFC and RNAS, and Dallas was posted to command 40 Squadron, flying S.E.5as. Flying with 40 Squadron, Dallas notched up another nine victories in S.E.5a B4879.

The exact number of enemy aircraft that Dallas brought down is uncertain, but is around 40. On 19 June 1918 he took on three Fokker

Above: Major Dallas, DSC and Bar.

Left: Major Roderic Stanley Dallas, (3rd from right) with members of 40 Squadron.

Dr Is over Lievin, but was shot down and killed. So died a gallant Australian ace, who so typified his country.

Marshal of the Royal Air Force William Sholto Douglas, 1st Baron of Kirtleside, GCG, MC, DFC (1893–1969)

Born 1893 and qualified as an aviator in 1913, Douglas was commander of 43 and 84 Squadrons during World War One. Post-war he became a test pilot with Handley Page Ltd, but he returned to the RAF in 1920, serving in the Sudan 1929–32.

Douglas replaced Air Chief Marshal Dowding as AOC Fighter Command after the Battle of Britain, officially as Fighter Command was going on the offensive. In 1944 he assumed command of RAF Coastal Command, holding this post until 1945 when he became Military Governor of the British Zone of Germany after the war. He retired from the RAF in 1948 and entered civil aviation.

Air Chief Marshal Hugh Caswall Tremenheere Dowding, 1st Baron of Bentley Priory and 1st Baron Dowding, GCB, GCVO, CMG (1882–1971)

'Stuffy' Dowding – as he came to be nicknamed – was one of the greatest air commanders of World War Two. He commanded and directed Fighter Command during the Battle of Britain, when Great Britain and the Royal Air Force saved civilisation from Nazi German tyranny.

Dowding was born in 1882 and enlisted in the Army in 1900. He transferred to the RFC in 1914 and to the RAF in 1918. During 1929–30 he was in command of the Air Defence of Great Britain, becoming AOC-in-Chief of RAF Fighter Command in 1936.

He foresaw the German aerial threat and pressed the politicians to develop the Spitfire and Hurricane fighters that earned immortality in the Battle of Britain. He also encouraged the development of radar, both in fighter direction and in night fighters. His air defence policies in practice won the Battle of Britain, although it was by a narrow, close-run margin.

Lord Dowding died in 1971 – a great commander, to whom the free world owes much.

Sergeant Ernest John Elton, DCM, MM, Italian Bronze Medal (dates unknown) 16 victories

Ernest John Elton enlisted in the RFC in 1914 as an air mechanic and in 1915 was with 6 Squadron in France, servicing Martinsyde S.1s, Bristol Scouts, B.E.2ds and B.E.2es. He assisted Major Lanoe Hawker in fitting an offset machine-gun to Hawker's Bristol Scout.

Elton was accepted for pilot training late in 1917, and promoted to sergeant and posted to 22 Squadron, flying Bristol Fighters. His first success came on 26 February 1918 when, flying a Bristol with Sergeant J. C. Hagen as observer/gunner, he accounted for two Albatros D Vs at 10.30 hours over Lens. Flying Bristol B 1162 with 2nd Lieutenant G. S. L. Hayward as gunner/observer on 6 March 1918, he scored another double when two more Albatros D Vs were destroyed.

Sergeant Elton was the most successful NCO pilot in the RFC as he and his observers/gunners – Hagen, Hayward, Sergeant S. Belding and Lieutenant R. Critchley

– shot down sixteen enemy aircraft in 32 days' action. Elton shot down ten with his front machine-gun and his gunners six with the rear-mounted machine-gun.

Captain Philip Fletcher Fullard, DSO, MC and Bar, AFC (1887–1984) 40 (46) victories

Philip Fullard was born at Hatfield on 27 June 1887 and educated at Norwich. He loved football and played centre-half for Norwich in 1914.

Fullard learned to fly at his own expense and, after a spell in the Army, transferred to the RFC in 1916. He proved to be an exceptional pilot and marksman, maintaining his aircraft guns himself. This proved invaluable in combat as – unlike so many other airmen's – his guns never had a stoppage.

In April 1917 he was posted to 1 Squadron, flying Nieuport Scouts and S.E.5as, and scored his first victory, over an Albatros D III, on 26 May 1917 when flying Nieuport B1559. Another victory over an Albatros D III followed on 28 May. On 4 June, on an early patrol, he shot down an Albatros D V at 08.00 hours, then another at 08.15 hours. His aircraft then came under fire from an all-red Albatros D V – the trade mark of Jasta 18 (and others). Fullard rolled his Nieuport away and the Albatros was shot down by an S.E.5 flown by Flight Commander T. F. N. Gerrard of 1 Squadron, with whom he shared the kill.

During July 1917 Fullard continued to score victories at an amazing rate: eight downed, all but one Albatros D Vs: the eighth was a C-type. August 1917 was even more productive for Fullard: twelve enemy went down, eight of them Albatros D Vs. In September, Fullard was awarded the Military Cross and Bar, followed a month later by the award of the Distinguished Service Order.

October 1917 saw Fullard continue his success with eleven more enemy downed – his last two confirmed victories came on 15 November 1917 when he shot down one Albatros D V at 11.55 hours then another at 11.56 hours! As is often the case, there are differences of opinion as to how many aircraft Fullard downed: 40 or 46 seems to be the approximate total. He is sometimes credited with two balloons, but these are unconfirmed.

Major John Inglis Gilmour, DSO. MC and two Bars. Gained three victories with 27 Squadron flying Martinsyde G.100 'Elephants', the only pilot to do so with this ungainly aircraft.

Captain Fullard broke his leg playing football and was returned to England. He did not score any more victories before the war ended in November, but remained in the RAF on a permanent commission, gaining air rank and the CBE and AFC. He died on 24 April 1984.

Major John Inglis Gilmour, DSO, MC and 2 Bars (dates unknown) 39 (44) victories

John Gilmour joined the Argyll and Sutherland Highlanders (the 'Thin Red Line'), then transferred to the RFC and was posted to 27 Squadron (with which this author later served) and flew Martinsyde G.100 'Elephants', which were initially used as scouts but lacked agility and so were used for reconnaissance and bombing.

Gilmour scored three victories in September 1916 flying G.100s – unusual for this type of aircraft. He was awarded the Military Cross in 1917.

In November 1917, he was posted to 65 Squadron as a flight commander flying Sopwith Camels, and scored two victories on 18 December, flying Camel 9166, followed by three more victories on 4 January 1918. By 29 June 1918 his victory tally had reached 31 confirmed, including one balloon. On 1 July 1918 he downed three Fokker D VIIs, one Pfalz and an Albatros D V, all within 45 minutes; the next day he downed a Pfalz D III then on 3 July 1918 another two Pfalz D IIIs, bringing his confirmed total to 39.

Gilmour received the Distinguished Service Order and two Bars to his Military Cross, and was promoted to the rank of major. In October 1918 he was posted to Italy in command of 28 Squadron, flying Camels from Treviso, but did not add to his victory score.

Major Arthur Travers Harris AFC (1892–1984) 5 victories

'Bomber' Harris – as he was to be nicknamed – was born in Gloucestershire on 13 April 1892 and went to West Africa at an early age.

He served in the Rhodesian Regiment as a boy bugler and enlisted in the RFC in 1915. Qualifying as a pilot, he served with 70 (Home Defence) Squadron, which was formed at Farnborough on 22 April 1916 flying Sopwith 1½ Strutters. He was then posted to 51 Squadron, a Home Defence squadron using bases in East Anglia to combat the German Zeppelin menace, flying B.E.s as night-fighters. After a spell with 51 Squadron he was posted as a flight commander to 45 Squadron, again flying Sopwiths.

Taking off from Fienvillers in a Strutter on 5 July 1917, he intercepted an Albatros D V and sent it down out of control at 17.20 hours – his first victory. Four more Albatros aircraft were confirmed victories for Harris; his last, on 3 September 1917 while flying a Camel, was an Albatros D V sent down in flames over Ledeghem. In 1918 Harris was posted to England in command of No.44 (Home Defence) Squadron, stationed in Essex to combat Zeppelin and bomber attacks. 44 Squadron flew Camels on night patrols with success and Major Harris was awarded the Air Force Cross.

After World War One ended Harris remained in the RAF and commanded squadrons in India and Iraq. He joined the staff of the Air Ministry in 1934, and then commanded 4 Bomber Group in 1937–38 and 5 Bomber Group 1939–40. He came into his own in 1942 when he took command of RAF Bomber Command and began the great bombing offensive against Germany, which was supported by the great mass of the British (and other) people as it meant that the Allies were fighting back against Nazi tyranny.

'Bomber' Harris retired from the RAF as Marshal of the Royal Air Force Sir Arthur Harris, GGB, OBE, AFC LL.D, also holding many foreign decorations. A statue in his memory was placed in London and unveiled by H.M. Queen Elizabeth the Queen Mother, a fitting tribute to a great commander.

Major Lanoe George Hawker, VC, DSO (1890–1916) 7 victories

Hawker is acknowledged to be the first British ace; he was one of the RFC's first fighting pilots to receive the Victoria Cross.

Hawker was born on 30 December 1890 into a military family at Longparish, Hampshire. In June 1910 he joined the Royal Aero Club and on 4 March 1913 gained

Flying Certificate No.435. Commissioned in the Royal Engineers, he requested attachment to the Royal Flying Corps and moved to the CFS at Upavon on 1 August 1914. Passing out from Upavon on 3 October 1914, Hawker was sent to 6 Squadron at Farnborough.

On 6 October 1914 Hawker flew to France in Henri Farman No.653. Two days later he was in action, flying as observer in B.E.2a No.492 to observe the German advance. On 31 October 1914 he fired his first airborne shots at the enemy – six rounds from his Webley service revolver. His other airborne armament was a .303in service rifle.

On 18 April 1915 Hawker took off alone to bomb the German Zeppelin airship LZ.35 in its hangar at Gontrode. His bomb load was only three 20lb Hales bombs and some hand grenades. He scored two hits on the hangar and threw his grenades at the crew of a captive balloon who were firing machine-guns at him. The hangar proved to be empty as LZ.35 had crashed five days before Hawker's attack. For this raid and previous good work he was awarded the Distinguished Service Order and promoted to captain.

On 3 June 1915 Hawker was allocated a new aircraft – a single-seat Bristol Scout C, No.1609 –

Major Lanoe George Hawker, VC. The first British ace with seven victories. Shot down by Manfred von Richthofen on 23 November 1916, Richthofen's eleventh victory.

which he promptly modified for air fighting. A Lewis machine-gun was fixed to the left side of the cockpit, pointing forward and outwards to clear the propeller arc. On 7 June he fired on a German two-seat reconnaissance aircraft, causing it to spin earthwards. On 21 June he attacked a DFW C-type which also spiralled earthwards. The next day Hawker made a bad landing when he ran out of petrol and 'broke' his aeroplane. Eager to get back into action, he acquired another Bristol Scout C, No.1611, and fitted it with his 'local mod' Lewis gun.

On 25 July 1915 Hawker took off in No.1611 on a combat patrol and spotted an Albatros C-type over Passchendaele. Closing, Hawker fired an entire drum of ammunition at the Albatros, causing it to force-land. He then turned his attention to a second enemy aircraft and opened fire, again forcing the enemy to land. Continuing his fighting patrol Hawker saw another Albatros C-type. Closing to within 100 yards, he riddled it with Lewis gun fire, causing it to burst into flames and crash. The Albatros was later found to be from Flieger Abteilung 3, piloted by Oberleutnant Ubelacker with Hauptmann Roser as observer; both German officers were killed.

Captain Hawker was recommended for the Victoria Cross for this, his previous air combats and his gallantry over the months he had been in France. The recommendation was approved and gazetted on 24 August 1915: the first VC awarded for air combat.

On 2 August 1915, while flying F.E.2b No.4227, he forced down a C-type at Wulverghem, bringing his official total to four; his unconfirmed total was many more. On 11 August, while flying the same aircraft with Lieutenant Noel Clifton as gunner/observer, he scored two more victories: an Aviatik C-type and a Fokker E-type. His last victory was on 7 September 1915, when he shot down a German scout over Bixschoote, while flying Bristol Scout 1611.

On 20 September 1915 Hawker was posted back to England, recommended for promotion to major and command of a new squadron, No.24. On 5 October he was decorated by King George V with the Victoria Cross and Distinguished Service Order. On 3 February 1916 he was promoted to major.

On 7 February 1916, 24 Squadron moved to St. Omer in France to work up into a fighting unit flying D.H.2 fighters – the first such squadron to reach the Western Front. On 12 February the squadron moved to Bertangles, near Amiens. As Commanding Officer, Major Hawker was forbidden to fly, but he continued to do so. At 13.00 hours on 23 November 1916, Hawker took off in a four-aircraft patrol. One D.H.2 was forced to return to base with engine trouble but the three others carried on. At about l4.00 hours German two-seater reconnaissance aircraft were spotted – it was a trap laid by the Richthofen Geschwader. Albatros D IIs from Jagdstaffel 2, led by Manfred von Richthofen, swooped on the D.H.2s.

Hawker was outclassed in his D.H.2 against the Albatros D II of von Richthofen but, circling, gave combat to the 'Red Baron' over the German lines, waving at one time to acknowledge his adversary. Hawker's aircraft ran out of petrol and he tried to reach British lines – von Richthofen seized his chance and poured machine-gun fire into the D.H.2. It is recorded that he fired over 900 rounds during the combat. Hawker was killed by a single bullet which went through his head – his only injury. His aircraft went down two miles south of Bapaume, and German grenadiers buried his body next to his aircraft. Major Hawker was Manfred von Richthofen's eleventh victim.

Major Tom Falcon Hazell, DSO, MC, DFC and Bar (?–1946)
43 victories

Born in Galway, Ireland, Hazell joined the Army when World War One broke out and was commissioned as a 2nd lieutenant in the 7th Battalion, Royal Inniskilling Fusiliers ('The Skins') on 10 October 1914, serving with them until June 1916, when he transferred to the RFC.

After flying instruction – and a bad crash – he was posted to 1 Squadron in France, equipped with Nieuport 17s in January 1917, Nieuport 27s in August 1917 and S.E.5as in January 1918. At 16.10 hours on 4 March 1917 Hazell scored his first victory: flying Nieuport A6604 he sent a German HA type down out of control over Westhoek. It was not until 24 April that he had his next victory, an Albatros C-type destroyed over Grenier Wood at 12.00 hours that day, while flying Nieuport A6738. Another Albatros C-type was sent spinning out of control on 9 May 1917. His fourth and fifth victories were two Albatros D IIIs destroyed over Hollebeke at 07.00 and 07.02 hours on 4 June; two more victories followed the next day – an Albatros D III and a C-type.

On 8 and 9 June 1917, Hazell sent two Albatros D IIIs down out of control, and on 12 July an Albatros D II met a similar fate. On 22 July 1917 he scored a hat-trick when he destroyed a DFW C-type and two Albatros D Vs, whilst flying Nieuport B3455. With his victory total at 14, he was now made a flight commander in No.1 Squadron.

On 13 August Hazell destroyed an Albatros D V at 07.10 hours and shared an Albatros C with Lieutenant H. G. Reeves at 09.20 hours. On the 14th Hazell repeated his feat of the previous day, downing two Albatros D Vs within five minutes. Another Albatros D V was sent out of control on 16 August 1917, making Hazell's total twenty victories and bringing the award of the Military Cross (which had been gazetted on 26 July 1917).

Hazell was sent back to England as a flying instructor at Upavon, returning to France in command of 'A' Flight, 24 Squadron, on 28 June 1918. Now flying S.E.5as, Hazell scored a further 23 victories with 24 Squadron: six victories in July, of which four were balloons, eleven in August, of which three were balloons, three in September, of which two were balloons, and lastly three in October, of which one was a balloon.

Hazell was promoted to major and left 24 Squadron on 18 October 1918, moving to the Sopwith Camel-equipped 203 Squadron as Commanding Officer. He served with No.203 Squadron until 2 April 1919, and was granted a permanent commission in the Royal Air Force. Hazell died in 1946: his total awards had been the Distinguished Service Order, the Military Cross and Distinguished Flying Cross and Bar.

Captain Leslie Norman Hollinghurst, DFC (1895–1971)

11 victories

'Holly', as he came to be known to servicemen (including this author), was born on 2 January 1895 and enlisted in the Royal Engineers in 1914, but transferred to the RFC in 1916. Completing his pilot training with distinction, he was 'creamed off' to instruct new entrants in flying.

Captain Leslie Norman Hollinghurst, DFC. During WW2 became an Air Chief Marshal.

He managed to get to battle in April 1918 with 87 Squadron, flying Sopwith Dolphin aircraft, and opened his score on 6 July when he sent a Fokker D VII down out of control at Bapaume. On 9 August he downed a Pfalz D III and an LVG C-type within minutes, sending the Pfalz down in flames. Next day he destroyed a Fokker D VII which brought his score to five victories. By 4 October 1918 his score had risen to eleven, including another five Fokker D VIIs. The November Armistice brought an end to the air war, with a DFC being awarded to Captain Hollinghurst.

Hollinghurst remained in the RAF after the war and reached high rank within the service, being made an OBE in 1932. During World War Two he became Commanding Officer of No.38 Group (with which the author served) on 6 November 1943, with the rank of Air Vice Marshal. Against orders (he was in possession of airborne battle plans) he flew on Operations 'Overland' (the 'D-Day' invasion) and 'Market Garden' (the Arnhem airborne landings).

He was knighted in 1948 and retired from the RAF in 1952 (as did the author!) as Air Chief Marshal Sir Leslie Norman Hollinghurst, GCB,

KCB, OBE, DFC. Sir Leslie died suddenly on 8 June 1971 after attending a D-Day reunion in Normandy, a well-liked officer, gentleman and commander.

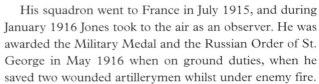

Captain James Ira Thomas Jones, DSO, MC, DFC and Bar, MM, Order of St George (?–1960) 40 (37) victories

Welsh-born Jones enlisted in the RFC on the outbreak of World War One: he had been serving in the Territorial Army since 1913 but decided to join the new service. After training he was posted to 10 Squadron as an Air Mechanic (Wireless).

Captain James Ira Thomas Jones, DSO, DFC and Bar, who scored 37 victories in SE5As of 74 Squadron. An aggressive Welsh fighter pilot who flew again during WW2.

His squadron went to France in July 1915, and during January 1916 Jones took to the air as an observer. He was awarded the Military Medal and the Russian Order of St. George in May 1916 when on ground duties, when he saved two wounded artillerymen whilst under enemy fire.

Jones began his flying career in earnest when he gained his observer's flying brevet in October 1916, flying in B.E.2cs, -ds and -es. He was detached to England for pilot training on 27 May 1917, and commissioned.

He was returned to 74 Squadron on 30 March 1918, flying S.E.5as; his flight commander was Captain Edward Mannock. He scored his first victory on 8 May, while flying S.E.5a C6406 over Bailleul, when he shot down in flames a German C-type. On 12 May he sent an Albatros D V down out of control and on 17 May he shot a Hannover C-type out of the sky in flames at 09.30 hours, followed within a minute by sending an Albatros C-type down out of control.

On 18 May he shot down another Albatros C-type, followed by a kite balloon the next day, making his total six victories, with none shared. By 31 May his total was fifteen and he was awarded the Military Cross. He scored a double victory on 27 May, another double on 30 May and yet another on 31 May.

During June 1918 he shot down seven enemy aircraft, three of them in flames. This aggressive fighter pilot was elevated to flight commander and went at the enemy with vigour. On 24 July he scored three victories over DFW C-types in one day, one at 07.20 hours the other two at 17.30 hours.

On 30 July 1918, by which time he had 28 kills, he scored another triple victory during an afternoon's flying.

On 3 August he was gazetted with the Distinguished Flying Cross for destroying six enemy aircraft in just eleven days. On 3 and 4 August he increased his score by two, then on 6 August he shot down in flames two Fokker D VIIs.

The next day he scored his final victories – another double – at 12.25 and 17.15 hours. His confirmed total was now 37, but the actual total was probably several more. On 25 August he was awarded the Distinguished Service Order and a Bar to his DFC for scoring 21 victories in but three months.

After the Armistice he remained in the RAF, becoming Officer Commanding 74 Squadron, the squadron he had first served with as an NCO – a splendid achievement. He served in the RAF until 1936, leaving as time expired. He was recalled to the colours in August 1939 in the rank of Group Captain and put in charge of fighter Operational Training Units (OTUs). He flew Spitfires – probably without permission – over occupied France on operational sorties. His indomitable, aggressive spirit was still to the fore, as was shown when he was flying an unarmed Hawker Henley target tug and attacked a German Ju 88 bomber with the only weapon he had, a Verey flare pistol.

Group Captain Jones survived World War Two but died on 30 August 1960, at 65 years of age.

Captain Robert Alexander Little, DSO and Bar, DSC and Bar, CdeG (1895–1917) 47 victories

Robert Little was born in Melbourne, Australia, on 19 July 1895. He was one of the many colonials who flocked to the British colours during World War One, and enlisted in the Royal Naval Air Service (RNAS) during 1915. He qualified as a naval pilot on 27 October 1915 and was commissioned as a flight sub-lieutenant early in 1916 at RNAS Eastchurch.

Late in June 1916 he was posted to No.1 Naval Wing at Dunkirk, flying Bristol Scouts and Sopwith 1½ Strutters. On 26 October 1916 he was posted to No.8 (N) Squadron, flying Sopwith Pups. Little gained his first victory on 11 November 1916 when he shot down an Aviatik C I on the Western Front while flying Sopwith Pup N5182. By March 1917 his score stood at four and he had received the Distinguished Service Cross.

8 (N) Squadron converted to Sopwith Triplanes and, flying N5469, Little gained his fifth victory on 7 April 1917 south-east of Lens, downing an Albatros D III during a dogfight. Little continued to score victories, gaining eight during the remainder of April. On April 30 he and three others attacked twelve Albatros D IIIs – Little shot down two of them and the other pilots accounted for three more. Another eight of the enemy went down during May 1917 and on 25 May 1917 his score had reached twenty.

From 16–29 June 1917 he shot down two C-types and two Albatros D Vs and by 10 July he had added another four victories in N5493, before switching to Sopwith Camel N6378, in which he shot down an Albatros D V over Vitry on 12 July. By 27 July 1917 his score had risen to 38, 24 of them while flying triplanes. In August 1917 he received the Distinguished Service Order and a Bar to his DSC – a Bar to his DSO followed on 14 September 1917.

Little was then posted to 3 (N) Squadron. On 1 April 1918 – the day on which the Royal Air Force was formed, 3 (N) Squadron becoming No.203 Squadron RAF – and while flying Camel B7198, he brought down a Fokker Dr I triplane over Oppy. Five more enemy aircraft went down in April and then three more in May, bringing his victory tally to 47 enemy aircraft downed.

On 27 May Little took off at night to try to intercept a Gotha bomber over Noeux. He found the Gotha and made an attack on its rear. Ground searchlights caught the Gotha in their beams and ground gunners opened fire: Little was hit by either the Gotha's rear gunner or by ground fire, the bullet passing through his thighs. Bleeding heavily, he crash-landed his aircraft, but later succumbed to his wounds. He was the highest scoring Australian ace of World War One.

Opposite page: Captain D. R. MacLaren DSO, MC and Bar, DFC.

Major Donald Roderick MacLaren, DSO, MC and Bar, DFC, LdH, CdeG (1893–1989) 54 victories

Donald MacLaren was born at Ottawa, Canada, on 28 May 1893. On 8 May 1917 he enlisted in the Royal Flying Corps as a trainee pilot, qualifying and receiving his pilot's brevet six months later.

On 23 November 1917 he was posted to 46 Squadron, flying Sopwith Camels on the Western Front. He gained his first victory on 6 March 1918 when he shot down a Hannover C-type over East Douai. Four days later, flying Camel B9153, he downed an Albatros D V.

On 21 March 1918, flying alongside seven others from 46 Squadron, he bombed and crippled a German long-range gun six miles behind enemy lines. En route to his base he encountered two German LVG C-types and shot down both. Minutes later he brought down an observation balloon too; for this action he was later awarded the Military Cross.

The Germans' great Spring Offensive was in full flow, and MacLaren scored daily until 25 March 1918, increasing his score to twelve. He made it thirteen on 27 March 1918 when he downed a Junkers J 1 During April 1918 he scored three more victories – a balloon, a C-type and an Albatros D V – and was promoted to captain.

By the end of May 1918 he had destroyed another sixteen enemy aircraft, bringing his total to 32. June was somewhat quieter – two more victories. Nine more aircraft went down to his machine-guns during July – he was a deadly marksman, as were most of the Canadian pilots. Four more victories were gained during August, bringing his total to 45. From 15 September to 2 October he shot down no fewer than eight Fokker D VIIs, a remarkable tribute to his shooting skill.

At 14.30 hours on 9 October 1918 he scored his final victory – a C-type over Ricqueval Wood – making his total 54, including six balloons. He was promoted to major before the Armistice on 11 November. He died in July 1989.

Major Edward Mannock VC, DSO and 2 Bars, MC and Bar (1887–1918) 73 victories

Edward Mannock was born at Preston Cavalry Barracks, Brighton, on 24 May 1887, into a military family of Irish parentage. As a youngster he developed astigmatism in his left eye, leaving him poorly sighted in that eye.

He was working in Turkey when World War One broke out and – as the Turks were allied to Germany – was interned until 1 April 1915. Returning to Britain, he was commissioned 2nd lieutenant into the Royal Engineers on 1 April 1916. In August 1916 he transferred to the Royal Flying Corps and was taught to fly at Hendon and Upavon, qualifying on 28 November with Aero Club Flying Certificate No.3895. He was sent to

Major Edward (Mick) Mannock, VC, DSO and Bar, who served with 40, 74 and 85 Squadrons. One of the top British aces before his death on 26 July 1918.

France on 1 April 1917 and posted to 40 Squadron at Aire five days later.

On 7 April 1917, Mannock flew one of 40 Squadron's Nieuport Scouts on his first sortie, but it was not until 7 May that he opened his score by downing a kite balloon. On both 25 May and 1 June he downed enemy two-seater observation aircraft, but he did not claim them as victories.

On 7 June he 'officially' shot down his first enemy aircraft, an Albatros D III scout, with a mere 30 rounds from his machine-gun. Two more enemy aircraft followed on 9 June over Douai. On 12 July Mannock – flying his Nieuport, B1682 – shot down a DFW C V of Schusta 12. This was followed next day by another DFW C V over Montigny.

Mannock was awarded the Military Cross on 22 July 1917 and promoted captain and flight commander. Between 28 July and 15 August he shot down five enemy single-seaters, including the German ace Leutnant von Bertrab of Jagdstaffel 30 on 12 August. During the next week he began to score victories steadily – five victories in seven days – exhibiting the hallmark of the finest fighter pilot: the desire to be at the throat of the enemy and shoot them out of the sky.

On 4 September 1917 Mannock – in spite of being practically blind in one eye – downed three DFWs in one day. During the rest of September another seven two-seater reconnaissance aircraft were added to his score. A Bar to his Military Cross followed on 18 October 1917. On 1 January 1918 Mannock shot down another two-seater – a Hannover C13 of Flieger Abteilung A 28 – and the next day he left 40 Squadron for a month's leave to England with his victory score at 23.

Mannock returned to France on 31 March 1918 as a flight commander with 74 Squadron, a new squadron equipped with S.E.5a scouts. On 12 April Mannock scored the squadron's first victory, an Albatros Scout over Carvin, and shared another victory. Most of the time he flew into battle with his squadron, but on occasion went on a lone hunt for the hated enemy.

Amazingly, he downed another six German aircraft by the end of April 1918. His hunting skill was now coming to its zenith: during May he gained another 24 victories.

85 Squadron with a captured Fokker D.VII. 1918.

On 19 May he was awarded the Distinguished Service Order. On 1 June 1918 he scored an incredible triple victory, shooting down three Pfalz D III Scouts over Estaires. By 18 June Mannock had downed another eight German aircraft and on 21 June he was promoted to major. He was then placed in command of 85 Squadron, also equipped with the S.E.5a.

By 3 July 1918 Mannock was airborne again with his new squadron, flying with his pilots as a formation, not as individuals. This method had brought great success to Mannock with 40 Squadron, and he now brought it to 85 Squadron.

On 7 July 1918 Mannock was out in formation with his squadron and clashed with Fokker D VIIs, causing mayhem. He shot one Fokker down and drove another down in a spin; two more collided, with fatal results. Mannock scored another victory on 8 July 1918, another on the 10th, two more on the 19th, two more on the 20th, and a Fokker Dr I triplane on 22 July.

On 26 July 1918 a two-plane dawn sortie took off at 05.00 hours from St. Omer and flew low to the Front. Mannock had as wingman – or rather tailman – 2nd Lieutenant Donald Inglis. Mannock and Inglis attacked a DFW C V at 50 feet and sent it down in flames over the German trenches. At 05.30, as Mannock and Inglis flew over the enemy trenches they met a hail of ground machine-gun fire. Mannock's aircraft was hit and set on fire. and he met his end in a ball of flames near Pacaut. The Germans buried the top ace's remains at La Pierre au Beure.

On 18 July 1919 Edward Mannock was awarded the Victoria Cross for valour.

Captain Frederick Robert Gordon McCall, DSO, MC and Bar, DFC (1896–1949) 35 (37) victories

McCall was born on 4 December 1896 at Vernon, British Columbia, Canada. He enlisted in the Alberta Regiment in February 1916, arriving in England with his regiment that December.

He was commissioned and transferred to the RFC in March 1917, being posted after training to 13 Squadron on 4 December that year. No.13 Squadron was flying the slow and ungainly R.E.8 (nicknamed 'Harry Tate') two-seater reconnaissance aircraft.

McCall crewed up with 2nd Lieutenant F. C. Farrington as observer/gunner and between them they scored several victories in R.E.8 B6523, an amazing feat for this slow and awkward aircraft, and a nasty shock for attacking German airmen. Other victories were scored in R.E.8 B5090.

On 4 March 1918 McCall was awarded a Military Cross, and two weeks later – after another two victories – a Bar to it. After a short leave he was posted to 41 Squadron, flying S.E.5as, and by 1 June he had scored three more kills, bringing him a well-deserved DFC. June 1918 was an excellent month for McCall but not for the Germans whom he met in aerial combat – four went down on 28 June and five on 30 June, bring his total to twenty victories confirmed, all in S.E.5a D3927. His five victories in one day (30 June 1918) brought him the Distinguished Service Order, with his score standing at 24 victories.

On 17 August 1918, with his tally at 35, he and William Gordon Claxton were on patrol with other airmen from 41 Squadron when they clashed with a large force – some say 40–60 – of German aircraft. McCall and Claxton are believed to have shot down three enemy aircraft each, but this was unconfirmed (though probably correct).

Claxton was shot down behind German lines but McCall returned to base. He was taken ill and returned first to England, then home to Canada where he was when the war ended. McCall died on 2 January 1949. A gallant, aggressive fighter pilot and a credit to his country, he was one of the illustrious band of colonial airmen who came to Britain's aid in the Great War – their descendants would return in World War Two and carry on the splendid tradition.

Major James Byford McCudden VC, DSO and Bar, MC and Bar, MM, CdeG (1895–1918) 57 victories

Born at Gillingham, Kent, on 28 March 1895 of an army family, McCudden enlisted in the Royal Engineers as a boy on 26 April 1910. He transferred to the RFC as an air mechanic, second class, with service number 892, on 28 April 1913.

On 16 June 1913 he moved to 3 Squadron RFC at Netheravon, and went to France with the Squadron on 13 August 1914. By April 1915 he was a sergeant air mechanic. In June 1915 McCudden began to fly as an unofficial observer in Morane-Saulnier two-seater monoplanes, and on 19 December 1915 saw his first dogfight. On 1 January 1916 he became an official observer and continued to see action. He was awarded the Croix de Guerre on 21 January 1916, and on 25 January was accepted for pilot training with promotion to flight sergeant.

After flying training at Farnborough and Gosport, he was sent to the Central Flying School at Upavon; he was awarded his RFC pilot's brevet on 30 May 1916. Posted back to France on 7 July, he joined 20 Squadron at Clairmarais, equipped with F.E.2b two-seater bombers.

On 7 August he joined 29 Squadron's C Flight at Abeele, flying D.H.2 fighters. On 6 September, flying D.H.2 5985, he had his first victory – an all-white C-type two-seater which he sent down on the Menin Road. He was awarded the Military Medal on 1 October 1916.

Major James McCudden, VC, in an S.E.5a of 56 Squadron.

On 1 January 1917 McCudden was commissioned 2nd lieutenant, remaining with 29 Squadron. On 26 January he brought down another C-type over Ficheaux and by 15 February 1917 his victories totalled five. On 16 February he gained his third gallantry decoration – the Military Cross – and was sent back to RFC Maidstone in England on a rest tour. On 1 June 1917 he was promoted to captain and the following month joined 66 Squadron, downing an Albatros D V over Gheluwe and, when on a brief spell with 56 Squadron, another Albatros D V over 'Polygon' Wood. On 14 August 1917 he returned to 56 Squadron, equipped with the new S.E.5a fighter, as commander of B Flight. During August he shot down four Albatros D Vs in S.E.5a B519: his score now stood at eleven victories.

On 14 September 1917 he forced down an Albatros D V flown by Leutnant Weigand of the famous Jasta 10 of

Richthofen's 'Flying Circus'. By 23 September he had three more enemy to his credit, and during the evening of that day his flight became involved in a famous dogfight: the German ace Werner Voss, with 48 victories, flying a new Fokker triplane and accompanied by two other scouts, was shot down and killed by 56 Squadron. On 3 October McCudden was awarded a Bar to his Military Cross.

By the beginning of December 1917 McCudden's official score was 23 victories; by the end of the month it had risen to 37. On 15 December 1917 he received the Distinguished Service Order; a Bar to the DSO followed on 3 January 1918.

January 1918 saw his score mount steadily to 46 victories. His 50th victory came on 16 February: at 10.35 hours he downed a Rumpler C-type; at 10.45 hours a DFW C V; at 11.10 hours another Rumpler C-type; then at 12.30 hours yet another Rumpler C-type. By 26 February his score stood at 57 victories, 52 of them scored with 56 Squadron.

McCudden flew his final combat mission on 1 March 1918 before returning to England on leave. On 29 March 1918 the award of the Victoria Cross was gazetted, with which he was invested on 6 April 1918, together with the DSO and Bar and a Bar to his Military Cross.

On 15 June McCudden flew again with 56 squadron in France but not on a combat rôle. However he badgered higher authority for a return to air combat. He succeeded in winning his battle to get back into the war, and was given command of 60 Squadron at Boffles in France with effect from 9 July 1918, in the rank of major.

McCudden left Hounslow on 9 July 1918, in S.E.5a C.1126, to take up his new command; he crossed the Channel and landed in France at 17.30 hours at Auxi-le-Châteaux. He found he was five miles short of his destination at Boffles and took off again, but as he climbed the engine cut out and the aircraft side-slipped downwards and crashed into trees. McCudden died of his injuries and was buried next day at Wavans, where he still rests, a gallant fighter pilot.

Captain G.E.H. McElroy, MC, DFC, in front of his aircraft.

Captain George Edward Henry McElroy, MC and 2 Bars, DFC and Bar (1893–1918) 46 victories

Born at Donnybrook, Dublin, on 14 May 1893, McElroy enlisted in the Royal Irish Regiment in August 1914 and was sent to France in October 1914, where he saw action. He transferred to the RFC during February 1917 and after pilot training joined 40 Squadron in France, flying Nieuport Scouts.

In October 1917, 40 Squadron was re-equipped with S.E.5as and on 28 December 1917 – flying S.E.5a B598 – 'McIrish', as he was nicknamed, shot down a LVG C-type over Vitry. His second victory – a Rumpler C-type – was on 13 January 1918 over Vendin Bridge. Two more victories followed during January, then between 2–26 February 1918 his score reached thirteen.

Eight more were confirmed during March, then another six during April, taking 'McIrish' up to 27 victories. On 7 April he shot down three enemy aircraft between 10.40 hours and 11.15 hours!

Three more victories followed in June 1918 – a DFW C-type and two balloons – to bring his score up to 30 confirmed. July 1918 proved incredible for 'McIrish': he accounted for no fewer than sixteen enemy up to the 25th, making his final confirmed score 46.

On 31 July 1918 'McIrish' took off from Bryas airfield at 08.15 hours on what proved to be his last flight, in S.E.5a E1310. He shot down a Hannover C-type over Laventie (which was unconfirmed by the RFC but confirmed by the German Air Service), but was hit by ground fire and died in the crash that followed. He was buried by the German Air Service at Laventie.

Captain McElroy was awarded the Military Cross in February 1918, then a Bar to the Cross in March, then a second Bar in April. The Distinguished Flying Cross was awarded in July, followed by a Bar to the DFC in July.

Majors Donald Roderick MacLaren, 54 victories (left) and Andrew Edward McKeever, 31 victories.

Lieutenant-Colonel Andrew Edward McKeever, DSO, MC and Bar (1895–1919) 30 (31) victories

Yet another outstanding ace from Canada, Andrew McKeever was born in Listowel, Ontario, on 21 August 1895 and came to Britain with the Canadian Army in 1914. In 1916 he transferred to the RFC, and was sent to 11 Squadron on 28 May 1917, flying Bristol Fighter two-seaters.

He was to become the leading and outstanding ace of two-seater aircraft, scoring a confirmed 31 victories, mostly with Sergeant L. F. Powell as his gunner/observer. Sergeant Powell is credited with shooting down eight German aircraft. McKeever scored his first victories on 26 June 1917 when he downed two Albatros D Vs within minutes of each other, Lieutenant E. Oake being his gunner/observer on this occasion. On 7 July 1917 he shot down three Albatros D Vs within ten minutes while flying Bristol Fighter A7144 with Sergeant Powell. By 13 July he had shot down another three Albatros D Vs. On 5 August he downed three Albatros D Vs with Sergeant Powell, again within minutes of each other.

By 28 September 1917 he had downed another seven Albatros D Vs, making his score eighteen victories. During October he accounted for another eight aircraft: one C-type and seven Albatros D Vs. During November he had five more victories – one C-type and four Albatros D Vs – bringing his total score to 31. McKeever was awarded the Military Cross on 17 September 1917. A Bar to his MC followed on 27 October and the Distinguished Service Order on 30 November. Sergeant Powell was awarded a richly deserved Distinguished Conduct Medal.

Lieutenant-Colonel McKeever survived the war, but was injured in a road traffic accident and died from his injuries on 25 December 1919.

Major Keith Rodney Park MC, French CdeG (1892–1975)
20 victories

A New Zealander, Keith Park was born on 15 June 1892 and served with the New Zealand Artillery, gaining his commission in July 1915. He served in France with the Royal Artillery during 1916, being wounded in October.

He transferred to the RFC in December 1916, underwent pilot training and then became an instructor. He was posted to 48 Squadron, flying Bristol Fighters, on 7 July 1917 and by 11 September was a flight commander.

On 24 July 1917 he sent an Albatros D III down out of control off Ravensdyke. August proved a good month for Park, who scored nine victories – on 17 August he and his observer downed four Albatros D IIIs in 30 minutes. Two Albatros D Vs went down on 21 August, followed by another Albatros D V on 25 August. He was awarded the Military Cross and the French Croix de Guerre.

By the end of September 1917 he had accounted for another six Albatros D Vs, taking his score to 16 confirmed. He was shot down once by anti-aircraft fire and once in aerial combat – on 3 January 1918 by Unteroffizer Ungewitter of Schlachtstaffel 5 – but managed to crash-land his Bristol, A7229, safely. On 10 April 1918 he assumed command of 48 Squadron with seventeen confirmed victories to his credit. He scored three more victories, the last two of them on 25 June, making his final confirmed score twenty.

Park remained in the RAF on a permanent commission and achieved high rank – during World War Two he became Air Officer Commanding 11 Group, Fighter Command, during the Battle of Britain. He later became AOC Fighter Command Malta and Burma, and retired as Air Chief Marshal Sir Keith Park, GCB. KBE, MC, DFC, DCL. He returned to New Zealand and died on 6 February 1975 aged 83 years.

Lieutenants Croye Rothes Pithey (?–1919) and Hervey Rhodes (?–1987) 10 victories

Lieutenant Pithey was born in South Africa and Lieutenant 'Dusty' Rhodes enlisted in the Yorkshire Regiment before transferring to the RFC. Pithey was the pilot and Rhodes the observer/gunner in an R.E.8 observation and reconnaissance aircraft; very different to a fast fighter aircraft. However, the R.E.8 had two Lewis machine-guns in the rear cockpit for the observer/gunner, and the pilot had a Vickers machine-gun fixed on the port side of the fuselage; 260lb of bombs could also be carried. By September 1917, sixteen squadrons were flying the R.E.8 on the Western Front. Slow and cumbersome, it was regarded as an easy kill by the Germans, but was not always so. On 21 August 1917 Oberleutnant Dostler (26 victories) was killed by an R.E.8 gunner.

Pithey and Rhodes joined forces during March 1918, flying the R.E.8 with 12 Squadron. They scored their first victory on 7 May 1918 when they destroyed a balloon, followed by another balloon on 4 June. Incredibly, on 7 June, at 09.20 hours, they shot down out of control three Pfalz D IIIs. On 8 May, while flying with another officer, Lieutenant Rhodes shot down another enemy aircraft.

By 3 September 1918 the two officers had taken their total to ten enemy aircraft (including the two balloons) in their R.E.8, F6097, making them the top-scoring R.E.8 pilot and gunner/observer crew. But on 27 September their partnership came to an abrupt end when they were both shot up and wounded. Both of these splendid airmen survived the war – Pithey died in 1919 and Rhodes in 1987.

Captain Francis Grainger Quigley, DSO, MC and Bar, (1894–1918) 34 (33) victories

Canadian Captain Francis Grainger Quigley, DSO, MC and Bar, of 70 Squadron.

Quigley – another of that gallant band of Canadians who flocked to the colours – was born 10 July 1894 in Toronto. He arrived in England in May 1915 with Canadian Army Engineers and was sent to France. He transferred to the RFC in the spring of 1917 and after flying training he was posted to 70 Squadron in France. This squadron was equipped with Sopwith 1½ Strutters until July 1917, then Sopwith Camels for the rest of the war.

Quigley's first victory was an Albatros D V, destroyed on 10 October 1917 while flying Camel B2356 at 08.05 hours; twenty minutes later he sent another Albatros D V down out of control. Both victories were confirmed. A German C-type was destroyed on 20 October, then on 12 November he attacked an Albatros D V and sent it spinning out of control. He was awarded the Military Cross and Mentioned in Despatches several times during the autumn of 1917. By the year's end he had nine victories to his credit.

A brief spell of inactivity followed, but on 3 January 1918 he was back in action, sending a C-type out of control earthwards. Three days later he destroyed two Albatros D Vs within fifteen minutes over Stadenberg and Passchendaele, while flying Camel B2447. The first Albatros was shared with two other pilots of 23 and 70 Squadron; the German pilot was Leutnant Walter von Bülow Bothkamp, of Jasta 2 'Boelcke', with 28 victories to his credit. On 22 January 1918 Quigley shared in the destruction of three Albatros D Vs, upping his total to fifteen; by 17 February it was up to eighteen.

Between 8–23 March 1918 Quigley had another fifteen confirmed victories, making his score 33. On 9 March, over Menin and Quesnoy, he destroyed or sent down out of control four Albatros D Vs between 09.30 hours and 13.10 hours, while flying Camel B7475. On 11 March he had another four victories: a balloon and three Pfalz D IIIs over

Menin/Passchendaele; the next day he accounted for three Albatros D Vs within five minutes over Dadizeele. During this month he received the Distinguished Service Order, in part due to his offensive action in attacking German ground troops during the last German offensive of the war. He fired more than 3,000 rounds at the enemy on the ground and dropped bomb after bomb, flying almost non-stop during the short daylight hours of March.

On 22 March 1918 Quigley destroyed an Albatros D V and a Fokker Dr I Triplane. The next day he scored his final victory, a Pfalz D III, sending it down to crash at Morchies. He was now promoted to captain. On 27 March he was wounded in the ankle, hospitalised and sent home to Canada. In September he managed to get himself back to England, with a view to returning to combat. However, he contracted the deadly influenza virus prevalent at the time. and died in hospital at Liverpool on 20 October.

2nd Lieutenant Indra Lal Roy DFC (1899–1918) 10 victories

Roy was born in Calcutta, India, and educated in England. He enlisted in the RFC in July 1917 and, after training, was sent to 56 Squadron on 30 October 1917. On 6 November he made a bad landing in an S.E.5a and was medically downgraded. Determined to get into the fight, Roy managed to get back to France and combat in June 1918.

Posted to 40 Squadron, he joined the high-scoring Captain George McElroy's flight and began his brief but valiant career as a fighter pilot, flying S.E.5a B180. Between 6–19 July 1918 he scored ten victories (two of them shared): on the 8th he downed three enemy aircraft in less than four hours, on the 13th two: and then on the 15th he destroyed a Fokker D VII and sent another Fokker D VII out of control in minutes.

His final victory was a Hannover C-type shot down on 19 July, and then on the 22nd he was shot down in flames and killed in B180, aged nineteen years. He was awarded a posthumous DFC in September 1918. He was – and still is – the only Indian fighter pilot ace.

2nd Lieutenant Indra Lal Roy, DFC, of 40 Squadron RAF, in 1918. The first and as far as is known the only Indian fighter ace.

Captain Robert Henry Magnus Spencer Saundby MC (1896–1971) 5 victories

Born on 26 April 1896 and educated at St. Edward's School, Saundby served with the Royal Warwickshire Regiment during 1914 and was seconded to the RFC in January 1916. He went to France during 1916, flying D.H.2s with 24 Squadron, and scored his first victory – over a Fokker *Eindecker* – on 31 July. Wounded during this dogfight, he continued flying and scored two more victories in September and November. The victory in September was shared.

Saundby was posted to 41 Squadron on Home Defence duties on 31 March 1917. On 17 June he and Lieutenant L. P. Watkins attacked the German Zeppelin L48 over Theberton, Suffolk, at 03.30 hours. Bringing the massive airship down, Saundby and Watkins returned to base in their D.H.2, A5058. Saundby was awarded the Military Cross for destroying the L48. With the destruction of the L48 Saundby's score now stood at five.

After the war Saundby remained in the RAF and was awarded the DFC. During World War Two he became Deputy Commander-in-Chief Bomber Command, was knighted in 1944 and promoted to Air Marshal in 1945. He retired as Air Marshal Sir Robert Saundby, KCB, KBE, MC, DFC, AFC, DL, in 1946 and died on 25 September 1971

Marshal of the Royal Air Force Lord Trenchard, GCB, DSO, DCL, LL.D (1873–1956)

Born in 1873 and known as the 'Father of the Royal Air Force', Trenchard was awarded Aviator's Certificate No.270 in 1912 and became an instructor at the CFS at Upavon. He was selected to command the RFC in 1915 and was Chief of the Air Staff in 1918–29. He died in 1956 and was buried in Westminster Abbey.

Captain Henry Winslow Woollett, DSO, MC and Bar, CdeG, LdH, (?–1969) 35 victories

Suffolk-born Henry Woollett was commissioned into the Army when the war broke out, transferring to the RFC in 1916. He passed out as a pilot after only a few hours' dual instruction and was posted to 24 Squadron at Bertangles on 30 November 1916.

Captain Henry Winslow Woollett, DSO, MC.

24 Squadron was flying D.H.2s when Woollett joined them, but it was not until 5 April 1917 that he gained his first victory, an Albatros D III over Honnecourt that he claimed as destroyed. 24 Squadron then converted to the superior D.H.5s and Woollett – flying D.H.5 A9165 – shot down an Albatros D V and a C-type within a few minutes on 23 July 1917. A Rumpler C-type was destroyed on 28 July and an Albatros D V on 17 August.

Lieutenant Woollett was promoted to captain with effect from 13 July and made 'A' Flight commander. He returned to England where he was awarded the Military Cross and became a flying instructor. He returned to France in March 1918, being posted to 'C' Flight of 43 Squadron, flying Sopwith Camels. On 8 March 1918 he reopened his score by sending an Albatros D V down in flames over La Bassee, this bringing him up to six confirmed.

Between 11–27 March he destroyed six aircraft and two balloons, scoring a double on the 24th and two balloons on the 27th. On 2 April he shot down three balloons, followed on 12 April by an incredible feat of arms. Taking off on an early fighting patrol in Camel 6402, he met an Albatros D V and a C-type over La Gorgue. Minutes later the two were downed – the

Albatros in flames. Ten minutes later, at 10.40 hours, he shot down another Albatros in flames. Landing to refuel and reload his guns, he took off and met three Albatros D Vs over La Gorgue at 17.00 hours: he destroyed all three within minutes. All were confirmed, Woollett becoming the second RFC pilot to claim six victories in a day (the first was Captain J. L. Trollope, also of 43 Squadron). He was awarded the Distinguished Service Order and received a Bar to his MC, as well as the French Legion of Honour and Croix de Guerre.

Woollett returned to the offensive on 22 April with two balloons destroyed, then an Albatros D V and a balloon on 9 May 1918. This brought his total to 27 confirmed, but it is thought he scored several more unconfirmed. By 9 August he had 35 confirmed victories, making his official total twenty destroyed, four driven down out of control and 11 balloons; his unofficial total was around 43 to 51.

Captain Woollett survived the war and remained in the new RAF. He became commanding officer of his old squadron – No.23 – during 1930–31. He died on 31 October 1969.

BRITISH ACES 1914–19

Figures in parenthesis are from latest research which suggest different totals. Many kills were shared and many were officially unconfirmed.

* Indicates Americans

** Indicates later prominent persons

Fighter Aces

73 kills Major E. Mannock

72 kills Lieutenant-Colonel W. A. Bishop

60 kills Lieutenant-Colonel R. Collishaw

57 kills Major J. T. B. McCudden

54 kills Captain A. Beauchamp Proctor

54 kills Captain D. R. MacLaren

53 kills Major W. G. Barker (50)

47 kills Captain R. A. Little

46 kills Captain P. F. Fullard (40)

46 kills Captain G. E. H. McElroy (47)

44 kills Captain A. Ball

44 kills Captain J. Gilmore (39)

43 kills Major T. F. Hazell

39 kills

Captain W. G. Claxton

Major R. S. Dallas (32)

Captain W. L. Jordan

38 kills

Captain A. C. Atkey

37 kills

Captain J. I. T. Jones

Captain F. R. McCall (35)

36 kills

F/Commander J. S. T. Fall

35 kills

Captain H. W. Woollett

34 kills

Captain F. G. Quigley (33)

32 kills

Major G. H. Bowman

31 kills

Major A. D. Carter (29)

30 kills

Captain M. B. Frew (23)

Captain S. M. Kinkead (35)

Captain A. E. McKeever (31)

Captain S. F. H. Thompson

29 kills

Major C. D. Booker

Captain P. J. Clayson

Captain A. H. Cobby

Captain L. H. Rochford

28 kills

Captain J. E. Gurdon

Captain D. Latimer

27 kills

Captain R. Hoidge (28)

Captain H. E. Luchford (24)

Lieutenant C. M. McEwan

Major G. Maxwell (26)

Captain T. P. Middleton

Captain F. O. Soden

Captain A. T. Whealy

26 kills

Captain W. C. Campbell (23)

Captain W. F. Harvey

Captain E. R. King

Captain W. E. Staton**

Captain W. McKenzie Thomson

25 kills

Major K. L. Caldwell

Major R. J. O. Compston

Major J. Leacroft (22)

Captain R. A. Mayberry (21)

Lieutenant A. Rhys Davids

Captain S. W. Rosevear

24 kills

Major J. O. Andrews (12+)

Captain P. Carpenter

Captain W. E. Shields

Captain J. A. Slater

23 kills

Captain W. M. Alexander

Captain W. C. Campbell

Captain H. P. Lale

Captain E. J. K. McCloughry (21)

Captain A. A. N. D. Pentland

Major Charles Dawson Booker, DSC, Croix de Guerre. 29 victories. Killed in action 13 August 1918.

Captain H. A. Whistler
22 kills
Major W. Cochrane
  Patrick (21)
Captain L. F. Jenkins
Captain C. F. King
Captain B. Roxburgh-
  Smith
Captain J. L. White
21 kills
Captain C. R. R. Hickey
Captain R. P. Minifie
Captain G. E. Thomson
20 kills
Captain J. D. Bell
Lieutenant K. B. Conn
Captain F. W. Gillett★
Captain T. S. Harrison
  (22)
Captain E. C. Johnston
Captain C. F. King (22)
Captain C. H. R.
  Lagesse
Captain I. D. R.
  McDonald
Major K. R. Park★★
Captain C. G. Ross
Captain W. A. Southey
19 kills
Captain H. D. Barton
Captain W. Beaver
Captain A. B. Bradfield
Captain A. B.
  Fairclough
Captain C. E. Howell
Lieutenant H. A.
  Kullberg★
Major S. M. Miles
Lieutenant A. E. Reed
Captain H. W. L.
  Saunders (15)
Major A. Wilkinson
18 kills
Lieutenant L. M.
  Barlow (20)
Captain J. D. Belgrave
Lieutenant C. F. Collet
  (11)
Captain A. K. Cowper
  (19)
Captain F. R. Cubbon
Captain F. L. Hale★
Captain W. C. Lambert★
Captain G. C. Mackay
Captain M. A.
  Newnham
Lieutenant E. V. Reid
  (19)
Captain F. J. H. Thayre
  (20)
Captain J. Todd
Captain J. L. Trollope
17 kills
Captain R. B.
  Bannerman

Captain H. J. Burden
  (16)
Major A. W. Carter
Captain C. F. Falken-
  berg
Captain G. E. Gibbons
Major F. P. Holliday
Lieutenant A. T.
  Iaccaci★
Lieutenant P. T.
  Iaccaci★
Lieutenant E. G.
  Johnstone
Lieutenant R. M.
  Makepeace
Captain J. W. Pinder
Captain E. Swale
Captain E. R. Tempest
Captain W. A. Tyrell
16 kills
Captain O. M. Baldwin
Major C. G. Bell
Captain J. S. Chick
Lieutenant E. S. Coler★
Captain S. T. Edwards
Sergeant E. J. Elton
Captain R. M. Foster
Captain G. B. Gates
Captain A. Hepburn
Sergeant F. Johnson
Captain H. T. Mellings
  (15)
Major K. Oxspring
Captain O. W. Redgate
Captain O. R. Rose★
Major S. F. Pender
Captain F. R. Smith
Captain E. W. Springs
Captain D. A. Stewart
Captain C. J. Venter
15 kills
Captain L. P. Coombes
Major C. M. Crowe
Captain C. W.
  Cudemore
Lieutenant R. L. Curtis
Captain M. H. Findley
  (14)
Captain J. A. Glen
Lieutenant H. K. Goode
Captain J. E. Greene
Captain R. A.
  Grosvener (16)
Captain E. T. Hayne
Captain F. H. Hobson
Captain A. C. Kiddie
Major R. C. Phillips
Lieutenant H.
  Richardson
F/Sublieutenant H. F.
  Stackard
Lieutenant F. G. C.
  Weare
14 kills
Captain C. M. Clement

Major A. Coningham★★
Captain E. Dickson
Captain M. H. Findlay
Captain J. Fitz Morris
Lieutenant F. G.
  Gibbons
Major G. E. Gibbs (10)
Captain A. E. Godfrey
Captain F. C. Gorringe
Captain S. W.
  Highwood (16)
Major A. W. Keen
Captain F. Libby★
Captain N. McEwan
Captain R. T. Mark
Captain J. D. Payne
Lieutenant W.
  Sidebottom
Captain J. V. Sorsoleil
Lieutenant K. R. Unger
Captain A. W. Vigers
Lieutenant H. G.
  Watson
Captain T. F. Williams
13 kills
F/Commander F. C.
  Armstrong
Captain R. C. B.
  Brading
Captain C. P. Brown
  (14)
Captain G. H. Cock
Captain D. G. Cooke
Captain J. Cottle
F/Commander W. A.
  Curtis
Captain R. A. Delhaye
  (9)
Captain A. J. Enstone
Lieutenant G. L.
  Graham
Captain H. A.
  Hamersley
Lieutenant T. M.
  Harries
Captain J. Hedley
Captain O. A. P. Heron
Captain S. B. Horn
Lieutenant G. R.
  Howsam
Captain E. C. Hoy
Lieutenant H. B.
  Hudson
Captain A. Jones
  Williams (11)
Captain S. C. Joseph
Captain R. McNeil
  Keirstead
Captain J. H. T. Letts
Captain S. T.
  Liversedge
Captain W. E. G. Mann
Captain J. G. Manuel
Lieutenant N. W. Mawle
  (12)

Captain W. R. May
Captain G. P. Olley
Captain T. L. Purdom
Captain H. G. Reeves
Lieutenant G. R. Riley
Captain F. R. Smith
Captain S. Stanger
Captain E. J. Stephens
Lieutenant F. S.
  Symondson
1st Lieutenant G. A.
  Vaughn
Captain O. H. D.
  Vickers
Lieutenant D. J. Weston
Lieutenant W. B. Wood
12 kills
Major J. O. Andrews
Captain C. C. Banks
Captain B. E. Baker
Captain T. C. R. Baker
Lieutenant L. Bennett
Lieutenant G. A. Birks

*Lieutenant Walter
Bertram Wood, MC
and Bar, 29 Squadron,
RFC, 13 (18) victories.
He died in an air crash
on 11 November 1917.*

Captain A. R. Brown (5)
Captain R. J. Brownell
Captain O. C. Bryson
Captain W. F. Carlaw
Captain R. W. Chappel
Captain E. A. Clear
Captain F. J. Davies
Major C. Draper (9)
Captain H. S. Drewitt
Lieutenant A. Gerrard
Lieutenant F. D. Gillette
Captain W. L. Harrison
Major P. Huskinson (11)
Captain W. H. Hubbard
Captain J. E. L. Hunter
Captain G. B Irving
Lieutenant W. S. Jenkins
Captain F. E. Kindley
Major R. G. Landis
Captain G. H. Lewis
Major F. I. Lord★

Captain Arthur Clunie 'Snowy' Randall, DFC and Bar, 32 and 85 Squadrons.

Captain D. U. McGregor
Captain R. L. Manuel
Lieutenant M. E. Mealing
Lieutenant K. B. Montgomery
Captain W. E. Molesworth
Lieutenant-Colonel R. Mulock
Captain I. P. R. Napier
Captain James Parson★
Captain G. W. Price
Major C. Quintin Brand
Captain J. S. Ralston
Lieutenant H. C. Rath
Lieutenant C. R. Richards
Captain A. W. Saunders
Captain R. R. Soar
Major F. Sowrey
Major A. M. Shook
Captain W. S. Stephenson
Lieutenant L. T. E. Taplin
Lieutenant C. W. K. Thompson
Captain R. M. Trevethan
Lieutenant C. W. Warman★
Captain N. W. W. Webb (14)
Major J. T. Whittaker
Captain J. B. White
Captain P. Wilson
11 kills
Lieutenant G. F. M. Apps
F/Commander F. E. Banbury
Captain H. F. Beamish
Captain A. Beck
Captain P. S. Burge
Captain S. Carlin
Captain R. W. Chappell
F/Commander A. J. Charwick
Captain C. F Collet
Captain T. Colvill-Jones
F/Lieutenant H. Day
Lieutenant H. F. Davison
Captain W. J. A. Duncan
Captain F. J. Gibbs
Lieutenant C. B. Green
Captain J. C. B Firth
Captain W. M. Fry
Captain H. A. Hammersley (13)
Lieutenant L. N. Hollinghurst★★
Captain G. H. Hooper

Lieutenant F. J. Hunt
Lieutenant W. R. Irwin
Captain M. R. James
Captain G. O. Johnson
Captain H. J. Larkin
Captain K. M. G. Leaske (8)
Captain W. H. Longton
Captain C. N. Lowe
Lieutenant E. J. Lussier★
Captain A. McCudden (8)
Captain M. C. McGregor
Lieutenant R. W. McKenzie (6)
Captain N. McMillan
Captain R. Manzer
Captain C. M. Maud
Captain J. H. Mitchell
Lieutenant A. J. Morgan
Lieutenant S. A. Oades
Captain H. A. Oaks
Captain H. A. Patey
Captain L. A. Payne
Lieutenant C. W. Payton
Captain J. W. Pearson (12)
Lieutenant G. E. Randall
Captain C. B. Ridley
Captain W. W. Rogers (9)
Lieutenant I. C. Sanderson
Captain M. D. G. Scott (12)
Captain J. Sharman (8)
Captain R. M. Smith
F/Sublieutenant A. W. Wood
Major W. E. Young
10 kills
Lieutenant E. O. Amm
Captain E. D. Atkinson
Major B. Barker
Lieutenant H. H. Beddow
Captain H. B. Bell
Captain Oliver C. le Boutillier ★
Major L. S. Breadner
Captain A. Roy Brown
Captain F. E. Brown
Captain A. J. Boswell
Captain R. A. Birbeck
Captain R. L. Chidlaw Roberts
Captain C. C. Clark
Lieutenant-Colonel J. A. Cunningham
Lieutenant D. A. Davies
Lieutenant E. G. Davies
Captain R. E. Dodds

Lieutenant A. B. Ellwood
Lieutenant W. H. Farrow
Captain H. G. Forrest
Captain C. V. Gardner
Major T. F. N. Gerrard
Major G. E. Gibbs
Major S. J. Goble
1st Lieutenant L. A. Hamilton
Lieutenant G. S. Hodson
Lieutenant T. S. Horry (8)
Captain R. W. Howard
Captain W. Hubbard
Lieutenant W. E. Jenkins
Captain V. Kearley
1st Lieutenant D. Knight★
Lieutenant A. Koch
Captain P. A. Lamgan Byrne
Lieutenant A. E. McKay
F/Sublieutenant J. J. Malone
Captain G. B. Moore
Lieutenant R. F. S. Mauduit (9)
Sergeant G. P. Olley
Captain J. de C. Paynter
Lieutenant C. R. Pithey and Lieutenant H. Rhodes (R.E.8 crew)
Captain A. C. Randall
Lieutenant H. B. Redler
Lieutenant L. Richardson (7)
Captain H. N. C. Robinson
Lieutenant T. Rose (11)
Captain R. H. Rusby
Captain J. Scott
Lieutenant A. S. Shepherd
Captain S. P. Smith (5)
Captain St Cyprian C. Tayler
Lieutenant F. H. Taylor
Captain A. Tonks (12)
Captain J. H. Tudhope
Captain S. H. Wallage
Lieutenant W. L. Wells
Lieutenant R. Winnicott
Major W. E. Young (11)
9 kills
Lieutenant C. H. Arnison
Major H. H. Balfour
Lieutenant R. G. Bennett
Lieutenant J. A. W. Binnie
Lieutenant C. G.

Boothroyd
Captain J. D. Breakey
Captain F. J. S. Britnell
Lieutenant S. MacG.
Brown
Lieutenant W. H. Brown
F/Commander F. D.
Casey
Captain E. D.
Cummings
Captain D. C. Cunnel
Captain R. J. Dawes
Captain R. A. Del'haye
Captain G. C. Dixon
Captain J. E. Doyle
Major C. Draper
Captain A. T.
Drinkwater
Captain J. H. Forman
Lieutenant H. A. F.
Goodison
Lieutenant F. S. Gordon
Lieutenant R. M.
Gordon
Captain G. H. Hackwill
Captain J. D. I.
Hardman
Major L. G. Hawker VC
(7)
Lieutenant J. A. Hone
Lieutenant R. L. Johns
Captain H. S. Kerby
Captain F. M. Kitto
Lieutenant J. F. Larsen*
Captain S. S. I. Lavers
Captain J. L. Leith
Major S. H. Long
Captain J. S. McDonald
Lieutenant C. McEvoy
Captain D. M. McGoun
Captain N. Macmillan
Captain F. McQuistan
(10)
Captain C. J. Marchant
Major R. S. Maxwell
Captain J. T. Milne
Lieutenant B. H.
Moody
Captain C. G. D.
Napier
Major E. W. Norton
Captain S. C. O'Grady
F/Lieutenant E. Pierce
Captain F. C. Ransley
Captain W. E. Reed
Major G. R. M. Reid
Captain O. J. Rose (16)
Captain R. M. Ross
Smith
Captain H. V. Rowley
Lieutenant I. L. Roy
(10)
Captain E. J. Salter
Lieutenant J. H. Siddall
Lieutenant C. J. Sims

Lieutenant R. H. Sloley
Captain A. N. Solly
Lieutenant A. G. A.
Spence
Lieutenant G.
Thompson
Captain R. R. Thornley
Lieutenant F. D. Travers
Lieutenant H. L.
Waddington
Captain G. W. Wareing
Lieutenant K. B. Watson
Captain T. M. Williams
Lieutnant A. Williamson
8 kills
Lieutenant G. F.
Anderson
Captain E. B. Betts
Captain B. P. G.
Beanlands
Lieutenant E. L.
Benbow
Lieutenant D. W. Beard
Captain C. A. Brewster
Joske
Captain G. H. Blaxland
Captain E. W.
Broadberry
Captain A. J. Brown
Lieutenant W. H. Brown
(9)
Lieutenant G. W.
Bulmer (10)
Lieutenant H. Burdick
Captain A. A. Callender
Captain J. M. Child
1st Lieutenant H. R.
Clay
Lieutenant R. D. Coath
Captain A. T. Cole
Lieutenant E. S. T. Cole
Captain J. G. Coombe
Lieutenant W. B. Craig
Captain H. C. Daniel
(9)
Captain J. D. DePencier
Captain A. Dover
Atkinson
Captain G. M. Duncan
Captain T. Durrant (11)
Lieutenant W. Durrand
Major R. M.
Drummond
Lieutenant H. R. Eycott
Martin
Captain J. H. Forman
(9)
F/Lt D. F. Fitzgibbon
Captain G. C. Gardiner
(6)
Lieutenant R. Gordon
(9)
Lieutenant J. S. Griffith
(7)
Captain V. E. Groom

Captain R. G. Hammer-
sley
Lieutenant F. G.
Harlock
Captain J. Harman
Lieutenant H. G.
Hegarty
Captain A. S. Hemming
Lieutenant G. R. Hicks
Lieutenant D. A. F.
Hilton
Captain I. V. Hind
Lieutenant D. Ingalls (6)
Lieutenant K. W. Junor
Captain N. Keeble (6)
Captain R. K. Kirkman
Captain A. G. Knight
(8)
Lieutenant D. Lamb
Major G. L. Lloyd
Captain D. Lloyd Evans
Captain C. A. Lewis
Lieutenant W. M.
Macdonald
Lieutenant P. A.
McDougall (7)
Lieutenant J. A. Mann
Lieutenant G. I. D.
Marks
Captain H. Meintjes
Major G. W. Murlis
Green
Lieutenant A. Mussared
Captain T. W. Nash
Captain E. Oliver
Lieutenant E. C.
Pashley
Captain A. H. Peck
Lieutenant L. F. Powell
Lieutenant A. H.
Pritchard
Captain P. B. Prothero
Major J. B. Quested
Lieutenant-Colonel L.
W. B. Rees VC**
Captain W. V. T. Rooper
Captain W. J. Ruther-
ford
Captain F. G. Saunders
Captain O. J. F. Scholte
Lieutenant H. W. Sellars
Lieutenant W. K.
Simon*
Captain G. G. Simpson
Lieutenant J. H. Smith
F/Sublieutenant L. F. W.
Smith
Captain J. K. Summers
Lieutenant A. G. Vlasto
Lieutenant J. W. Warner
Lieutenant C. M.
Wilson
Captain W. A. Wright
7 kills
Lieutenant F. Allberry

Captain C. P. Allen
Captain J. W. Aldred (8)
Lieutenant T. H. Barkell
Major R. R. Barker
Corporal A. Beebee
Captain A. Bell Irving
Captain T. H. Blaxland
(8)
Captain W. A. Bond (5)
Captain A. J. Bott (5)
Captain E. W.
Broadberry (8)
Lieutenant A. Buchanan
Captain L. Campbell
Captain A. Claydon
Lieutenant J. C.
Courade
Lieutenant R. N.
Chandler
Major C. M. B
Chapman
Captain R. M. Charley
F/Lieutenant W. H.
Chisam
Captain S. Cockerell
Captain A. Cole (6)
Captain G. K. Cooper
Captain E. D. Crundall
Lieutenant A. S.
Cunningham Reid
Lieutenant J. E. A. R.
Daly
Lieutenant R. W. Daly
Captain E. E. Davies
Lieutenant E. F. H.
Davis
Lieutenant P. R.
Dennett
Lieutnant J. H.
Dewhirst
Lieutenant C. H.
Dickens
Lieutenant H. E. Dolan
Captain J. O. Donaldson
Lieutenant T. A. Doran
Captain H. F. S. Drewitt
Lieutenant C. G.
Edwards
Lieutenant H. E. O. Ellis
Captain C. Mc. G.
Farrel
Lieutenant R. M.
Fletcher
Captain M. M. Freehill
Captain C. B. Glynn (8)
Captain W. B. Green
Captain F. L. Hale
Lieutenant F. V. Hall
Captain H. J. Hamilton
(6)
Lieutenant H. H.
Hartley
Lieutenant-Colonel H.
E. Hartney
Captain I. H. D.

Henderson
Captain W. C. Hilborn
Lieutenant P. K. Hobson
Lieutenant F. J. Hunt (9)
Lieutenant N. W. Hustings
Captain L. W. Jarvis
Lieutenant A. Jenks
Lieutenant A. Jerrard
Captain W. Fielding Johnson (6)
Lieutenant A. L. Jones
Captain G. Jones
Major H. W. G. Jones
Lieutenant H. W. Joslyn
Lieutenant E. P. Kenney
Captain A. S. G. Lee
Captain A. A. Leitch
Lieutenant R. K. McConnell
Lieutenant H. O. Macdonald
Lieutenant W. M. McDonald
Lieutenant P. J. McGinness
F/Lt N. M. Macgregor
Captain M. C. McGregor (11)
Captain W. Maclanachan
Lieutenant M. P. Macleod

Captain H. H. Maddocks
Captain H. M. Moody (8)
Major R. B. Munday
Major A. Murray Jones
Lieutenant W. J. B. Nel
Captain C. W. Odell
Captain A. H. Orlebar
Lieutnant R. J. Owen
F/Lieutenant J. A. Page
Lieutenant A. J. Palliser
Captain W. D. Patrick
Captain W. R. G. Pearson
Lieutenant G. C. Peters
Lieutenant-Colonel C. F. A. Portal★★
Lieutenant J. C. Preston
Lieutenant W. T. Price
Lieutenant L. W. Ray
Captain J. M. Robb★★
Lieutenant E. M. Roberts
Captain H. L. Satchell (8)
Lieutenant D. A. Savage
Lieutenant H. Scandrett
Lieutenant K. G. Seth Smith
Captain L. H. Slatter
Lieutenant E. A. L. F. Smith
Lieutenant F. C. Stanton
Captain C. R. Steele

Lieutenant C. O. Stone
Captain G. J. Strange
Major W. V. Strugnall (6)
Lieutenant C. L. Stubbs
Captain O. M. Sutton
Captain A. G. V. Taylor
Lieutenant M. S. Taylor
Captain D. M. Tidmarsh
Captain S. T. Todd
Captain T. C. Traill
Lieutenant N. Trecowthick
Captain H. E. Walker
Lieutenant H. J. Walker-dine
Captain H. L. Wallis
Captain H. A. White★
Captain P. Wilson
Lieutenant F. C. Wilton
Captain J. W. Woodhouse
Major A. M. Vaucour
6 kills
Captain J. V. Aspinall
Lieutenant L. A. Ashfield
Lieutenant G. C. Bailey (8)
Sergeant J. M. Bainbridge
1st Lieutenant H. L. Bair
Lieutenant J. L. Barlow
Captain F. L. Barwell
Captain C. L. Bissel
Lieutenant C. A. Bissonette
Captain H. A. R. Biziou (8)
Lieutenant W. H. Bland
Lieutenant N. S. Boulton
Major C. Brand
Lieutenant C. G. Brock
Captain E. G. Brooks
Lieutenant J. C. Bush
Captain D. H. DeBurgh
Captain W. J. Cairns
Lieutenant G. G. S. Candy
Captain H. G. Clappison
Captain S. E. Cowan (7)
Lieutenant J. H. Colbert
Lieutenant R. E. Conder
Captain M. L. Cooper
Lieutenant N. Cooper
Captain E. D. Clarke
Lieutenant H. G. Clements
Lieutnant E. F. Crabb

F/Sublieutenant T. G. Culling
Captain W. G. S. Curphey
Captain H. B. Davey
Lieutnant C. R. Davidson
Captain H. G. W. Debenham
Captain J. E. Drummond
Captain D. L. Evans
Lieutenant G. S. J. Evans
F/Commander C. A. Eyre
Lieutenant R. W. Farquhar
Lieutenant J. P. Findlay
Captain G. B. Foster (7)
Lieutenant H. H. S. Fowler
Lieutenant A. W. Franklyn
Lieutenant R. W. Fumer
Captain D. M. B. Galbraith
Lieutenant R. C. A. Gifford
Captain G. H. D. Gossip
Sergeant J. Grant
Captain R. Gregory
Captain D. Grinnel Milne
Captain E. D. Gundall
Lieutenant. A. J. Haines
Captain H. J. Hamilton
Lieutenant L. Hamilton
Lieutenant G. S. L. Haymard
Lieutenant R. A. Hewat
Captain W. C. Hilburn
Captain W. G. R. Hinchliffe
Captain F. N. Hudson
Major V. H. Huston
Captain G. R. Jones
Gun Layer W. Jones
Lieutenant E. T. S. Kelly
Lieutenant H. C. Knotts
Captain O. C. LeBlanc
Lieutenant T. A. M. S. Lewis
Lieutenant G. A. Lingham
Captain A. T. Loyd
Captain T. C. Luke
Lieutenant M. McCall
Lieutenant C. R. McKenzie
Lieutenant R. W. McKenzie
Captain J. Mackereth
Captain R. McLaughlin

Captain Howard John Thomas Saint, DSC, of 10(N) Squadron in Sopwith Triplane N5380 during August 1917. He was later Chief Test Pilot for the Gloster Aircraft Company.

Lieutenant O. L.
McMaking
Captain R. G. Malcolm
(8)
Captain G. F. Malley
Lieutenant M. J. J. G.
Mare-Montebault
Lieutenant T. W. Martin
Captain F. H. M.
Maynard
Captain E. T. Morrow
(7)
Lieutenant A. W. B.
Miller
Captain N. C. Millman
Lieutenant D. J. W. M.
Moore
Lieutenant K. K.
Muspratt (8)
Lieutenant G. E. Nash
Sergeant A. Newland
Lieutenant A. Paget
G. A. H. Pidcock
Captain C. F. Pineau★
S. L. G. Pope
Lieutenant T. G. Rae
Major R. Raymond
Barker
Lieutenant A. Rice-
Oxley
Captain H. A. Rigby
Lieutenant H. R.
Rhodes
Lieutenant F. A.
Robertson
Lieutenant B. Rogers★
Captain H. S. T. Saint
(7)
Lieutenant T. Seaman
Green
Captain W. Selwyn
Lieutenant D. E. Smith
Lieutenant C. R.
Smythe
Major O. Stewart
Captain G. Strange (7)
Major R. Stuart Wortley
Captain O. M. Sutton
(7)
Lieutenant W. K.
Swayze
Captain H. L. Symons
Lieutenant C. R.
Thompson (6)
Lieutenant C. R. J.
Thompson
Lieutenant G. L. Trapp
Lieutnant P. M.
Tudhope
Lieutenant A. H. Turner
(6)
Lieutenant H. E. Watson
Lieutenant J. J.
Wellwood
Captain W. G.

Westwood
Lieutenant W. A.
Wheeler
Lieutenant H. A. White
Lieutenant W. O. B.
Winkler
Captain A. B. Yuille

5 kills

Lieutenant J. A.
Aldridge
Captain L. W. Allen
G. F. Anderson
Captain D. V.
Armstrong
Major A. R. Arnold
Captain M. H. Aten
Lieutenant F. Babbage
Captain L. D. Baker
Captain L. D. Bawlf
Captain M. A.
Benjamin
Lieutenant R. M.
Bennett
Captain F. Billinge
Lieutenant A. W. Blake
Lieutenant A. V.
Blenkiron
Captain G. Blennerhas-
sett
Captain G. H. Boarman
Captain W. O. Boger
Lieutenant R. Bollinds
Lieutenant E. B. Booth
Captain W. A. Bond
Captain A. J. Bott
Lieutenant F. S. Bowles
Lieutenant H. K.
Boysen
Lieutenant G.
Bremridge
Captain A. R. Brown
Lieutenant S. M. Brown
Captain W. J. Cairnes
Major J. C. Callaghan
1st Lieutenant L. K.
Callahan
2nd Lieutenant D. E.
Cameron
Captain D. H. M.
Carberry
Lieutenant R. N.
Chandler
Lieutenant J. E. Childs
Captain A. G. Clark
Lieutenant E. D. Clark
(6)
Lieutenant H. G.
Clements (6)
Captain S. Cockerall (7)
Lieutenant H. N.
Compton
Lieutenant. H. A.
Cooper
Captain N. Cooper (6)
Lieutenant G. J. Cox

Captain G. M. Cox
Captain K. Crawford
Captain J. B. Crompton
Lieutenant K. Crossen
Lieutenant R. C.
Crowden
Lieutenant H. G. Crowe
Captain G. B. Crole
1st Lieutenant J. O.
Creech
Captain G. L.
Cruikshank
Lieutenant R. J. Cullen
Captain L. Cummings
Captain F. J. Cunning-
hame
Captain S. Dalrymple
Captain C. J. W. Darwin
F/Commander M. J. G.
Day
Lieutenant P. A. De
Fontenay
Major B. P. H.
DeRoeper
Captain E. B. Drake
Major C. S. Duffus
Lieutenant R. Dunston
Lieutenant E. C. Eaton
Captain H. J. Edwards
Lieutenant H. W. Elliot
F/Sublieutenant S. E.
Ellis
Lieutenant H. C. Evans
Captain W. R. Fish
Major E. L. Foot
Lieutenant J. V.
Gascoyne
Lieutenant G. W. Gauld
Lieutenant H. R. Gauld
Lieutenant W. B. Giles
Lieutenant D. H. S.

Gilbertson
Lieutnant W. B.
Gillespie
Lieutenant C. G. Glass
Lieutenant M. E.
Gonne
Lieutenant H. A. F.
Goodison
Captain E. R. Grange
Lieutenant W. E. Gray
Sergeant J. H. R. Green
Captain E. C. Gribben
Captain J. P. Hales
Captain J. E. Hallon-
quist (6)
Major A. T. Harris★★
Lieutenant R. B. Hay
Lieutenant E. S.
Headlam
Captain R. G. Hewitt
Captain O. Horsley
Lieutenant P. F. C.
Howe
Lieutenant M. G.
Howell
Captain D. J. Hughes
Captain E. Y. Hughes
Sergeant E. C. Hunt
Captain T. V. Hunter
Lieutenant C. E. Hurst
Captain G. A. Hyde
Captain A. G. Jarvis
Lieutenant E. R. Jeffree
Lieutenant C. H. Jeffs
Captain O. C. W.
Johnsen
Captain C. Kingsford
Smith★
Lieutenant K. J. P. Laing
Lieutenant D.
Langlands

Major H. G. White,
Commanding Officer of
29 Squadron, who later
became an Air Vice-
Marshal in the RAF.

Captain J. D. Latta
Captain F. H. Laurence
Captain G. E. B.
  Lawson (6)
Lieutenant J. S. Lennox
Lieutenant E. W.
  Lindeberg
Lieutenant J. D.
  Lightbody
Lieutenant E. Lindup
Lieutenant R. H. Little
Captain G. L. Lloyd
Lieutenant F. E. Luff
Lieutenant C. G. O.
  Macandrew
Lieutenant R. K.
  McConnel (7)
Captain E. Mc Hand
Lieutenant R. M.
  Macdonald
Captain L. J. Maclean
Major R. St. Clair
  McLintock
Captain J. H.
  McNearney
Lieutenant J. F. N.
  Macrae
Lieutenant R. F. McRae
Lieutenant P. S. Manley
Captain L. M.
  Mansbridge
Lieutenant W. S.
  Mansell
Lieutenant F. P. Magoun
Lieutenant W. D.
  Matthews
Lieutenant A. Matthews
Lieutenant W. H.

Maxted
Lieutenant H. W.
  Medlicott
Captain E. S. Meek
Lieutenant W. G.
  Meggit (6)
Lieutenant F. J. Mellersh
Lieutenant F. T. S.
  Menendez
Lieutenant K. C. Mills
Captain H. A. S.
  Molyneux
Lieutenant J. T. Morgan
Lieutenant L. L.
  Morgan
Captain W. J. Mostyn
1st Lieutenant D. F.
  Murman
Captain R. H. G.
  Neville
Lieutenant T. H.
  Newsome
Captain T. A. Oliver
Lieutenant O. J. Orr
Lieutenant E. E. Owen
Captain A. R. Oxley
Captain W. J. Pace
Captain E. R. Pennell
Lieutenant E. H.
  Peverell
Major C. E. M.
  Pickthorne
Lieutenant G. R. Poole
Lieutenant D. S. Poller
Lieutenant H. J. Pratt
Lieutenant. W. A. Pritt
1st Lieutenant O. A.
  Ralston★
Captain J. W. Rayner
Lieutenant G. P. S. Reid
Major G. R. Mc. Reid
Lieutenant A. G. Riley
Lieutenant N. Roberts
Lieutenant A. E.
  Robertson
Major H. A. van
  Rynveld
Lieutenant-Colonel W.
  D. S. Sanday
Captain R. H. M. S.
  Saundby★★
Lieutenant-Colonel A. J.
  L. Scott
Captain J. P. Seabrook
Captain O. J. F. Selous
Lieutenant F. Sharp
Captain T. S. Sharpe
  (6)
1st Lieutenant H. G.
  Shoemaker
Major W. Sholto
  Douglas★★
Captain E. L. Simonson
Lieutenant W. A. Smart
Lieutenant H. C. Smith

Captain S. P. Smith
Captain N. R. Smuts
Lieutnant W. H. Sneath
Lieutenant A. R.
  Spurling
Lieutenant I. O. Stead
Sergeant T. F.
  Stephenson
Captain F. D. Stevens
Major O. Stewart
Captain V. R. Stokes
Lieutenant E. Taylor
Captain M. Thomas
1st Lieutenant W. D.
  Tipton
Lieutenant G. Tod
2nd Lieutenant R. M.
  Todd
F/Commander H. G.
  Travers
Lieutenant J. S. Turnbull
Lieutenant J. H. Umney
Lieutenant E. R. Varley
Lieutenant R. B.
  Wainright
Captain A. G. Waller
Lieutenant K. M.
  Walker
Lieutenant G. A. Welsh
Lieutenant M. S. West
Lieutenant F. Westing
Captain L. E.
  Whitehead
Lieutenant R. K.
  Whitney
Lieutenant E. G. H. C.
  Williams
Captain F. J. Williams
Lieutenant C. F. C.
  Wilson
F/Commander R. R.
  Winter
Captain J. H. G.
  Womersley
Major H. A. Wood
Captain C. H. C.
  Woolven
Lieutenant A. E.
  Woodbridge
Lieutenant C. E.
  Worthington
Lieutenant V. M. Yeates
Lieutenant G. C. Young
Captain E. L. Zink

Bomber and Gunner Aces

To cover – as far as is possible – all aces, fighter, bomber and gunner, it is necessary to categorise bomber pilots and gunners in a separate section for exact information as to

flying brevet status.
Some names may
therefore appear twice
in the overall lists.

Bomber Pilots
16 kills Captain D. A.
  Stewart
14 kills Captain E.
  Dickson
11 kills Captain A. G.
  Waller
10 kills Lieutenant C. R.
  Pithey (H. Rhodes)
9 kills Lieutenant G.
  Darvill
8 kills
CPO Bartlett
Captain L. R. Warren
Captain W. E. Green
Major E. G. Joy
Captain J. S. Stubbs
7 kills
Captain J. Gamon
Captain G. Fox Rule
F/Commander T. Le
  Mesurier
Captain A. Roulstone
Captain F. M. C. Turner
6 kills
Lieutenant L. A. Ashfield
Lieutenant R. L. M.
  Barbour
Captain G. Bowman
Lieutenant R. Chalmers
Sergeant D. E. Edgley
Captain H. R. Gould
Captain D. S. Hall
Lieutenant C. J.
  Heywood
Lieutenant J. Keating★
Captain A. McGregor
Captain L. Minot
Lieutenant P. O'Leiff
Lieutenant A. R.
  Spurling
Lieutenant F. C. Wilton
5 kills
Lieutenant P. E.
  Appleby
Captain E. D. Asbury
Captain R. Atkinson
Captain D. H. M.
  Carberry
Lieutenant W. Clarke
Lieutenant W. B. Elliot
Lieutenant W. Grossart
Captain O. C. W.
  Johnsen
Lieutenant C. I. Lally
Captain C. R. Lupton
Captain L. H. Pearson
Captain W. J. Pace
Captain J. E. Pugh
Captain C. H. Stokes

Lieutenant Walbanke Ashby-Pritt, MC. His youthful looks belied his gallant, aggressive, dashing combat in the air. He said he was 20 years of age!

Bomber Gunners/ Observers

13 kills Gunner Naylor

11 kills Lieutenant H. Rhodes

9 kills Lieutenant L. Christian

8 kills

Lieutenant G. Blenner-hasset

Corporal L. Emsden

Sergeant J. Grant

Lieutenant F. Leathley

7 kills

Lieutenant D. L. Burgess

Gunner C. Robinson

6 kills

Sergeant F. W. Bell

Lieutenant F. A. Britton

Lieutenant S. H. Hamblin

Lieutenant P. Holligan

Gunner L. Jackson

Lieutenant F. T. S. Menendez

Sergeant W. Middleton

Lieutenant W. Miller

Lieutenant R. Scott

Lieutenant E. A. Simpson

Lieutenant E. Walker

5 kills

Captain L. Collins

Sergeant L. S. Court

Lieutenant F. C. Craig

Lieutenant C. G. Dance

Sergeant W. Dyke

Lieutenant C. E. Eddy

Lieutenant H. C. T. Gompertz

Lieutenant C. P. Harrison

Lieutenant E. P. Hartigan

Sergeant M. B. Kilroy

Sergeant S. F. Langstone

Lieutenant H. Mackay

Lieutenant L. L. T. Sloot

Lieutenant J. R. Smith

Lieutenant C. N. Whitham

Gunners/Observers

39 kills Lieutenant C. G. Cass

26 kills Sergeant R. M. Fletcher

25 kills Lieutenant G. S. L. Hayward

24 kills Lieutenant T. C. Noel

21 kills Captain F. R. Cubbon

21 kills Lieutenant H. L. Edwards

21 kills Sergeant A. Newland

20 kills Lieutenant L. A. Powell

16 kills Captain A. H. Wall

16 kills Sergeant J. J. Cowell

15 kills

Sergeant E. A. Deighton

Lieutenant J. R. Gordon

Sergeant J. Jones

Lieutenant A. Mills

Lieutenant B. D. Worsley

14 kills

Lieutenant G. Thomson

Captain F. Libby

13 kills

Lieutenant F. J. Ralph

Lieutenant J. H. Umney

Lieutenant D. P. F. Uniacke

12 kills

Lieutenant C. G. Boothroyd

Lieutenant P. V. G. Chambers

Captain F. Godfrey

Lieutenant E. Hardcastle

Lieutenant G. H. Kemp

Lieutenant J. L. Morgan

Lieutenant W. Noble

Lieutenant J. Scaramanga

Lieutenant M. W. Waddington

Captain D. E. Waight

11 kills

Captain H. Claye

Lieutenant T. E. Elliot

Captain J. H. Hedley

10 kills

Lieutenant V. S. B. Collins

Lieutenant C. A. Hoy

Lieutenant J. Rudkin

9 kills

Lieutenant C. Angelasto

Lieutenant W. Barnes

Sergeant W. Beales

Lieutenant G. V. Learmond

Lieutenant J. McDonald

Lieutenant A. W. Merchant

Lieutenant H. E. Merrit

Lieutenant A. R. Ness

Lieutenant S. Parry

Corporal V. Reed

Lieutenant I. Thompson

Lieutenant R. W. Turner

Lieutenant A. E. Wear

8 kills

Lieutenant S. W. Bunting

Lieutenant H. G. Crowe

Lieutenant P. Douglas

Lieutenant C. Gladman

Sergeant W. Holmes

Sergeant H. C. Hunt

Lieutenant A. N. Jenks

Lieutenant S. A. W. Knight

Lieutenant A. D. Light

Corporal M. Mather

Lieutenant L. E. Mitchell

Lieutenant W. O'Toole

Lieutenant C. C. Robson

Lieutenant W. W. Smith

Lieutenant L. W. Sutherland

Lieutenant C. J. Tolman

7 kills

Lieutenant I. W. F. Agabeg

Lieutenant L. W. Allen

Sergeant D. Antcliffe

Lieutenant T. Birmingham

Lieutenant G. A. Brooke

Captain L. W. Burbidge

Lieutenant A. C. Cooper

Lieutenant R. Critchley

Lieutenant A. S. Draisey

Lieutenant H. E. Easton

Lieutenant G. Finlay

Lieutenant E. C. Gilroy

Lieutenant W. Grant

Lieutenant R. F. Hill

Private J. Hill

Air Mechanic E. Hoare

Lieutenant A. W. Kirk

Corporal F. J. Knowles

Lieutenant H. Owen

Private F. A. Potter

Lieutenant I. H. Scott

Lieutenant B. H. Smyth

Lieutenant J. Tennant

Lieutenant W. Tinsley

Lieutenant A. Tranter

Lieutenant P. S. Williams

6 kills

Lieutenant M. A. Benjamin

Lieutenant W. C. Cambray

Lieutenant T. S. Chiltren

Sergeant C. Hill

Air Mechanic B. Jackson

Lieutenant T. Lewis

Air Mechanic H. Lingfield

Lieutenant L. H. McRobert

Lieutenant E. S. Moore

Lieutenant M. K. Parlee

Sergeant E. H. Sayers

Lieutenant T. C. Tuffield

Lieutenant W. U. Tyrell

Lieutenant V. R. S. White

5 kills

Lieutenant A. E. Ansell

Sergeant W. G. Benger

Lieutenant R. G. Bennet

Lieutenant G. W. Blacklock

Lieutenant J. Bruce Norton

Lieutenant E. Caulfield Kelly

Lieutenant C. W. Davies

Lieutenant H. R. Eldon

Lieutenant H. Fysh

Lieutenant W. T. Gibson

Sergeant J. H. Hall

Lieutenant R. S. Herring

Sergeant G. F. Hines

Lieutenant W. Hodgkinson

Lieutenant P. G. Jones

Lieutenant F. J. Kydd

Lieutenant R. Lowe

Lieutenant G. McCormack

Lieutenant M. A. McKenzie

Lieutenant S. H. P. Masding

Corporal J. Mason

Lieutenant H. E. Moore

Lieutenant J. G. Murison

Lieutenant E. A. Mustard

Air Mechanic S. H. Platel

Private T. Proctor

Lieutenant J. H. Robertson

Sergeant G. Shannon

Lieutenant A. J. H. Thornton

Lieutenant E. H. Vessey

Lieutenant E. H. Ward

Lieutenant W. J. A. Weir

Captain J. L. L. Williams

FRANCE

French military aviation truly began in 1909 when the War Ministry bought an American Wright aircraft. The French War Minister then ordered that French industry produce French-designed and -built aircraft. By 1913 the French were exporting over 400 aircraft a year.

Two Farman biplanes, one Wright biplane and one Blériot monoplane were bought and delivered in spring 1910; by the end of the year this force had expanded to eleven Henri Farmans, four Maurice Farmans, five Wrights, four Summers, four Blériots and two Antoinettes. In March 1910, ten French military officers were sent to private flying schools and eventually formed the nucleus of the embryo French Air Service. The first airman to pass out as a military pilot was Lieutenant Camerman, with Aéro Club de France Brevet No.33. A military pilot's brevet came into service use in March 1911, with the first holder being Capitaine Trocornet de Rose.

Initially, military aviation was divided into two parts, half under the artillery, half under the engineers. In March 1912 the French Air Service was formally constituted and formed into three branches, as the French military saw the use of aircraft: fighter, reconnaissance and bombing.

When World War One began in August 1914 the French Air Service comprised 21 Escadrille (squadrons), the names of each reflecting the aircraft used: Blériot BL; Henri Farman – HF; Maurice Farman – MF; Deperdussin – D; Dorand – DO; Bréguet – BR; Voisin – V; Caudron – C; Nieuport – N; and REP – R. There were also four cavalry Escadrilles, making a total strength of 138 aircraft.

At war with the German Air Service in the new dimension – the sky – the French (and the Germans) had to work out aerial combat: there was no convenient handbook of rules laid down yet. The first bombing raid of the war was made by Lieutenant Ce'sari and Caporal Pindhommeau in a Voisin of the French Air Service against the German Zeppelin hangars at Metz-Frescaty on 14 August 1914. The first aerial combat with firearms was on 5 October when a Voisin of Escadrille V24, piloted by Sergent Joseph Frantz with Caporal Louis Quenault as observer. shot down an Aviatik of Flieger Abteilung 18, using rifle fire.

It was not long before airmen began to fit machine-guns to their aircraft. Caporal Stribick, piloting a Henri Farman with Observer David, shot down a German spotter aircraft using a Hotchkiss heavy machine-gun. fired from the rear cockpit. Both airmen were awarded the Médaille Militaire for this exploit.

The first French single-seater fighter to down a German aircraft, with a machine-gun firing forward through the propeller arc, was a Morane-Saulnier Type G of Escadrille MS23, piloted by Roland Garros. On 1 April 1915. Garros fitted deflector plates to the wooden propeller to protect it from bullets from the machine-gun. Eventually machine-guns were fitted to fire forward through the arc of the propeller. using synchronising interrupter gear. This changed the tactics of air fighting wholesale. and the aggressive fighter pilot came into his own, being able to fly and fire his guns at the same time.

This new development was put to good use by far-sighted French commanders, who began to use fighters to keep away German reconnaissance and spotter aircraft from their troop movements during the Verdun offensive of 21 February 1916. Success was achieved by flying near-continuous fighting patrols that cleared the enemy from the front.

The same tactic was used by the French during the July 1916 Battle of the Somme – again with excellent results from the Nieuport Scouts of Escadrilles Nos. N3, N26, N37, N62, N65, N73 and N103. This grouping of large numbers of aircraft resulted in the formation of permanent combat groups (groupes de combat), each composed of four chasse Escadrilles. By 4 February 1918 there were 21 combat groups. and these began to be amalgamated into larger units: three combat groups comprised an Escadre de Combat, with No. 1 Escadre coming into being that day, made up of Combat Groups 15, 18 and 19. Three weeks later another Escadre de Combat was formed, comprised of Combat Groups 11, 13 and 17. Bombing Groups (Groupes de Bombardment) 5, 6 and 9 were amalgamated into Escadre de Bombardment No. 12, and Bombing Groups 3 and 4 into Escadre de Bombardment No. 13. On 14 May 1918 the 1st Air Division (Division Aérienne) was created – consisting of the units listed above – under the command of General Duval.

The Division Aérienne was used to great effect during the Battle of the Marne – on 15 July 1918 – when great numbers of French aircraft were switched from one part of the offensive front to any other as directed and required. During the great US Army offensive at St. Mihiel in August the French air division was used, again with great effect. The US commander – Colonel 'Billy' Mitchell – requested and got the French air division to fight alongside his air power. Opposing the Allies were the best German squadrons, but by 26 September 1918 the St. Mihiel offensive was won and the final push forward began. However the German Air Service could still do damage, and September 1918 was the worst month for Allied air casualties since 'Bloody April' in 1917.

During World War One the French aircraft industry produced some excellent aircraft as the following alphabetical list demonstrates:

Blériot XI Unarmed single-seater reconnaissance type; two- and three-seater XI-2 Genie (engineer) and XI-2 Artillerie (artillery) marques were used until mid-1915.

Bréguet The Bréguet biplane had a metal-covered fuselage with a tractor engine. Prior to World War One the Bréguet was in service with Escadrille BR17 only.

The Bréguet 2, 4 and 5 were two-seat 'pusher' biplane bombers that came into service during 1915. Some 45 were bought by the British RNAS and used with success.

The two-seat reconnaissance/bomber Bréguet 14 biplane had an advanced – for its time – metal fuselage. The pilot's seat was armoured to protect against ground fire. The A2 reconnaissance version and B2 day bomber came into service during 1917.

Caudron Type G2 single-seater reconnaissance biplane had twin-boom tails. It was followed by the improved G3 two-seater with an 80hp Gnome engine that served as an unarmed reconnaissance/bomber until 1917. When war broke out the French Air Service had but one six-strong Caudron G3 unit – Escadrille C11 – which was used by the Army for artillery spotting. The G3 was used in Mesopotamia by the RFC and in Italy, Belgium, Russia; the USAS used it as a trainer.

The next marque was the twin-engined G4 bomber, armed with one or two machine-guns and used for daylight formation bombing raids on the German Rhineland. The more powerful G6 came after the G4 but the later (June 1915) R4 was successful as a heavily armed photo-reconnaissance aircraft, and Escadrille C46 shot down 34 German aircraft. The French ace Capitaine Lecour Grandmaison was shot down and killed with one of his gunners, Caporal Crozet, whilst flying an R4 on 10 May 1917; the second gunner, Sergent Boye, took the controls and crash-landed the aircraft in French territory.

The R11 was armed with five machine-guns, one of them firing downwards. This heavy firepower proved successful in a bomber escort role during the French bomber offensive in July 1918.

Deperdussin TT These two-seater shoulder-wing monoplanes were used in small numbers for reconnaissance at the beginning of the war. Escadrilles D4 and D6 were the only units equipped with the TT; the British Royal Navy bought several for evaluation, but the aircraft was out of date with its wing-warping flying controls, and it was soon obsolete.

Dorand The DO1 two-seater reconnaissance biplane was used in the early part of the war by Escadrille DO22. It was not successful and was replaced. Later models were the AR1 and AR2 used in 1917 to 1918 – eighteen Escadrilles were equipped with these models.

Farman The British-born but France-based Farman brothers – Henri and Maurice – designed and produced a series of successful two-seater pusher biplane aircraft. Each brother produced his own designs, using their names independently but using the same factory. Farsightedly, they had their factory up and running just prior to the outbreak of World War One.

Henri Farman produced the F.20, F.21, F.22 and F.27. These were underpowered, pusher-type, two-seater reconnaissance biplanes which could also be used as light bombers. By 1915 they were relegated to training duties. The F.27 was a metal-skeletoned four-wheel aircraft of which 80 were bought by the British and used in Africa, the Middle East and the Dardanelles by the RNAS and RFC.

The Maurice MF.7 (Type 1913) and MF.11 (Type 1914) were early aircraft, two-seaters with the observer in front with a Lewis or Hotchkiss machine-gun. Power units were De Dion or Renault engines. The MF.7 was nicknamed the 'Longhorn' and the MF11 the 'Shorthorn' due to their appearance, outriggers and frontal elevators being used.

In 1915 the Farman brothers pooled the best parts of their designs and came up with the Farman F.30, F.40, F.41, F.56, F.60 and F.61 aircraft. The F.40 was a two-seater pusher biplane armed with a Lewis gun, and occasionally with Le Prieur rockets fitted to the wings. A few light bombs could be carried. The F.30 was used mainly by the Russian Aviation Service. The F.50 Bn2. was a two-seater twin tractor-engined heavy night bomber carrying 1,000lb of bombs that saw action in September 1918, with Escadrilles F.110 and F.114.

Early in 1917 most Farmans (though not the F50.Bn2) were made obsolete by the French Government.

Hanriot Built by M. Hanriot and designed by Dupont, the Hanriot HD-1 single-seat biplane fighter came into service in 1916. Strangely, the aircraft proved most popular with the Belgian and Italian Air Services. Major Willy Coppens (37 victories) was the outstanding exponent of the HD-1.

Morane-Saulnier aircraft Morane-Saulnier and Saulnier began to design and build aircraft in 1911, and their Type L Parasol monoplanes were considered to be the first fighters. The first Morane-Saulnier aircraft to come into service with the RFC, in small numbers, was the MS BB biplane, in 1915.

The Type L was fast and nimble, and took a great toll of the German Albatros and Aviatik aircraft. The then Caporal Guynemer of Escadrille MS3 made his first kill in a Type L, with his mechanic/gunner Guerder, on 15 July 1915. Flight Sub-Lieutenant Warneford, RNAS, destroyed Zeppelin LZ37 on 7 June 1915, flying Type L number 3253. This exploit won him the Victoria Cross.

The Morane-Saulnier Type N – known to the British as the 'Bullet' – was a mid-wing single-seater fighter monoplane. The first French ace, Navarre, shot down several German aircraft in a Type N before he was shot down and killed in action. Another ace, Pegoud, downed six German aircraft in them before he too was killed in action.

Nieuport Edouard de Nieuport began to design and produce monoplane aircraft before World War One broke out. He had broken the world's air speed record on 21 June 1911, but was killed in an air crash on 16 September that year. However, his first designs of small, well-built monoplanes were used in World War One – outstanding being the Nieuport Type 6M (M standing for Militaire) which saw service with Escadrille N12 and with Italian squadrons. Some were used by the Russian Aviation Service. During 1914 the Nieuport company acquired the services of designer/engineer Gustave Delage and retained them during the duration of the war.

The first World War One design was the Nieuport 10 two-seater biplane, which due to its lack of power was flown as a single-seater when two guns were carried. The N12 was larger and more powerful, with a Lewis gun for the observer and a fixed Vickers for the pilot. The Nieuport 11 and 16 marques followed, both single-seater biplane fighters. The N11, in service from 1915–17, was known as the Bébé from its small size. The N16 was bigger and better, with a 100hp Le Rhône engine.

The outstanding Nieuport was the N17, which came into service in 1916. Fitted with either the 110hp Le Rhône or 130hp Clerget engines. the Type 17 was one of the outstanding fighter aircraft of the war. Nieuport Marks 21 and 23 were also produced. The Nieuport line continued with the 24, 27, 28C1, and the Nieuport Delage 29 in 1918.

Letord The Letord Marks 1, 4 and 5 reconnaissance bombers were developed by Colonel Dorand from the Caudron R.4 twin-engined biplane. The Letord 1 three-seater, carrying a pilot and two Lewis gunners, went into production late in 1916 and came into service in 1917. The Letord 5 came into service in 1918 and was used for long-range photography.

REP Robert Esnault-Pelterie designed the Type N two-seater reconnaissance monoplane, which was used in small numbers between 1914–15 by Escadrille 15 and later by REP27. Another design, the REP Parasol, was a two-seater reconnaissance aircraft, twelve of which saw service in the RNAS only. There was no French use of the REP Parasol.

Salmson Emile Salmson formed the Société des Moteurs Salmson in 1909 and produced the Salmson Type 2 late in 1916, the prototype flying in April 1917. This two-seater biplane was a solid, well-made machine, and well liked as a reliable reconnaissance aircraft. Fitted with one Vickers and two Lewis machine-guns, it could give a good account of itself. One US Air Service pilot – Lieutenant W. P. Erwin – destroyed eight German aircraft whilst flying the Salmson 2A2. Some 22 French Escadrilles were equipped with the Salmson, as were eleven US Air Service Squadrons. Exactly 3,200 Salmson 2A2s were produced.

Paul Schmitt French, in spite of his German name, Paul Schmitt's Type 7 was a big, single-engined biplane heavy bomber. This type was developed from his Aérobus design of 1913 which could carry nine passengers. The Type 7 B2 had a 200hp Renault engine and could carry 200lb of bombs with a pilot and an observer/gunner armed with two machine-guns. Schmitt's Type 7/4 design had four instead of two wheels.

The design quickly became obsolete, and by 1917 no more were made. Escadrilles PS125, PS126, PS127 and PS128 were equipped with Schmitt Types 7 and 7/4s.

SPAD The most famous of French single-seat fighters was the SPAD. The acronym was derived in August 1914 from 'Société Pour l'Aviation et ses Dérives', though the original pre-war acronym was 'Société Provisoire de Aéroplanes Deperdussin'. The Deperdussin TT was the generic ancestor of the SPAD, Louis Blériot having taken over the Deperdussin name in 1914.

The first SPAD A2 was a two-seater biplane first flown on 21 May 1915, powered by an 80hp Le Rhône engine and armed with a forward-firing machine-gun: the observer/gunner sat in a nacelle forward of the propeller! The SPAD A4 had a more powerful 110hp Le Rhône.

The famous SPAD 7 single-seater followed in May 1916 with a 140hp Hispano engine: Hispanos of up to 200hp were later fitted. It was armed with a fixed Vickers machine-gun firing forward – some pilots had an extra Lewis machine-gun fitted on the top wing. The SPAD 7 arrived at the front in late 1916 and quickly proved popular with the dashing French pilots. It was the favourite of the Les Cigognes (Stork) Escadrilles, and was flown by aces such as René Fonck and Georges Guynemer. SPAD 7s were also used by Italy, Russia, Belgium, Britain and the USA.

Further marks of the SPAD were produced: the S.12, S.13, S.14 and S.17. By 1917 the S.7 had been replaced by the S.13. The S.14 was a seaplane variant of the S.12. The S.17 of 1918 was equipped with a large 300hp Hispano Suiza engine and fitted with twin Vickers machine-guns mounted to fire through the airscrew arc. By the end of the war all but one of the French fighter Escadrilles were equipped with the SPAD.

Voisin The French used the two-seater Voisin in great numbers as follows: Types 1 and 2 were unarmed reconnaissance/observation aircraft; Type 3 was armed with a machine-gun for reconnaissance and observation; Type 4 was used for ground attack; Type 8 was a night bomber; and Type 10 was a heavy bomber.

The Type 8 was fitted with 220hp Peugeot engine and was somewhat bigger than its forerunners. Unusually, the aircraft was fitted with four wheels on its undercarriage – which proved remarkably effective. Almost 400lb of bombs were carried. In 1918 the Mark 10 appeared with a bigger 300hp Renault engine enabling it to carry some 600lb of bombs.

26 Escadrilles were equipped with Voisins during World War One and the French used them to great effect in bombing raids.

By the November 1918 Armistice the French Military Air Service had scored 2,049 confirmed aerial victories with another 1,901 probables, plus 357 balloons destroyed making a grand total of 4,307 victories. Aircraft strength had risen to 336 Escadrille, of which 74 were equipped with single-seater SPAD fighters. Personnel strength had risen from about 8,000 in May 1915 to 52,000 in November 1918.

Aircraft losses were about 3,700, of which some 2,000 were during 1918.

Victory totals below are listed as accurately as is possible, but there is a wide difference in some totals. René Fonck is officially credited with 75 victories but his actual total is believed to be 127. Unofficial totals are in parenthesis.

FRENCH/BRITISH RANKS

French Air Service	Royal Flying Corps	Royal Air Force
Colonel	Colonel	Group Captain
Lieutenant-Colonel	Lieutenant-Colonel	Wing Commander
Commandant	Major	Squadron Leader
Capitaine	Captain	Flight Lieutenant
Lieutenant	Lieutenant	Flying Officer
Sous Lieutenant	2nd Lieutenant	Pilot Officer
Adjutant Chef	Warrant Officer I	Warrant Officer I
Adjutant	Warrant Officer II	Warrant Officer II
Sergent Chef	Staff Sergeant	Flight Sergeant
Sergent	Sergeant	Sergeant
Caporal	Corporal	Corporal
Soldat	Private	Aircraftman 1 and 2

Sous Lieutenant Marius Jean Paul Elzeard Ambrogi (1895–1971) 14 victories

Born in Marseilles on 9 June 1895, Ambrogi began his military service on 25 September 1914. He was sent to the 2nd Infantry Regiment, then applied for pilot training. He trained at Juvisy and Dijon and was awarded flying brevet No.4477 on 15 September 1916.

His advanced flying training was completed at Avord, Caz and Pau, and then he was posted to Groupe de Combat N507 in February 1917, flying Nieuport aircraft. On 10 April he was sent to Escadrille N90 flying Nieuports on the 7th Army Front, where he scored his first victory on 30 October, shooting down DFW C V no. 127/17 of FA 46 over Commercy. His next success came on 6 January 1918 when he shot down an enemy two-seater over Régneville; this was followed by another on 16 May over Nomeny.

On 17 May 1918 he began a run of attacks on enemy observation balloons, a dangerous pursuit as the balloons were heavily defended by ground and fighter forces. Balloons were vital to the German High Command as they gave vital information on Allied forces and dispositions. Between 25 June and 18 October 1918 Ambrogi shot

down another ten balloons – two balloons went down on 18 October within the space of five minutes – making his total war victories fourteen. He was awarded the Médaille Militaire on 2 February 1918 followed by the Légion d'Honneur (Chevalier) on 11 August, then the Croix de Guerre with 10 Palmes and a star.

Surviving the war, Ambrogi stayed in the French Air Force until 1920. He was back in the French Air Force in World War Two: he flew with Groupe de Chasse No.1/8 flying Bloch 125 fighters and shot down a Dornier Do-17 near Cambrai. He had scored victories in two world wars – a superb achievement. Sous Lieutenant Ambrogi died on 25 April 1971 and was buried at the village of d'Artignose sur Verdun, France.

Lieutenant Jean Pierre Léon Bourjade (1889–1924) 28 victories

Born at Montauban in the Garonne on 25 May 1889, Bourjade was destined to enter the priesthood then become a missionary, but the war intervened and he was drafted into the 23rd Regiment of Artillery with the lowly rank of brigadier (corporal in artillery or cavalry!). He fought in the Battle of the Marne and was promoted to Maréchal des Logis (sergeant in cavalry and artillery). After two years he was further promoted to sous lieutenant in the 125th Brigade de Bombardiers (Brigade of Bombardiers).

Bourjade applied for a transfer to the aviation service and won flying brevet No.7457 on 20 October 1917, after finishing his flying training at Avord. He was sent to Escadrille N152 (Escadrille SPA152), 'The Crocodiles', flying Nieuports and SPADs, and became the foremost exponent of shooting down enemy observation balloons. Between 27

Above left: Lieutenant Ambrogi.

Above: Lieutenant Bourjade.

March and 29 October 1918 he scored 28 victories, all but one of them balloons. On 15 July he shot down three balloons in the space of five minutes. 'Balloon busting' was a dangerous job: the German balloons were protected by heavy anti-aircraft fire and swarms of fighters. Bourjade was wounded in action on 19 July by ground fire.

Bourjade remained with SPA152 until the end of the war. He was awarded the Légion d'Honneur (Chevalier) and Légion d'Honneur (Officer), and the Croix de Guerre with 17 Palmes. Surviving the war, he became a missionary and died in New Guinea on 22 October 1924.

Capitaine Albert Louis Deullin (1890–1923) 20 victories

Born on 24 August 1890 in Epernay, Marne, Deullin began his military service at the age of 16 and by 1912 was an NCO in 31 Régiment de Dragons. In August 1914 he was posted to 8 Régiment de Dragons, and promoted to sous lieutenant in 1915.

Capitaine Deullin.

Deullin transferred to the aviation service in April 1915 and gained military flying brevet No.2078 on 14 June 1915, flying Maurice Farman aircraft. He underwent a course at the Chartres Ecole Militaire and was posted on 2 July to Escadrille MF62, engaged on artillery spotting, photography and bombing. On 11 February 1916 he was awarded the Médaille de St. Georges and his first citation for downing an enemy aircraft on 10 February.

He was posted to Escadrille N3, of the illustrious Cigognes (Storks) group, flying Nieuport aircraft and shot down another enemy aircraft on 19 March. His third victory was a Fokker *Eindecker* on 31 March 1916, but he was wounded in action on 2 April. Two weeks later he had recovered from his wound and flew again, bringing down his fourth enemy aircraft on 30 April. He was made Chevalier of the Légion d'Honneur on 4 June 1916 for this feat of arms.

He destroyed a balloon on 24 June, and then between 24 August and 23 November 1916 he downed another five enemy aircraft, making his total at the end of the year ten confirmed victories. Still with Escadrille N3 in 1917, he shot down his eleventh enemy aircraft on 10 February.

He was placed in command of another elite squadron – Escadrille SPA73 of Cigognes Group – on 22 February. SPA73 was equipped with the 150hp Hispano Suiza-engined SPAD S.7 aircraft which Deullin put to good combat use.

On 16 March 1917 he scored his 12th victory over Enville en Haye, and he continued to score heavily over the battlefields of Soissons, Flanders and the Somme. By the end of 1917 his tally of confirmed victories stood at nineteen.

The last year of the war dawned and on 7 February Deullin was in command of Groupe de Chasse No.19. He flew and fought in the great battles of St. Mihiel and Château Thierry, and scored his last confirmed victory on 19 May 1918 when he shot down an Albatros fighter. During his service he was decorated with the Légion d'Honneur (Chevalier) on 4 June 1916 and the Légion d'Honneur (Officer) on 23 June 1918. In addition he was awarded the Croix de Guerre with 14 Palmes. He was wounded in aerial combat three times. His total score was twenty confirmed and five probables.

Capitaine Albert Louis Deullin died on 29 May 1923 when flight-testing an aircraft at Villacoublay airfield.

Capitaine René Paul Fonck (1894–1953) 75 (127–144) victories

The highest scoring Allied ace of World War One was born on 27 March 1894 in the Vosges. When called up 22 August 1914 he was sent for five months to the 11th Regiment of Engineers, digging and building in the Moselle region.

However, on 15 February 1915 he was posted to the famous military academy at Saint Cyr for aviation instruction. By 1 April 1915 he was at Le Crotoy learning to fly, and within two weeks he had graduated as military pilot No.1979.

Posted to Escadrille C47 in the Vosges, flying Caudron G14s, on 15 June 1915, he clashed with a German reconnaissance aircraft on an observation mission. As both machines were unarmed it was a stalemate. On 2 July 1915 Fonck was flying again, but this time he was armed with a rifle. He was a crack shot and marksman, and when he came upon a German two-seater observation aircraft, he opened fire with his rifle. The German pilot turned tail and made for home as fast as he could fly. This aptitude for marksmanship was the key to Fonck's large total of victories. Some enemy aircraft went down for the expenditure of but a few rounds of properly placed ammunition. On the ground Fonck would practise with a Belgian-made Browning slide action rifle to enhance his prowess in aerial combat to deadly effect.

Studio portrait of the top French ace, René Fonck.

The top-scoring Allied ace, Capitaine René Paul Fonck, with 75 confirmed victories plus some 69 unconfirmed.

Escadrille C47 engaged in reconnaissance and bombing missions, together with hazardous gun spotting that provoked intense ground fire – on one occasion resulting in Fonck making a hasty forced landing.

Fonck's first aerial victory was a Rumpler over Estrée on 6 August 1916 and his first French decoration – the Médaille Militaire – followed on 30 August. He had been decorated with the British Military Medal on 16 August.

Fonck's Caudron GIV was fitted with an extra forward-firing machine-gun, which improved its lethal performance. On 14 October 1916 – whilst artillery spotting during the massive Somme offensive – he shot down a rival German artillery spotter, but like many of his victories this was unconfirmed. Escadrille C47 moved base to Fismes on 17 March 1917, and Fonck had his second victory, an Albatros, one of five that he and another French pilot, Sergent Raux, clashed with.

Fonck transferred to Groupe de combat No.12, the famous Cigognes (Storks), at Bonnemaison on 15 April 1917. This famous unit – commanded by Commandant Brocard – comprised four escadrilles: SPA3, SPA26, SPA73 and SPA103. These four escadrilles were the cream of French military aviators, led by some of the most illustrious pilots in the French Air Service: Guynemer, Dorme, Heurtaux, de la Tour, Garros, Auger and Deullin.

Fonck first saw action with the Storks on 3 May 1917 when he and another pilot attacked two German spotter aircraft over Berry au Bac. Fonck – the superb marksman – fired 20 rounds at one of the enemy, who spun earthwards out of control – but this was yet another unconfirmed victory. His first confirmed victory with the Storks was a Rumpler on 5 May. Another victory followed on 11 May: the doomed enemy aircraft fell in flames onto French lines, another confirmed kill.

During July the Storks moved base to Dunkerque but began to come under German night bombing raids and massed day attacks by swarms of Fokkers. The German attacks began to tell, the Storks losing many of their finest airmen. The French responded by putting an entire Escadrille into the air to give battle. On 9 August 1917 SPA 103 was put into the air with Capitaine d'Harcourt in the van. Spotting a formation of 32

FRANCE

Fokkers attacking French bombers, SPA103 gave battle. Fonck dived to the attack and put a Fokker down in flames; banking his aircraft, he shot down another Fokker. Yet again only one kill was confirmed, bringing his official score to seven. By 27 October 1917 Fonck's confirmed score stood at nineteen with many probables as well.

1918 came and Fonck began to score at a consistently amazing rate: on 19 January, two enemy downed; between 5 and 26 February, five more victories; March, seven kills; and April, three more downed, making a total of 36 victories.

Taking off in the afternoon of 9 May, Fonck downed an enemy two-seater at 16.00 hours followed by a second two minutes later and a third three minutes after that – three victories, all over two-seaters, in the space of five minutes! Refuelled and rearmed, Fonck took off again and at 18.20 hours shot down another two-seater; at 18.55 hours another followed and one minute later yet another, a total of six enemy aircraft downed in one day. His tally of confirmed victories now stood at 42 with many more probables unconfirmed. The award of the Croix d'Officier de la Légion d'Honneur followed in recognition of this amazing feat of arms.

On 25 June Fonck was back in the battle – three victories in the one day, followed by two victories on 27 June 1918 was remarkable: two kills on the 16th July, two on the 18th July and three on the 19th July, brought his total to 56 victories confirmed. Fonck's 57th victory was on 1 August – a two-seater over Hangard woods, at 11.00 hours. On the 14th came three more victories and a grand total of 60 confirmed. On 26 September Fonck scored six victories between 11.45 and 18.20 hours! 5–31 October saw another seven victories.

Fonck's last confirmed victory was on 1 November 1918 – ten days before the Armistice – a Halberstadt C-type going down east of Vouzières at 14.20 hours, making his final total 75 victories.

Capitaine René Fonck died in Paris on 18 June 1953 aged but 59 years. He was the top-scoring Allied ace with 75 confirmed victories, but with a probable total of between 127 and 144 victories.

His wartime awards included the Croix de Guerre with 28 Palmes, Military Cross and Bar (British), Military Medal (British), Belgian Croix de Guerre and the Cross of Karageorge (Czarist Russia).

Capitaine Paul Adrien Gastin (?–1976) 6 (10) victories

Gastin transferred to the Aviation Service from the Army on 24 February 1915 and was awarded his flying brevet, No.1484, on 1 September at the age of 29 years. He was posted to Escadrille N49 and on 22 May 1916 he downed an Aviatik, killing both pilot and observer.

Two more victories followed in October and November 1916, as did the award of the Légion d'Honneur. During 1917 he gained another three confirmed victories, with another four probables credited to his total.

Gastin took command of Escadrille N84 on 31 January 1917, was promoted to capitaine on 19 April 1918 and then given command of 23 Groupe de Combat on 24 August 1918. He was awarded the Croix de Guerre with eight Palmes and a Bronze Star.

He survived the war, reaching general rank and becoming a Commandeur de La Légion d'Honneur. He died on 23 August 1976.

Capitaine Georges Marie Ludovic Jules Guynemer (1894–1917)

53 (88) victories

A venerated name in French aviation, Georges Guynemer was born on 24 December 1894 in Paris. When World War One broke out he attempted to enlist but was turned down, perhaps because of his frail appearance and build. Determined to fight, he persisted and on the third application succeeded in enlisting, on 21 November 1914. He was posted to Aviation School to train as a mechanic, but this was not what he wanted and he applied for pilot training. He was posted to Avord to learn how to fly and on 26 April 1915 he graduated as military pilot No.1832 in the rank of caporal.

On 8 June 1915 he was posted to Escadrille M53 under the command of Capitaine Brocard at Vauciennes airfield. On 15 July 1915 he brought down his first enemy aircraft – an Aviatik – that fell in flames at Septmonts. This victory brought him the award of the Médaille Militaire and on 20 July 1915 he was promoted to sergent.

On 5, 8 and 14 December 1915 he downed another three enemy aircraft, and on his 21st birthday – 24 December 1915 – he was awarded the cross of the Légion d'Honneur. His citation stated that 'he had in six months taken part in thirteen aerial combats with great gallantry'.

Studio portrait of Capitaine Georges Marie Ludovic Jules Guynemer, who scored 53 confirmed victories plus 35 probables before his death in action in September 1917.

1916 came and on 3 February he engaged and downed two LVG C-types within 30 minutes. Another LVG C went down two days later – his score now stood at seven. On 15 July he was wounded over Verdun, but made a quick recovery and began to fly Nieuport Scouts. By 28 July another four LVG Cs went down and by 23 September 1916 Guynemer's confirmed score rose to 17 when he shot down two Fokker E-types. At the year's end his total had risen to 25 victories and he was promoted to lieutenant.

1917 dawned and he began to score at an incredible rate: two on 23 January 1917, two the next day and another on 26 January, making his grand total 30. He was promoted to capitaine on February 1917. His 31st victory was unusual – a Gotha G-type bomber – and on 16 March 1917 he downed three enemy aircraft in one day, with another next day.

By 14 April 1917 he had shot down 36 of the enemy. Seven more went down in May – four on 25 May 1917, two of them within one minute! On 5 June 1918 he was promoted Officer of the Légion d'Honneur when he scored another two kills in one day. Five more enemy were downed during July – one of them an Albatros shot down by 37mm cannon fire from Guynemer's SPAD. August came and two kills came on the 17th. His last official confirmed victory was on 20 August 1917 when he shot down a DFW C-type over Poperinghe. His score now read 53 kills, but he probably scored another 35 victories.

At 08.25 hours on 11 September Capitaine Guynemer took off and never returned. The French authorities issued a statement in which they said 'Capitaine Guynemer disappeared whilst in aerial combat with a German aircraft over Belgium.'

The Germans later stated that Leutnant Kurt Weissman of Jasta 3 shot Guynemer down behind German lines. The gallant Capitaine's body and SPAD aircraft were never located: a British rolling artillery barrage tore up the ground losing his body for ever.

So died one of France's greatest heroes – a truly gallant young fighter pilot. His valediction is inscribed on the wall of the crypt of the Pantheon in Paris: 'Fallen on the field of honour on 11 September 1917 – a legendary hero, fallen in glory from the sky after three years of fierce struggle.'

Georges Guynemer on a Belgian airfield on 9 September 1917, two days before he died in combat.

Capitaine Georges Félix Madon (1892–?) 41 (105) victories

Georges Madon was born in Tunisia, North Africa, on 28 July 1892, and qualified as pilot No.595 at the Blériot School of Flying, Etampes, on 7 June 1911. He enlisted in the French Army on 12 March 1912 and transferred to the flying school at Avord on 1 January 1913. He won military pilot's brevet No.231 and on 12 July 1913 was promoted to caporal.

Madon was posted to Escadrille B130 as a reconnaissance pilot and on 30 October 1914 was in airborne action when he was shot down over Chemin des Dames: a shell blew his Blériot's engine away, but Madon managed to land his stricken aircraft safely.

On 20 November 1914 Madon was promoted sergent. His unit was re-equipped with Maurice Farman aircraft and he was sent to Bourget to convert to the machine. On 5 April 1915 Madon and his observer/mechanic Chatelain lost their bearings in fog and inadvertently landed in neutral Switzerland. They were at once interned.

Chafing at the inaction, Madon and Chatelain escaped and tried to reach Italy, but were recaptured and sent back to their internment camp. The two fliers tried several

French ace Capitaine Georges Félix Madon. Madon died in a flying accident on 11 November 1924 in Tunis, North Africa.

times to escape and finally made it back to France on 27 December 1915, where they were promptly arrested and confined to camp for sixty days for getting lost in fog and being interned!

Sergent Madon was sent to Escadrille MF 218 as a reconnaissance pilot but applied for-and was granted – a transfer to train as a fighter pilot. On 1 September 1916 he was posted to Escadrille N38 in the Champagne area, flying Nieuports.

On 28 September 1916 Madon shot down a Fokker over Reims – his first victory – and soon two more Fokkers had gone down to Madon's remarkable marksmanship, earning him the Médaille Militaire and a reputation as a remarkable pilot. This reputation became known to the German opposition, as he specialised in attacking the enemy over their own airfields. Many of his probables were gained behind German lines and were unconfirmed.

Madon was promoted adjutant on 16 December 1916 with his confirmed score at four. His fifth victory came on 31 January 1917 when he destroyed an Albatros near Suippe. On 15 February, with his score at seven, Madon was forced to land behind German lines when his engine spluttered and cut out. Landing, he repaired the fault and took off before advancing German troops could capture him. He took off and machine-gunned the Germans who had tried to capture him!

On 5 May 1917 Madon was made a Chevalier of Légion d'Honneur and by 20 May 1917 he had 12 victories to his credit. On 2 July 1917 he rammed an enemy aircraft in the heat of combat – crippling his Spad. Maddon just managed to land his stricken aircraft almost unscathed. His opponent crashed nearby. At the end of 1917 his total kills were nineteen. On 24 March 1918 he was placed in command of Escadrille Spa38 and continued to score until his total stood at 41 victories on 3 September 1918. On 25 November 1918 he was made a Croix D'Officier de la Légion d'Honneur. Madon survived the war but was killed in an aviation accident on 11 November 1924 in Tunis.

Sous Lieutenant Pierre Marinovitch (1898–1919) 21 victories

Born in Paris on 1 August 1898, Marinovitch was the youngest of the French aces, only twenty years of age when World War One ended in 1918.

He entered military service on 12 February 1916 with 27 Regiment de Dragons but on 14 July applied for a transfer to the French Aviation Service. On 15 November 1916 he was awarded military pilot's brevet No.4910 and posted to Escadrille N38 flying Nieuports. He opened his score on 8 September 1917 when he downed an Albatros over St. Hilaire le Petit. Two Rumplers followed during December, and another on 1 January 1918. An Albatros D V brought his score to five on 19 January.

Between 15 May and 3 November 1918 he continued to add to his total which reached 21 confirmed victories and three probables, all with Escadrille SPA94. He was decorated with the Médaille Militaire on 10 January 1918 and the Légion d'Honneur on 11 August. He received a promotion to sous lieutenant on 20 October. Among his recorded victories were Prince von Bülow and Karl Schlegel. He survived World War One but died in a flying accident on 2 October 1919, aged 21 years.

Sous Lieutenant Jean Marie Dominique Navarre (1895–1919)

15 (27) victories

Sous Lieutenant Marinovitch.

Jean Navarre was born 8 August 1895 in Jouy en Morin. He enlisted in the Army in August 1914 and gained entry into France's embryo Air Service, gaining military pilot's flying brevet No.601 that September.

He was posted to Escadrille MF8 then as a caporal, to Escadrille MS12 Observation Unit, flying Morane-Saulnier Type L parasol-winged two-seater aircraft.

The observation aircraft were theoretically unarmed, but a variety of small arms were carried for self defence and possible offensive action. On 1 April 1915, at 06.25 hours, Navarre and his observer, Lieutenant Robert, attacked a German Aviatik north of Fismes. Three rifle rounds were fired by the Frenchmen, one of which injured the German pilot, forcing him to land. This was the third French Air Service victory of the war, gained by rifle fire! For this action, Lieutenant Robert was awarded the Légion d'Honneur and Caporal Navarre the Médaille Militaire.

Navarre was promoted to sergent and transferred to Escadrille N.67, flying the Morane-Saulnier Type N. When flying, Navarre always wore a lady's silk stocking instead of a flying helmet. By 26 October 1915 his victory score stood at

French ace Sous Lieutnant Jean Marie Dominique Navarre, wore a lady's silk stocking instead of a flying helmet.

three: two Aviatiks and one LVG C-type. On 26 February 1916 he scored two more victories, a Fokker E.III and a unidentified two-seater. Two more victories followed in March then two more each in April and May, making his total eleven.

Navarre's last confirmed victory was on 17 June 1916, bringing him up to 12, though he was also credited with another 15 probables, making his score 27. On 17 June he was shot down and badly wounded over Argonne.

Navarre did not fly in combat again and did not return to active duty until November 1918, when the war ended. He flew for the Morane-Saulnier company, testing aircraft, but was killed in an air crash on 10 July 1919.

Charles Eugène Jules Marie Nungesser (1892–1927) 43 (54) victories

Born on 15 March 1892 in Paris, Nungesser enlisted in the 2nd Hussars and by 21 January 1915 was engaged in hand-to-hand combat that earned him the Médaille Militaire. Nungesser personally accounted for four Germans in a staff car with his rifle, then seized the car, and drove it back to French lines at speed under German fire. He was allowed to keep the car as 'spoils of war'.

Nungesser asked to be transferred to the French Air Service as he had had two weeks of instruction before the war. On 22 January 1915 he was sent to Avord to receive flying instruction and on 17 March was awarded pilot's brevet No.1803. On 8 April 1915 he was posted to Escadrille VB106 at St. Pol, near Dunkerque. A month later he was promoted to adjutant. His first – and only – victory with VB106 was on 1 July when he downed an Albatros over Nancy.

In November 1915 he was posted to Escadrille N65, having converted to fighter aircraft. His aircraft's fuselage was blazoned with the 'emblems of mortality', a coffin with two lighted candles and a skull and crossbones. These symbols, which are Masonic, had also appeared on his Voisin 10 aircraft whilst with VB106. He was made Chevalier of the Légion d'Honneur in December. His

French ace Jean M. D. Navarre in 1915, with a Morane Type L Parasol of MS12.

second and last victory in 1915 was on 5 December when he shot down an enemy two-seater over Nomeny.

1916 arrived and Nungesser was injured in an accident on 6 February that kept him out of the air until 29 March. On 2 April 1916 he was airborne again and claimed a balloon downed over Septsarges. The next day he shot down an LVG reconnaissance aircraft and on 4 April another victory followed. On 14 April he was promoted to sous lieutenant.

On 25 April another LVG C-type went down, bringing his score to six victories. The next day another LVG C went down, but Nungesser was himself shot down by German anti-aircraft fire. By 22 May his score stood at nine confirmed kills. His tenth kill is thought to have been a German ace, Leutnant Otto Parschau of FA 32, a holder of the Pour le Mérite.

On 22 June 1916 Nungesser was severely injured whilst flying his Nieuport 23. Flying over Verdun, he clashed with two enemy aircraft and a furious hour-long dogfight ensued. Nungesser got the better of the two but had to crash-land his aircraft near his two opponents. By 23 November Nungesser had taken his score to eighteen confirmed with many probables; on 4 December he was awarded the British Military Cross and on the same day scored two more kills. His last victory of 1916 was an enemy two-seater over Touy le Grand, and he ended the year with 21 victories.

Forced to go into hospital to have his broken and bruised body repaired, he had all his injuries attended to and managed to convince the Air Ministry to allow him to fly in combat again. On 1 May 1917 he was back in action – now with Escadrille V116 – and scored two victories, both Albatros D IIIs.

Nungesser's fame and prowess had spread over German lines, and a German aircraft dropped a message on V116's airfield inviting Nungesser to single combat over Douai. Taking up the gauntlet, Nungesser took off, but over Douai he met not one German pilot but six! It was a trap in which the duplicitous Germans came off worst – two of their number, Leutnant Paul Schweizer and Gefreiter Ernst Bittorf, were sent down in flames.

Lieutenant Charles Eugène Jules Marie Nungesser, who scored 43 confirmed victories plus another 11 probables. This highly decorated pilot disappeared into the ocean on 8 May 1927 whilst attempting an Atlantic crossing.

Nungesser was then involved in a car accident in which his mechanic/driver, Soldat Pochon, was killed, but the injured Nungesser returned to duty with SPA65 on 31 December 1917 with 30 victories to his credit. He scored several victories behind German lines, but these could not be confirmed.

Nungesser resumed his combat score on 12 March 1918 and by 15 August he had 43 confirmed victories with some eleven probables to his credit, at which point ill-health forced the gallant Nungesser to retire from combat flying. He survived the war but disappeared over the Atlantic when he and a Capitaine Francois Coli attempted to fly to New York in a 120mph Levasseur two-seater biplane on 8 May 1927.

Charles Nungesser was awarded: the Croix de Guerre with 28 Palmes and two stars, the Belgian Croix de Guerre and Croix de Léopold, the US Distinguished Service Cross, the British Military Cross, the Portuguese Croix de Guerre, the Serbian Cross of Bravery, the Montenegro Order of Danilo and the Russian Order of Karageorge.

Capitaine Armand Pinsard (1897–1953) 27 victories

Born on 28 May 1897 in Mercillac, Charente, Pinsard began his military service during 1906 and saw service in Algeria where he was awarded two Moroccan decorations on 27 June 1910 when serving with No.2 Régiment de Spahis (Spahis being a locally raised Algerian native regiment).

In May 1912 Pinsard applied for and was granted a transfer to the embryo French Aviation Service as a trainee pilot with the rank of maréchal des logis (sergeant of artillery or cavalry). He graduated on 3 September 1912 with pilot's brevet No.210 – a very early military aviator indeed. In 1913, with France still at peace, he was decorated with the Médaille Militaire for outstanding skill as a pilot.

When the war broke out he was posted to Escadrille MS23 at St. Cyr as an adjutant (warrant officer) pilot. MS23 had only been formed on 4 August under command of Capitaine August le Révérend and equipped with Moranes. (Three years later, in September 1917, Pinsard was to command Escadrille MS23.)

In November 1914 promotion to sous lieutnant (2nd lieutenant) came together with two citations for bravery, but on 8 February 1915 he became a prisoner of war when he had to land his aircraft in German-held territory. A long 14 months as a POW followed and several attempts to escape from prison camp. On 26 March 1916 he and Capitaine Victor Menard made a successful escape from custody and on 10 April made it back to France.

On 8 July 1916 Pinsard was posted to Escadrille N26 where Capitaine Menard was commanding officer. A month later he was cited for the Légion d'Honneur (Chevalier) for his bravery in combat when he attacked at just 200m and machine-gunned massed German troops held in reserve for a major attack on Allied forces.

Capitaine Pinsard.

On 1 November Pinsard made his first kill whilst flying a Nieuport over Lechelle. He was put in command of Escadrille N78 during November. He was badly injured in an accident on 12 June 1917, but not before he had scored 15 more victories.

After recovering from his accident he returned to the Front in command of Escadrille SPA23 (the former MS23 and N23) where he scored another eleven victories and six probables. His final confirmed score was 27, including nine balloons. The Escadrille's total victories were 59. Pinsard was decorated with the British Military Cross on 17 April 1918 and made an Officier de la Légion d' Honneur on 30 August. He was also awarded the Croix de Guerre with 19 Palmes and the Italian Military Medal.

Armand Pinsard stayed in the French Air Service after the war and by 25 December 1939 was a grand officer of the Légion d'Honneur. During World War Two he flew with distinction on bombing raids with Groupe de Classe 21, but lost a leg in action on 6 June 1940. He reached the rank of general and died on 10 May 1953 at Ceyzeriat. France.

FRENCH ACES 1914–18

Figures in parenthesis indicate probable but unconfirmed victories. (Some figures in parenthesis indicate a lower score!)

★ Indicates other nationalities e.g. Russian.

75 kills Capitaine René Fonck (127)
54 kills Capitaine Georges Marie Ludovic Jules Guynemer (88)
45 kills Capitaine Georges Charles Eugène Jules Marie Nungesser (54)
41 kills Capitaine Georges Félix Madon (105)
35 kills Lieutenant Maurice Boyau
34 kills Lieutenant Michel Coiffard
28 kills Capitaine Jean Pierre Léon Bourjade
27 kills Capitain Armand Pinsard (33)
23 kills Sous Lieutenant René Pierre Marie Dorme (40)
23 kills Lieutenant Gabriel F. C. Guérin (29)
22 kills Sous Lieutenant Claude Marcel Haegelen (25)
21 kills Sous Lieutenant Pierre Marinovitch (24)
21 kills Capitaine Alfred Heurtaux (34)
20 kills Capitaine Albert Deullin (25)
19 kills Capitaine Henri de Slade (22)
19 kills Lieutenant Jacques L. Ehrlich
18 kills Lieutenant Bernard de Romanet
16 kills Lieutenant Jean Chaput

15 kills
Capitaine Armand de Turenne (20)
Capitaine Pavel V. d' Argueff
Lieutenant J. L. M. G. Sardier

14 kills
Lieutenant Marc Ambrogi

13 kills
Sous Lieutenant O. P. DeMeuldre
Lieutenant Hector Garaud (14)

Lieutenant Marcel Nogues (15)

12 kills
Sous Lieutenant B. Artigau
Lieutenant Jean H. Casale (13)
Sous Lieutenant G. Daladier
Capitaine Xavier de Sevin (23)
Sous Lieutenant F. F. Guyou
Lieutenant Marcel A. Hugues (16)
Sous Lieutenant L. Jailler (20)
Capitaine A. L. J. Leps (14)
Sous Lieutenant J. M. D. Navarre (27)
Lieutenant Paul A. P. Tarascon

11 kills
Adjutant Armand Berthelot
Sous Lieutenant Jean Bouyer
Lieutenant J. Bozon Verduraz
Sous Lieutenant William Herisson (15)
Adjutant M. Lenoir (19)
Sous Lieutenant Ernst Maunoury (12)
Adjutant René Montrion (19)
Sous Lieutenant C. Nuville (14)
Lieutenant J. Ortoli (12)

10 kills
Adjutant Maurice Bizot
Adjutant A. J. Chainat (13)
Adjutant L. Marcel Gasser (13)
Sous Lieutenant A. Herbelin (12)
Capitaine Auguste Lahoulle
Adjutant Charles Mace (15)
Adjutant Jean Pezon (18)
Sous Lieutenant Charles Quette (15)
Adjutant L. B. Ruamps (14)
Sous Lieutenant P. Y. R.

Waddington (12)

9 kills
Capitaine F. Bonneton (11)
Sous Lieutenant A. A. R. Bretillon
Sous Lieutenant A. M. M. Coadou
Sous Lieutenant T. H. Condemine
Sous Lieutenant C. de Guingard
Capitaine M. de la Tour (12)
Sous Lieutenant Marcel M. Dhome
Adjutant Gustave Douchy (14)
Sous Lieutenant René Dousinelle (12)
Sous Lieutenant L. P. Gros
Capitaine Georges Matton (11)
Sous Lieutenant M. Viallet (10)
Sous Lieutenant H. Peronneau

8 kills
Sous Lieutenant Paul Barbreau
Adjutant F. Chauvannes
Sous Lieutenant Dieudonne Costes
Sous Lieutenant C. M. DeGuingand (15)
Sous Lieutenant A. H. M. de Cordou (9)
Commdt Robert de Marancour
Capitaine Jacques Gerard (10)
Adjutant Chef A. Laplasse (10)
Adjutant Edmond Pillon (10)
Capitaine Roger Poupon
Sergent Paul J. Sauvage (14)
Sous Lieutenant Gaston Vial

7 kills
Capitaine Alfred Auger (14)
Sergent Andre Louis Bosson
Sous Lieutenant Roger Bretillion
Sous Lieutenant F. H.

Chavannes
Lieutenant P. DeCazenove Pradines
Adjutant François P. Delzenne
Sous Lieutenant N. DeRochefort (12)
Sous Lieutenant François, Prince de Tonnay Charante, De Rochechouart (9)
Maréchal P. D. A Ducornet
Sous Lieutenant F. de Mortemart
Capitaine René Doumer (11)
Capitaine Raul Echard
Sous Lieutenant C. Flachaire (10)
Capitaine G. M. Lachmann (9)
Lieutenant Henry Languedoc (9)
Lieutenant C. L. de Kerland
Lieutenant Jean A. P Poste
Lieutenant Alex Marty M. des L. Jean Moissinac (8)
Lieutenant P. Pendaris
Adjutant Chef H. A. Peroneau
Adjutant Paul Petit
Adjutant J. R. Roques (8)
Sergent Paul Santelle
Adjutant Victor Sayeret (10)
Sous Lieutenant Gabriel Thomas
Adjutant Marie C. Vitalis
Commdt. Joseph Vuillemin
Lieutenant E. Weismann

6 kills
Lieutenant F. M. N. Battesti
Sergent E. J. F. Camplan (7)
Lieutenant Alex C. Borzecki (5)
Lieutenant Louis F. Coudouret
Sous Lieutenant Jules Covin
Lieutenant Albert R. Chabrier

*Capitaine Georges
Pelletier D'Oisy.*

Capitaine Paul Gastin
(10)
Lieutenant Maurice
Roch Gond
Capitaine C. Lefèvre
Sergent A. R. Levy
Lieutenant J. A. P. J.
Loste (7)
Capitaine A. Mezergues
Adjutant G. Naudin
Sous Lieutenant
Adolphe Pegoud (9)
Sous Lieutenant R. A.
Pelissier (5)
Sous Lieutenant V. F.
M. A. Regnier (7)
Sous Lieutenant E. J.
M. Regnier (9)
Capitaine Georges
Raymond (7)
Maréchal des Logis A.
Rousseaux
Sergent Constant
Soulier (15)

5 kills
Capitaine Albert
Achard
Sous Lieutenant M.
Arnoux
Lieutenant J. M.
Arpheuil
Lieutenant Y. F. Barbaza
Sous Lieutenant A. J. L.
Barcat
Adjutant A. Baux
Adjutant G. P. Blanc
Lieutenant P. L. de
Boiseumarie
Adjutant Marcel R.
Bloch
Lieutenant Georges
Boillot
Adjutant A. Buisson
Adjutant E. E. H.
Callaux (8)
Maréchal P. M. J.
Cardon
Lieutenant L. E. Cayol
Sous Lieutenant L. A.
Chartoire
Sous Lieutenant A.
Cordonnier (9)
Lieutenant H. M. J. L.
G. DeBonald
Aspirant J. C. A. Dubois
de Gennes
Adjutant André L. F. D.
Degennes
Maréchal des Logis J. P.
M. J. De Gaillard de la
Valden (9)
Lieutenant Jean de
Tierenns
Lieutenant V. C.
Fedorov★

Lieutenant Pierre
Gaudermen (6)
Sous Lieutenant E.
Gilbert
Adjutant F. Guerrier
Lieutenant Julien
Guertiau (8)
Sergent Joseph Guiguet
(6)
Adjutant Georges
Halberger
Adjutant Paul Hamot
(6)
Sergent Marcel Hauss
(6)
Sous Lieutenant M.
Hasdenteufel (7)
Adjutant Marcel
Henriot (7)
Lieutenant Paul C.
Homo
Capitaine D. L.
Grandmaison (6)
Capitaine Jean
Jannekeyn
Adjutant Georges
Leinhart (6)
Lieutenant P. M. C. V.
E. Leroy de Boiseau-
marie (7)
Capitaine Paul L.
Malaville (7)
Soldat L. H. Martin (6)
Adjutant Maudin
Sergent Paul Montange
Adjutant A. Petit
Delchet (6)
Sous Lieutenant A.
Paillard
Sous Lieutenant P.
Pendaries
Lieutenant C. M. Plessis
(6)
Lieutenant F. Portron
Sous Lieutenant F.
Pulpe
Adjutant Charles A.
Revol-Tissot
Sous Lieutenant Louis
Risacher
Adjutant Maurice
Robert (7)
Sergent P. G. A. Rodde
Adjutant M. Rouselle
Capitaine J. V. Sabatier
(7)
Sous Lieutenant B. F.
Saune
Maréchal G. Uteau
Adjutant P. A. F. Violet
Marty (8)
Adjutant Paul Violet
Lieutenant Pierre
Wertheimer

Lieutenant J. D. B. de
Bonnefoy
Lieutenant F. F. M. A.
De Boigne
Adjutant Pierre Delage
(7)
Lieutenant Robert J.
Delannoy (7)
Sous Lieutenant André
J. Delorme (11)
Capitaine J. M. E.
Derode (10)
Lieutenant L. A. de
Marmier (9)

Lieutenant P. Dufaur de
Gavardie
Adjutant Pierre de
Pralines
Sous Lieutenant H. N.
Rochefort
Sergent A. Dubois
d'Aische (11)
Sergent André
Dubonnet
Sous Lieutenant J. P. J.
Favre de Thierrens
Sous Lieutenant Jean
Fraissinet (8)

ITALY

3

I talian military flying began when a flying school was created at Centocelle, outside Rome, in the spring of 1910. This school catered for both military and civil aircrew, and by December 1910 31 Italian military pilots had qualified.

During 1911 the Italians enthused over aviation, and flying schools began to proliferate. The airfield at Aviano opened in April, and became the hub of Italian aviation – during the 1999 Balkans war Aviano airfield would be the base of NATO operations.

Only ten aircraft were in use at this time – a motley collection of Blériots and Henri Farmans, a Nieuport and an Etrich. By 1913 thirteen military airfields were in service with twelve squadriglia (squadrons). By 1914 the far sighted Italians had fourteen military airfields, thirteen squadriglia and two military flying schools. The Naval Air Service (Aeronautica della Regia Marina) possessed two airships, fifteen seaplanes and flying boats, and several land aircraft.

When Italy entered the war on 24 May 1915, the Italian Corpo Aeronautica Militare (Military Aviation Corps) had 115 aircraft in service, but these were all observation types, not suitable for aerial combat.

Italy had a thriving aircraft industry and produced excellent aircraft:

Ansaldo Ansaldo built the A-1 Balilla (hunter) single-seat biplane fighter late in 1917.

Caproni Caproni produced the Ca2 three-engined biplane heavy bomber in 1915, then the Ca3 in 1917, followed by the Ca4 triplane night and torpedo bomber. The Ca5 was a successful day/night biplane bomber, used during 1918.

Macchi The L1, L2, L3, M3, M5, M7 and M8 were successful flying boats used from late 1915 onwards for coastal patrol and combat. The L-types were copied from the successful Austro-Hungarian Lohner flying boats. The Parasol was an observation monoplane used when war broke out, but soon replaced by the French Caudron G3.

Pomilio Pomilio produced two-seater observation aircraft – the PC, PD, PE, and PY. These were not very successful, but the later PD, PE and PY marques were extremely successful. Pomilio was taken over by Ansaldo in 1918

SAML (Societa Anonima Meccanica Lombardo) The SAML Aviatik was copied from the Aviatik B.I two-seater observation biplane and used mainly for training. This was followed by the SAML Types 1 and 2 observation biplanes.

SIA (Societa Italians Aviazone)
The 7B1 and 7B2 were two-seater reconnaissance biplanes made during 1917–18; they were taken out of service early in 1918. The 9B was used by the navy as a bomber. Fiat produced the Fiat R2, which was derived from the SIA 7B2, as an observation/light bomber. SIA became Fiat-Aviazone in 1918.

SP (Savoia-Pomilo Fiat) The SP2 and SP3 were two-seater pusher biplane reconnaissance/bombers which the aircrews detested, calling them 'two-seater coffins' from their lumbering low speed and heavy handling. The SP4 was a twin-engined bomber with a three-man crew used from December 1917 to the summer of 1918.

SVA (Savoia-Verduzio Ansaldo) SVA designed and produced the successful 220hp SVA 5 biplane fighter in the summer of 1917. However. it was found that the aircraft was more suitable as a very long range reconnaissance, bomber and observation aeroplane. During 1918 it made (for the time) an amazing flight of 625 miles. A seaplane version – the SVA Idro-AM – was developed and saw service. A total of 1,245 SVA5s and about 50 Idro-AMs were built, which testifies to the quality of the machine.

Although the Italians had excellent aircraft of their own, they were not averse to using foreign types. The standard Italian fighter was the Franco-British H. Hanriot, but Nieuport 10s, 11s and 24s, SPAD VIIs and even a German Taube were used. The Blériot XI, Voisin, Caudron G111 and Farman MF and 5B were also put to good use.

The Italian Air Service was reshaped early in 1916 with a strength of 35 squadrons equipped with Caproni Ca32s and -33s, Caudron GIVs, Italian-engined Voisins, Farmans, several Aviatiks, and Nieuport Bébé fighters equipping Nos. 70a and 71a Squadrons. By the spring of 1917 there were 62 squadrons in service; by November 1917 there were fifteen fighter squadrons, fourteen Caproni bomber squadrons and 30 reconnaissance and observation squadrons.

To bolster the strength of the Italian Royal Army Air Service, three RAF Squadrons – Nos. 28, 45 and 66 – were detached to Italy. They had 90 aircraft, of which 54 were Camels. In November 1918 Italian air strength stood at 68 squadrons, plus four British and three French squadrons – a total of 75 squadrons of which twenty were fighter units. The Italian Navy comprised 46 squadrons: nine fighter units, 37 reconnaissance and observation units, fifteen airships and a small unit – Squadra 'San Marco' – of SVA5s, odd Capronis and a few SIA9bs.

ITALIAN/BRITISH RANK EQUIVALENTS

Italian	British
Colonello	Colonel
Tenente Colonello	Lieutenant-Colonel
Maggiore	Major
Capitano	Captain
Tenente	Lieutenant
Sottotenente	2nd Lieutenant
Sergente Maggiore	Sergeant-Major
Sergente	Sergeant
Caparole	Corporal

Maggiore Francesco Baracca (1888–1918) 34 victories

Francesco Baracca was born near Ravenna on 9 May 1888, the son of a farmer. Not relishing the life of a farmer, he decided to go to the Scuola Militaire (Military School) near Modena, in October 1907. Two years later, in September 1909, he passed out as a Sottotenente (2nd lieutenant), and joined the 2nd Cavalry Regiment.

He applied for, and was granted entry into, the embryo Italian Aviation Service on 28 April 1912. With several other officers, he was sent to Reims, France, to learn to fly. Within nine weeks he qualified on a Hanriot two-seater aircraft and was awarded brevet

No.1037. Baracca was posted to the Battaglione Aviatori (Aviation Battalion), and then on 25 July 1912 to Somma Lombardo airfield, flying Nieuports. He qualified for his full military brevet on 8 December 1912.

When World War One started in 1914 Italy remained neutral – giving her time to strengthen her forces – until May 1915, when war was declared against Austria. Baracca was soon in the air war: early in September 1915 he saw his first enemy aircraft, a two-seater over Udine. Closing with the Austrian aircraft, he opened fire but to no avail due to repeated stoppages of his machine-gun. The machine-gun malfunctions continued and Baracca had no luck in aerial combat.

At New Year 1916 70a Squadriglia was equipped with Nieuports and Baracca flew a Nieuport 11 Bébé single-

Major Baracca, Italy's top ace, by his SPAD. The prancing horse refers to his cavalry service; it was given to Ferrari by Baracca's mother after his death.

seat fighter. On 7 April 1916 he scored his first victory over an Austrian Aviatik, forcing it down by determined, accurate bursts of machine-gun fire. Baracca landed his aircraft and engaged the Aviatik's pilot and wounded observer in conversation until Italian troops arrived: the observer died from his wounds and the pilot went to a POW camp.

Baracca continued in combat but his aircraft suffered machine-gun stoppages and he did not score again until 16 May, when he and his squadron fought an aerial duel with 14 Austrian bombers over Udine. Baracca scored another victory, bringing an enemy aircraft down over Goriza.

On 25 November Baracca scored his fifth victory – an Albatros – making him an ace. He had a prancing horse blazoned on the fuselage of his Nieuport, indicating his cavalry roots. (This prancing horse badge was given by Baracca's mother to the Italian motor racing driver Enzo Ferrari, who later put the badge on his racing cars.)

On 11 February 1917 Baracca shot down an Albatros 12,000 feet over Ozzano. He was promoted to capitano the next day and awarded his third Silver Medal. On 1 May, with his score now standing at ten victories, Baracca plus a battle-hardened flight of pilots formed 91a Squadriglia flying SPAD S.VIIs. The new fighter proved popular with the pilots and Baracca shot down three enemy aircraft in three weeks. In June 1917, Baracca was placed in command of 91a Squadriglia and moved base to Istrana. He continued to score and by September 1917 his total was nineteen victories.

Airborne in a SPAD on 21 October 1917, Baracca gave battle to five Albatros D IIIs. Breaking off the unequal contest, he flew off and then engaged two enemy two-seaters over San Gabriele. He shot down both aircraft, his first double victory. Four days later he and his squadron engaged in no fewer than five aerial combats with enemy aircraft

Baracca destroying an Albatros. On 26 October 1917 he scored his second double victory, over two German Aviatiks, making his total 24 victories.

The Italian Army retreat at Caporetto caused Baracca's squadron to move to Pordenone airfield. The squadron was re-equipped with new aircraft – the excellent SPAD S.XII – but the air war grew harder as 91a squadron were opposed by the Austrian fighter ace Hauptmann Godwin Brumowski and his squadron. Nevertheless, Baracca continued to up his score – on 6 November 1917 he downed two Aviatiks within 30 minutes. The next day he shot down another, bringing his total to 27 victories.

Within a short time his total had reached 30 victories and he was taken off combat flying and sent test flying at Ansaldo's factory in Turin. On 6 February 1918 Baracca was invested by King Albert of the Belgians with a Belgian decoration and in March he and two of his pilots were invested at La Scala, Milan, with Italy's highest honour. the Medaglia d'Oro al Valor Militare (Golden Medal for Military Valour).

On 3 May 1918, Baracca was back with his squadron and was soon in action. He clashed with six Austrian Albatros D IIIs, shooting one down. His 32nd victory came on 22 May and his 33rd and 34th (his last) were on 15 June.

On 19 June Baracca and two aircraft of 91a Squadriglia took off on a patrol and ground support mission. Flying low – at 100 feet – over enemy troops at Montello, the three Italian aircraft machine-gunned Austrian troops below. The Austrians returned fire with heavy machine-guns and all three Italian aircraft were hit. In the mêlée Capitano Baracca disappeared from his comrades' view and was never seen alive again. His body was found with a bullet hole in his forehead – next to his burned-out SPAD.

So died the gallant Capitano Francesco Baracca – Italy's highest scoring ace with 34 victories. His prancing horse fuselage badge is still carried by all Ferrari motor cars around the world – a fitting memento to a redoubtable, dashing fighter pilot.

Tenente Colonello Pier Ruggiero Piccio (1880–?) 24 victories

Tenente Colonello Piccio was born in Rome on 27 September 1880. He joined the Italian Army as a regular officer and rose to the rank of Capitano. He gained flying

91 Squadriglia, 'The Aces Squadron; Baracca sixth from right, Piccio seventh from right.

brevet No.256 on 12 July 1913, which made him one of the first aviators in Italy. He was awarded the Medaglia Argento al Valor Militare on 3 June 1913.

Piccio was an enthusiast in aviation and had set up an Italian altitude record of 3,800 metres. He also specialised in long-distance endurance flying and set up some remarkable (for the time) records. In 1914, still in the rank of capitano, he was placed in command of 5a Squadriglia at Arsizio (Italy's top ace, Francesco Baracca, was in the same squadron).

When Italy came into World War One on the Allied side Piccio was an experienced pilot and officer. He flew with 70a and 91a Squadriglias as a fighter pilot in spite of his promotion to tenente colonello. By 30 September 1917 Piccio had 12 confirmed victories and on 25 October 1917 he added two more: both Albatros shot down in flames.

Italian aces, from left: Major P. Piccio and Captain F. R. Di Calabria (7th Duke of Calabria).

Flying with 91a Squadriglia – known as 'The Aces Squadron' – in a SPAD S.13 he undertook many offensive strafing missions against Austrian troops, as well as reconnaissance operations, sometimes flying with Baracca and Calabria as wingmen. His victory total rose to 24 by the end of the war, making him Italy's second highest scoring ace. In March 1918, together with Baracca and Calabria, Piccio was invested with Italy's highest honour, the Medaglia d'Oro al Valor Militare. A proud, deserved moment for three of Italy's aces.

Capitano Fulco Ruffo di Calabria (dates unknown) 20 victories

Ruffo di Calabria was a member of 70a Squadriglia and became the fourth highest scoring Italian ace. He was an outstanding pilot, an excellent marksman and cool in combat.

His first victory was on 23 August 1916 when, with Baracca and Tenente Olivari (with whom he usually flew) he shot down an Austrian observation aircraft over the Tolmino sector of the front. His second victory was on 16 September 1916 – again on combat patrol with Baracca and Olivari – when he shot down an Austrian Lohner two-seater near Villach. The Lohner pilot was killed in the action and the observer wounded. On 1 January 1917, di Calabria scored another victory, over an Austrian two-seater observation aircraft.

He was selected to join Baracca in forming 91a Squadriglia, which became known as 'Squadron of Aces'. Ruffo di Calabria continued to score victories with his squadron until his grand total reached twenty aircraft downed. He was promoted to capitano and awarded the prestigious Medaglia d'Oro al Valor Militare, Italy's highest award.

Tenente Silvio Scaroni (dates unknown) 26 victories

Scaroni first served with 4a Squadriglia flying Caudron GIVs on reconnaissance and artillery spotting missions. It was not until the summer of 1917 that he applied for – and was granted – training as a fighter pilot. By November 1917 he had qualified as a pilot and was sent to 76a Squadriglia at Istrana. The squadron had both Nieuport and Hanriot fighters on charge, and Scaroni was soon in action.

On 15 November 1917, he closed with an Albatros two-seater and shot it down in flames onto Colberstadio. On the 17th he shot down another Albatros and on the 19th yet another. December arrived and on the 5th, 10th and 19th respectively he shot down three Albatros CIIIs, making him an ace.

On 26 December, Scaroni's airfield at Istrana was attacked by a strong force of Austrian aircraft – almost 30 bombers protected by swarms of fighters. Scaroni's 76a Squadriglia took off and gave battle with the raiders.

Scaroni, on his first sortie, made Italian aviation history by shooting down three of the enemy – two WKFs and one Gotha – in one sortie. Several other pilots accounted for Austrian aircraft, making a total of eight Austrian aircraft shot down. Two days later Scaroni shot down two Albatros reconnaissance aircraft over Montello, again on one sortie.

The last year of the war dawned and during January Scaroni destroyed two Brandenberg two-seaters. His victory total was now eleven. By 3 April 1918 he had

Tenente Silvio Scaroni, Italy's second ace pilot.

increased his total to sixteen and by 15 June it was nineteen. On 7 July, with his score at 21 victories and with Sergente Ticconi as wingman, he attacked a formation of Austrian aircraft, knocking out a Brandenberg within minutes. Sergente Ticconi shot down two Phonix aircraft, Scaroni another Brandenberg and then a Phonix: five enemy aircraft downed by just the two pilots in one battle!

On 12 July 76a Squadriglia was providing a fighter 'umbrella' to a flight of three Italian observation aircraft, when they were engaged by a strong formation of enemy Phonix and Albatros fighters. A classic dogfight ensued: Italian reinforcements arrived and joined the battle, followed by an RAF Camel flight. Still outnumbered, the Allied aircraft began to give a good account of themselves and Scaroni shot down an Albatros and a Phonix. He was hit by a machine-gun bullet and passed out, but luckily he came round and regained partial control before his Hanriot crashed. As the Hanriot hit the ground at speed Scaroni was thrown clear from the wreckage, badly wounded. Scaroni convalesced after treatment in hospital and some six months later was returned to his squadron, but the war was over and Scaroni did not fly in anger again.

Tenente Silvio Scaroni was awarded the Medaglia d'Oro al Valor Militare for his 26 victories during the war. He remained in the Air Service and attained the rank of generale in the Italian Air Force.

ITALIAN ACES 1914–18

Aces 1914–18

34 kills Maggiore
  Francesco Baracca
26 kills Tenente Silvio
  Scaroni
24 kills T/Colonnelle
  Pier Ruggiero Piccio
21 kills Flavio T.
  Barachini
20 kills Capitano Fulco
  Ruffo di Calabria
17 kills Sergente
  Marziale Cerutte
17 kills Tenente
  Ferrucio Ranza
12 kills Tenente Luigi
  Olivari
11 kills Tenente Gio
  Ancillotto
11 kills Sergente

Antonio Reali
8 kills
Tenente Flamino Avet
Sottotenente Ernest
  Cabruna
Sottotenente Alv
  Leonardi
Tenente Carlo
  Lombardi
Sottotenente Giovanni
  Nicelli
Tenente Gastone
  Novelli
7 kills
Tenente Leo Eluteri
Sergente Maggiore
  Guliemo Fornagiara
Tenente Mario Fucini
Sergente Orazio
  Pierozzi

Sergente Maggiore
  Cosimo Renella
Capitano Antonia Riva
6 kills
Sergente Aldo Bocchese
Sergente Attilio Imolesi
Sergente Cesare
  Magistrini
Sergente Guy Nardini
Tenente Luigi Olivi
Tenente Giilano Parvis
Sergente Cosimo
  Rizotto
Sergente Mario
  Stoppani
Sergente Romolo Ticoni
5 kills
Sottotenente Michel
  Allasia
Sottotenente Antonio

Amantea
Tenente Sabas Bedendo
Capitano Bortolo
  Constantini
Tenente Alessandro
  Buzio
Sergente Antonio Chiri
Capitano Giulio Lega
Tenente Guido Masiero
Tenente Amedo
  Mecozzi
Tenente Giorgio
  Michetti
Sottotenente Alessandro
  Resch
Tenente Giovanni
  Sabelli

Below left: Pilots of the Royal Italian Navy.

Below: Pola raid pilots, From left: Capitano Maurizio Pagliano and Tenente Luigi Gori.

Bottom: Tenente Luigi Olivari.

UNITED STATES OF AMERICA

4

The United States Aviation Section was originally just a part of the US Signal Corps, with an original establishment on 18 July 1914 of 60 officers and 260 other ranks. Late in 1915 the Chief Signals Officer, General Scriven, recommended an aviation service of eighteen squadrons, each of twelve aeroplanes. The National Defence Act of 1916 provided an increase in the overall strength of the Aviation Section, with a new reserve of officers and other ranks.

The 1st Aero Squadron saw service on the Mexican border in a punitive offensive by America against the revolutionary leader Pancho Villa; its strength at the time was ten pilots, 84 other ranks and eight aircraft.

20 April 1916 saw the appearance in France of the soon to be legendary Lafayette Escadrille. This French/American squadron, equipped with seven Nieuport fighters and flown by American volunteer pilots, began to make its presence felt while based near Luxeuil les Baines in the Vosges region. Several of the American pilots had already seen air- and ground action with the French Air Force and the French Foreign Legion.

The Lafayette Escadrille began as L'Escadrille Americaine, but after protests by pro-Germans in the United States the name was changed to Lafayette Escadrille. The official name of the Lafayette was Escadrille de Chasse Nieuport 124.

It was supported by many wealthy and influential Americans – The France-American Committee – who believed that the United States should be actively engaged in the war as an ally of Britain and France.

The original Lafayette Escadrille with pilots of the 4th Bombardment Group, USAS.

The first commanding officer was Captain Georges Thennault with, as his second-in-command, Lieutenant de Laage de Meux. The seven original American members were Norman Prince, William Thaw, Elliot Cowdin, Victor Chapman, Kiffin Rockwell, James McConnell and Bert Hall. All their equipment and needs were paid for, and they received a bonus of $250 for every enemy aircraft shot down.

The only black US aviator of World War One was Eugene Bullard, who had transferred from the redoubtable 170th Regiment of the French Foreign Legion. He qualified as a pilot, obtained a commission and flew with SPA85 and 93. His stay was brief: it was said that he was unable to cope with the discipline of the French Air Service, so he transferred back to the iron-disciplined Foreign Legion!

In total 180 American pilots flew with the Lafayette Escadrille and their names and feats have gone into American (and other) legend. Eventually, in February 1918, the Lafayette was absorbed into the United States Air Service as 103 Squadron.

The United States of America entered World War One on the Allied side on 6 April 1917. The US Aviation Section's strength was only 131 offcers, 1,087 other ranks and just under 250 aircraft – none of which were considered battle-worthy. In June 1917 the USAS became the Aeroplane Division of the US Army Corps, and then in August all American air units in France were grouped into the United States Air Service (USAS).

Above left: Lieutenant Norman Prince, founder of the Escadrille Lafayette.

Above: Former French Foreign Legion soldier Eugene Bullard, who flew with SPA 93 and 95. He was the only black American pilot of World War One.

On 3 September 1917 Brigadier General William L. Kenny was appointed Chief of the Air Service for the American Expeditionary Force (AEF).

The USAS came into the European war when 1st Aero Squadron, under the command of Major Ralph Royce, arrived in France in August 1917 to begin training. The squadron was equipped with French aircraft and trained as an observation unit at a French school. On 15 April 1918 the squadron flew its first combat mission.

Now at war, the USA found that Britain and France were way ahead of her in aviation. and then on 24 July 1917 the US Congress authorised $640m for military aviation. 345 combat squadrons were envisaged, with 263 squadrons intended for the European war. Pilot and observer training began to get into top gear, with training being carried out in the USA, Canada and Europe. By November 1918 the Aviation Service was operating seven Aviation Centres in France.

The area around Toul was the centre of operations for the American build-up. On 14 April 1918, the 94th Squadron – the famous 'Hat in the Ring' Squadron – had the honour of being the first to shoot down a German aircraft, when Lieutenants Douglas Campbell and Alan Winslow shot down two enemy aircraft.

In June 1918 the various squadrons were organised into one large group, the 1st Brigade under the command of General Billy Mitchell at Chateau Thierry, only 56 miles from Paris. American forces came under sustained heavy attack by the Germans: aerial battles were fought daily and the gallant, but inexperienced, Americans lost heavily. In August 1918 Mitchell retaliated with overwhelming air power: under his control he had 89 US squadrons plus nine British bombing squadrons – a total force of over 1,500 aircraft to attack the Germans at St. Mihiel.

The American assault was successful and on 26 September 1918, US forces pushed forward into the Meuse Argonne Front, again with heavy air power, this time of over

The 94th Aero Squadron pilots from left: Lieutenent Joe Eastman, Captain Jim Meissner. Captain Eddie Rickenbacker, Captain Reed Chambers and Lieutenant Thorne Taylor.

600 aircraft. On 9 October the heaviest USAS blow was struck: 200 bombers, 50 fighter-bombers and over 100 fighter escorts, flying in two streams, attacked German troop concentration areas. USAS aircrew shot down over 100 German aircraft and 21 balloons.

The most successful US pilot of the war was Captain Edward Vernon Rickenbacker, with a total of 26 victories; he served with 94 Aero Squadron, commanded by Major Gervais Raoul Lufbery (17 victories). On 19 March 1918 Rickenbacker made the first American patrol over enemy lines, with Major Lulbery and Lieutenant Douglas Campbell (six victories). His first victory came on 29 April and by 30 May his total was five, bringing him the award of the US Distinguished Service Cross. On 25 September 1918 he was awarded the Medal of Honor.

Many famous Americans served in the war. Quentin Roosevelt – son of the 27th President of the United States, Teddy Roosevelt – fought officialdom to get into a combat unit. He was posted to 95 Squadron at Villeneuve but was shot down and killed on France's Bastille Day, 14 July 1918.

By August 1918 USAS aircraft strength had risen to almost 1,500 aircraft and by the Armistice in November 1918 the USAS had 45 operational squadrons on the battle-front, with a strength of 740 aircraft. Aircrew strength was 800 pilots and 500 observers/gunners.

USAS losses were 289 aircraft and 48 balloons, against enemy losses of 781 aircraft and 73 balloons, all in eighteen months of war.

A total of 90 American airmen were 'aces', having from five to 26 victories. Four airmen were awarded the Medal of Honor: Rickenbacker, 2nd Lieutenant F. Luke, 2nd Lieutenant E. R. Bleckley and 1st Lieutenant H. E. Goettler.

Lieutenant Frank Lemon Baylies (1895–1918) 12 victories

Frank Baylies was born at New Bedford, Massachusetts on 23 September 1895. He enlisted in the US Ambulance Section and was sent to France, arriving there on 6 March 1916. He saw active service on the Somme, Verdun and the Argonne. He was sent to Serbia for three months and won the Croix de Guerre for bravery under fire.

On 20 May 1917 he enlisted in the French Air Service, and after training received his pilot's wings on 20 September 1917. He joined SPA73 at Dunkirk on 17 November 1917 and on 18 December transferred as a Sergeant to SPA3 which was part of the famous 'Storks' Group.

On 19 February 1918 he shot down an enemy two-seater over Forges, his first confirmed victory. Two more of the enemy went down in March and another two in April, making Baylies an ace. Between 2–31 May 1918 he downed seven more enemy aircraft, making his final total 12 confirmed victories.

Frank Baylies preferred to fly and fight with the French, refusing the rank of captain in the USAS. He did transfer in May with the rank of 2nd Lieutenant, but continued to fly SPADs with SPA3.

On 17 June 1918 he accepted combat from four German aircraft over Lassigny: outnumbered by the Fokker triplanes of Jasta 19, he was shot down in flames onto Rollet village. The chivalrous Germans delivered an airborne message to French lines informing SPA3 of the death of the highest-scoring American airman in French service.

Baylies was awarded The Médaille Militaire by the French. In 1927 he was reinterred at the Mémorial de L'Escadrille Lafayette in Paris.

Captain Wilfred Beaver (dates unknown) 19 victories

An American serving with 20 Squadron RAF (motto: 'Deeds not Words'), Captain Beaver flew Bristol F.2b two-seater fighters with observer/gunners Lieutenant C. I. Angelasto, Lieutenant H. E. Easton, Corporal M. Mather and Sergeant E. A. Deighton.

20 Squadron had been re-equipped with Bristol Fighters in August 1917 at St. Marie-Cappel and Beaver and his gunners used this excellent aircraft to best advantage. Beaver and Angelasto opened their victory score on 13 November 1917 when they destroyed an Albatros D V over Houthulst.

Beaver and his observers began to destroy enemy aircraft on a regular basis: two victories in December 1917, two more in January 1918 and five in February 1918. This made their total ten enemy destroyed or sent down out of control.

Beaver's eleventh and twelfth victories followed in March and April; May saw him and his gunners score six victories. On the 27 May Captain Beaver and Sergeant Deighton downed three enemy aircraft – an Albatros and two Fokker Dr I triplanes – in just three minutes over Armentieres. The Albatros was sent down out of control at 11.25 hours, the first Dr I destroyed at 11.27 hours and the second Dr I destroyed at 11.28 hours.

Beaver and Deighton destroyed another Dr I on 29 May followed by their last victory, an Albatros D V, on 13 June 1918.

Captain Beaver was awarded the British Military Cross on 22 June 1918. His RAF gunners/observers are credited with victories as follows:

Sergeant Deighton	15 shared victories
Lieutenant Angelasto	9 shared victories
Corporal Mather	8 shared victories
Lieutenant Easton	7 shared victories

Lieutenant Douglas Campbell (1896–1990) 6 victories

Douglas Campbell was the first American pilot to shoot down a German aircraft during World War One, a Pfalz D III on 14 April 1918, and then the first American pilot to become an ace, having downed five enemy aircraft in aerial combat, on 31 May 1918.

Of Scottish descent, Douglas Campbell was born in California on 7 June 1896. Educated at Harvard and Cornell Universities, he learned to fly in America on a Curtiss JN4 'Jenny'. He was posted to France and completed his flying training at Issoudon.

On 1 March 1918 he was posted to 94th Aero Squadron, Villeneuve le Vertus sur Marne, which was awaiting its quota of Nieuport 28 fighters. The 94th was under the command of Major Raoul Lufbery and its insignia was the famous 'Hat in the Ring', symbolising 'Uncle Sam' throwing his hat into the ring of World War One. America's top ace Eddie Rickenbacker was also a member of the 94th (he became its commanding officer in September 1918).

On 19 March 1918 Douglas Campbell, accompanied in formation by Eddie Rickenbacker and Raoul Lufbery, took off on the first American patrol over enemy lines.

On 14 April Campbell and Alan Winslow took off in a hurry at 07.15 hours and closed in combat with two enemy two-seaters over Toul. Campbell opened fire and shot one of them down in flames – the first American pilot to score a victory in World War One. Alan Winslow shot down the other two-seater seconds later.

On the 18th and 19th May 1918, Campbell destroyed another two enemy aircraft, both Rumpler C-types. On 27 May 1918 he downed a Pfalz D III of Jasta 65 over Montsec. His American 'ace'-status qualifying victory was on 31 May 1918, when he shot down a Rumpler C-type of Fleiger Abteilung 242 over Lironville, making him the first American World War One ace.

Campbell scored his final victory on 5 June 1918, when he shared a victory over

Lieutenant Douglas Campbell.

a Rumpler C-type over Mailly with Lieutenant James A. Meissner, also of 94th Aero Squadron. The next day Campbell was in combat with a Rumpler, when he was wounded in the back by fire from the gunner of the opposing aircraft. In great pain from his wound, he landed his aircraft and was taken to hospital. He convalesced in America and returned to France in November, after the Armistice.

Campbell was promoted to captain in spring 1919. His decorations were the US Distinguished Service Cross with Four Oak Leaves, the Légion d'Honneur and the Croix de Guerre with two Palmes.

Douglas Campbell left the USAS and went into civil aviation. He died in Greenwich, Connecticut, aged 94 years on 16 December 1990. A grand innings for a famous, gallant American ace.

Lieutenant David Sinton Ingalls (1899–1985) 6 victories

Lieutenant Ingalls scored six victories during August and September 1918, making him the only United States Navy ace of World War One.

Ingalls was born 28 January 1899 at Cleveland, Ohio, where he went to school before entering Yale University. He joined the 1st Yale Unit (Flying School), graduating as Naval Aviator No.85. When he was 18, he enlisted in the 3rd Yale Unit for active service.

In November 1917 he was sent to France with a coastal protection squadron but – in his own off-duty time flew Camels of 13 Naval Squadron, RNAS. 13 Naval Squadron was renamed 213 Squadron on the formation of the RAF in April 1918.

On 11 August 1918 he scored his first victory with 213 Squadron, an Albatros C-type which he destroyed over Dixmunde. His excellent skills as a pilot were recognised and he was detached officially to 213 Squadron, where on 21 August 1918 he destroyed

an LVG C-type over Zevecote. He flew D.H.4 bombers for two months with 217 Squadron, and then returned to 213 Squadron in August. Between the 15th and 24th September 1918 he destroyed three more enemy aircraft and a balloon, making his final total six confirmed victories.

David Ingalls was Mentioned in Despatches and awarded the Distinguished Flying Cross by the British; he also received the American Distinguished Service Cross and the French Légion d'Honneur.

Lieutenant Ingalls survived the war and was recalled to duty as a Lieutenant Commander in the US Navy during World War Two. He served in the Pacific and was awarded the Bronze Star and Legion of Merit. He died on 26 April 1985, aged 86 years.

Lieutenant David Sinton Ingalls, the only US Navy Ace.

American ace Gervais Raoul Lufbery.

Major Gervais Raoul Lufbery (1885–1918) 16 (29) victories

Lufbery was born 14 March 1885 in central France of an American father and a French mother. At the age of seventeen he travelled the world, and in 1907 he enlisted in the US Army, seeing active service in the Philippines, where he became an expert marksman.

When World War One erupted, Lufbery tried to enlist in the French Aviation Service but as an American he had to join the French Foreign Legion first and then transfer to the Air Service. He gained Military Pilot's Brevet No.1286 on 29 July 1915, at Chartres, and was posted to the Voisin-equipped VB106, joining them on 7 October 1915. For several months the Voisins of VB106 carried out daily bombing missions, but Lufbery wanted to be a pilot de chasse (fighter pilot), and was sent for fighter pilot training.

Completing his fighter pilot training, Lufbery was sent to N124, the Lafayette Escadrille, which had been formed on 20 April 1916, at Luxeuil les Bains. He was promoted to adjutant in June 1916 and a year later to sous lieutenant.

On 30 July 1916 he shot down his first enemy aircraft, a two-seater over the Foret d'Etain. The next day he shot down another two-seater over Vaux. On 12 October he became an ace when he shot down his fifth enemy aircraft, a Roland C11, and was awarded a citation. His next victory was an Aviatik C-type over Chaulnes, on 27 December.

On 12 June 1917 he was awarded the British Military Cross – a rare honour for an American; he also brought down his tenth enemy aircraft the same day. Promotion to 1st lieutenant followed and by the end of 1917 his score had reached 16 victories. His decorations included the Médaille Militare, Légion d'Honneur, Croix de Guerre and the British Military Cross.

America had by now entered the war on the Allied side and Lufbery was commissioned as a major in the USAS. In January 1918 he transferred to 95th Aero Squadron, later joining the 94th Aero Squadron. In spite of illness he continued to fly with the 94th and had two further victories on the 12th and 27th April 1918, though these two were unconfirmed.

Lufbery took off in a Nieuport on his last offensive combat on 19 May 1918, with the 94th Aero Squadron. An enemy reconnaissance aircraft was approaching and Lufbery took off to attack. He engaged the enemy and scored hits, but his Nieuport caught fire. Rather than be burned to death the gallant major jumped to his death from the burning aeroplane. His broken body was found by French workers and immediately covered with flowers, as he lay crumpled in a garden at Maron.

Major Gervais Raoul Lufbery was buried with full military honours next day.

Lieutenant Frank Luke (1897–1918) 18 victories

Lieutenant Frank Luke.

Frank Luke was born in the western town of Phoenix, Arizona, on 19 May 1897, of German descent. He was brought up in a western environment and could handle a revolver and rifle with excellence.

He enlisted in the US Signal Corps 25 September 1917 at Tucson, and applied to transfer to the Aviation Section. He trained as a pilot at Rockwell Field, California, and was promoted to 2nd lieutenant in the Aviation Section on 23 January 1918. He sailed from New York in the SS *Leviathan* on 4 March 1918, bound for France. Luke was posted to 3 Aviation Instruction Centre for advanced flying training, then to Cazeau for a course in aerial gunnery, in which he excelled – perhaps his Western background helped!

Luke continually badgered the authorities to get him into aerial combat and on 26 July 1818 he was posted to the 27th Aero Squadron. He scored his first victory on 16 August, but as he had left his formation without permission it was not confirmed.

Chagrined at not having his victory officially confirmed, Luke began to attack heavily defended enemy observation balloons. His first confirmed victory was a balloon on 12

September 1918. This was the beginning of an incredible series of victories: 14 September, two balloons; 15 September, three balloons; 16 September: two balloons; and on 18 September, two balloons, two Fokker D VIIs and one Halberstadt C-Type – five victories in the space of ten minutes! He brought down one balloon and one Hannover CT on 28 September, and finally three balloons on 29 September, bringing his confirmed score to eighteen victories.

This last was, however, his final flight. Whilst attacking the heavily defended balloons he was shot down and wounded by ground fire. Struggling out of his crashed SPAD, Luke was called upon by advancing German troops to surrender but, true to his Western upbringing, he refused, drew his Colt .45 revolver and gave battle. The odds were against him, and he fell dead from rifle fire. He was buried in Murvaux Cemetery.

He was cited for the Distinguished Service Cross and Oak Leaf Cluster by his commanding officer, Major Harold Hartney, but it was felt that a higher honour was needed for the brave Frank Luke. Major Hartney – on being appraised of Frank Luke's last moments – recommended him for America's highest honour, the Medal of Honor. Luke became the only wartime pursuit pilot to receive this award posthumously.

On 3 January 1919 Luke's grave was found by US officials, and later his body was removed to the American Military Cemetery at Romagne.

Captain Edward Vernon Rickenbacker (1890–1973) 26 victories

America's top ranking ace – Captain Edward V. Rickenbacker – was born at Columbus, Ohio, on 8 October 1890. His Swiss parents' name was Reichenbacher, but the name was changed to Rickenbacker when America entered World War One on the Allied side. Rickenbacker was then a sergeant driver for General Pershing, and went to France. He was a trained engineer and a famous racing driver, so when he applied to transfer to the Aviation Section, he was accepted and sent to 2 Aviation Instruction Centre, at Tours.

Qualifying as a pilot, he expected to get into the air war where his racing car skills would serve him well in split-second decisions needing quick reflexes. The Air Service was more interested in his engineering skills, however, and sent him as Chief Engineering Officer to 3 Aviation Instruction Centre at Issoudun. Not pleased, Rickenbacker learned advanced flying and gunnery skills in his own time, and then bombarded his superiors with requests to fly on combat duty.

Officialdom relented, and on 4 March 1918 Rickenbacker was sent to the 94th Aero Squadron, on the Marne. On 19 March 1918, in formation with Major Raoul Lufbery and Lieutenant Douglas Campbell, he made the first aerial combat patrol over German lines by an American squadron.

Rickenbacker scored his first victory at 18.10 hours on 29 April 1918, over Baussant, when he downed a Pfalz D III. By 30 May 1918 his score stood at six confirmed victories, another Pfalz and four Albatros having fallen to his guns. He was now – officially – an ace. In June 1918, however, he suffered a severe ear infection and entered hospital in Paris for a mastoid operation. Returning to flying duty in September, he shot down another six enemy aircraft that month, and eleven aircraft and three balloons in October, making his final total 26 victories.

Captain Rickenbacker was awarded the Distinguished Service Cross, the French Croix de Guerre, and the Légion d'Honneur. Amazingly America's highest award – the

America's top ace, Eddie Rickenbacker of the 94th Aero Squadron.

Medal of Honor – was not awarded and presented until 6 November 1930, by President Hoover.

Eddie Rickenbacker returned to business life after the November Armistice – but rejoined the US Army Air Corps when World War Two broke out. He undertook worldwide missions for the American Secretary of State and was awarded the Certificate of Merit. On one mission his aircraft ditched in the Pacific, and he and his crew had to survive in a life raft on the open ocean for 21 days with sparse rations.

The highly respected American ace finally passed away in 1973, aged 82 years. His name is in American (and other) history for ever.

Captain Elliot Springs (1896–1959) 15 (17) victories

One of the outstanding ace fighter pilots of World War One, Elliot Springs was born in Lancaster, South Carolina on 31 July 1896. He was educated at Culver Military School and Princeton University, where he learned to fly with the university flying school.

In September 1917 he was posted to England to fly with the RFC, to gain flying experience. Early in 1918 he was sent to France and joined 85 Squadron, RAF, flying the S.E.5a. His first victory was over a Pfalz D.III, which he sent down out of control on 1 June 1918; by 25 June he had destroyed three more enemy aircraft. He was shot down in action on 27 June 1918, and was injured in the crash-landing.

Recovering from his injuries, he was sent to 148th Aero Squadron, USAS, which was flying Sopwith Camels under the overall command of RAF 65th Wing. On 3 August 1918 Springs began to add to his victory score by destroying a Fokker D VII over Ostend; this made him an ace. Another Fokker D VII went down under his twin machine-guns on 13 August, making his total six confirmed victories.

His next three victories, all Fokker D VIIs, came within minutes of each other at 10.10 hours. He was awarded the British Distinguished Flying Cross and the US Distinguished Service Cross.

The next three victories were also Fokker D VIIs, two of which he destroyed, the other being

Captain Elliot White Springs, OC B Flight, 148th Aero Squadron.

sent down out of control. His final victory was on 27 September 1918 when he destroyed a Halberstadt C-type over Fontaine Notre Dame, bringing his final score to sixteen.

Captain Springs survived the war and became a prolific writer on aviation themes, and entered his father's cotton business. He was recalled to the US Army Air Corps in 1941 and promoted to Lieutenant Colonel. He died on 15 October 1959, aged but 63 years.

85 Squadron RAF at Hounslow, England, about to fly to France. From left: E.W. Springs, Horn, Longton, Callaghan, Dymond, Thomson and Brown.

AMERICAN ACES 1917–18

Kill totals given are those officially confirmed; those in parenthesis refer to totals suggested by more recent research. 'RAF' or 'RN' in parenthesis indicates that the pilot served with the Royal Air Force or Royal Navy, respectively.

26 kills Captain E. V. Rickenbacker
21 kills 2nd Lieutenant Frank Luke (18)
20 kills Captain Frederick W. Gillet (RAF)
19 kills Captain Wilfred Beaver (RAF)
18 kills Captain William C. Lambert (RAF)
17 kills
Captain August T. Iaccaci (RAF)
Lieutenant Paul T.

Iaccaci (RAF)
Captain Howard A. Kullberg (RAF)
16 kills
Major Raoul Lufbery (29)
Lieutenant Eugene S. Coler (RAF)
Captain Oren J. Rose (RAF)
15 kills
Captain Elliot W. Springs (RAF and USAS)

14 kills
Captain Frederick Libby (RAF)
Lieutenant Kenneth R. Unger (RAF)
13 kills
1st Lieutenant George Vaughn
12 kills
Captain Field E. Kindley
1st Lieutenant David Putnam (13)
2nd Lieutenant Frank

Baylies (SPA3)
Major Reed G. Landis (RAF)
Lieutenant Louis Bennett (RAF)
Captain Frederick I. Lord (RAF)
Captain James W. Pearson (RAF)
Captain Clive W. Warman (RFC)
11 kills
Captain Emile J. Lussier (RAF)

Lieutenant Henry Robinson Clay Jnr of C Flight, 148th Aero Squadron.

10 kills

Lieutenant Duerson Knight (RAF)

Captain Oliver C. Le Boutillier (RN/RAF)

Captain Jacques Michael Swaab

9 kills

Captain Thomas G. Cassady

Lieutenant L. A. Hamilton (10)

Captain Frank Driscoll Hunter

Lieutenant Jens F. Larsen (RAF)

Lieutenant Chester Ellis Wright

8 kills

Lieutenant Paul F. Baer (9)

Major Charles J. Biddle (7)

Captain Alvin A. Callender (RAF)

Captain Hamilton Coolidge

Lieutenant Henry R. Clay

Leutenant Jesse Orin Creech (7)

Lieutenant William P. Erwin

Lieutenant D'Arcy Fowlis Hilton (RAF)

2nd Lieutenant Clinton Jones

Captain Gorman de Larner (7)

Major James A. Meissner

Lieutenant Walter K. Simon (RAF)

Lieutenant Joseph F. Wehner (6)

Lieutenant Wilbur W. White

7 kills

Lieutenant Harold A. White (RAF)

Lieutenant Archibald Buchanan (RAF)

Lieutenant Howard Burdick (8)

Major Reed Chambers

Lieutenant Harvey W. Cook

Captain John O. Donaldson (RAF)

Lieutenant John Sharpe Griffith (RAF)

Captain Frank L. Hale (RAF)

Lieutenant Lancing C. Holden

Major John Huffer

Lieutenant John K. McArthur

Lieutenant Wendel A. Robertson

Lieutenant Leslie J. Rummell

Lieutenant Karl J. Schoen

Captain Sumner Sewell

Lieutenant John S. Sharpe

6 kills

Lieutenant William T. Badham (5)

Lieutenant Hilbert L. Bair (RAF)

Lieutenant Byrne V. Baucom

Lieutenant James D. Beane

Captain Clayton L. Bissell

Lieutenant Charles A. Bissonette (RAF)

Captain Arthur R. Brooks

Lieutenant Charles G. Catto (RAF)

Captain Douglas Campbell

Lieutenant Norman Cooper (RAF)

Captain Edward P. Curtis

Lieutenant Murray K. Guthrie

Captain James N. Hall

Captain Leanard C. Hammond

Lieutenant-Colonel Harold E. Hartney (7)

Lieutenant Frank Kerr Hays

Captain Donald Hudson

Lieutenant Howard C. Knotts

Major James Alfred Keating (RAF)

Lieutenant Robert O. Lindsay

Lieutenant John K. Macarthur

Lieutenant Ralph A. Neill

Major D. Peterson

Lieutenant Cleo F. Pineau (RAF)

Lieutenant William T. Ponder

Lieutenant Kenneth L. Porter (5)

Lieutenant Bogart Rogers (RAF)

Captain Martinus Stenseth (8)

Lieutenant William H. Stovall

Lieutenant-Colonel W. Thaw (5)

Captain Edgar G. Tobin

Captain Jerry C. Vasconcells

Lieutenant Remington Deb Vernam

5 kills

Lieutenant Hilbert L. Blair

Captain C. L. Bissel

Lieutenant Howard K. Boyson (RAF)

Lieutenant Sydney M. Brown (RAF)

Lieutenant L. K. Callahan

Captain Everett R. Cook

Captain Charles R. D'Olive

Lieutenant Arthur E. Easterbrook

Lieutenant H. C. Ferguson

Lieutenant George W. Furlow

Lieutenant Harold H. George

Captain Charles G. Grey

Lieutenant Edward M. Haight

Captain James A. Healy

Lieutenant Malcolm G. Howell (RAF)

Lieutenant David S. Ingalls (RAF)

Lieutenant James Knowles

Lieutenant Frederick E. Luff (RAF)

Lieutenant Francis P. Magoun (RAF)

Lieutenant Zenos R. Miller

Lieutenant John S. Owens

Lieutenant Orville A. Ralston (RAF)

Lieutenant John J. Seerley

Lieutenant Harold G. Shoemaker (RAF)

Lieutenant Francis M. Simonds

Major Victor H. Strahm

Lieutenant Francis M. Symonds

Lieutenant Edgar Taylor (RAF)

Captain William D. Tipton

Lieutenant Robert M. Todd

Lieutenant R. de B. Vernon

Lieutenant Rodney D. Williams

The six American aces listed below served with French air services only:

12 kills

Second Lieutenant Frank L. Baylies (SPA3)

8 kills

Lieutenant Edwin C. Parsons (N124)

Lieutenant James J. Connelly (SPA157)

Lieutenant Ewart S. Miller (SPA49)

5 kills

Lieutenant Norman Prince (VB108, VB113, N124)

Lieutenant Charles H. Veil (SPA150)

BELGIUM

With World War One looming, Belgium mobilised its small air arm, the Compagnie des Aviateurs, on 1 August 1914. Only Nos. 1 and 2 Escadrilles became fully operational, with Nos. 3 and 4 working up. Thirty-seven military pilots were on strength, with eight more civilian pilots volunteering their services to their country. Three pilots brought their own aircraft to fight the coming battle.

Early in 1915 the Air Arm was renamed the Aviation Militaire. During the next three years the Aviation Militaire fought well and produced five aces (using the yardstick of five victories to be an ace).

By September 1918 the Aviation Militaire had built up to a strength of 11 Escadrilles. Nos. 9, 10 and 11 were fighter Escadrilles equipped with Hanriot HD.1s, SPAD S.13s and Camels. No.8 Escadrille was a night bombing unit equipped with Farman F.40s. Nos. 2 to 7 Escadrilles were used for observation and equipped with Bréguet A2s, SPAD S.11s and Henri Farmans. No.1 Escadrille had a maintenance role. Total aircraft strength was 69 single-seater and 58 two-seater aircraft.

Chevalier Willy Coppens de Houthulst (1892–?) 37 victories

Belgium's top scoring fighter pilot was born in Brussels in 1892. After army service he joined the Belgian Air Arm as a trainee pilot in early September 1915. He trained at Hendon, England, graduating as a pilot in December 1915, then returned to Etampes. He continued with flying training and by July 1916 had qualified as a fighter pilot.

His first posting was to 6me Escadrille at Houthem, flying British B.E.2cs and Farmans, but this reconnaissance squadron soon re-equipped with ex-Royal Navy Sopwith 11/2 Strutters. On 1 May 1917 Coppens was flying a Sopwith when he was 'bounced' by four German fighters: he retreated from the unequal dogfight and landed his bullet-riddled fighter safely. This first brush with the enemy brought him a Mention in Despatches.

On 15 July Coppens was posted to a fighter squadron equipped with single-seater Nieuport Scouts, based at les Moeres airstrip. Six days later he was in action, but failed to score. The squadron was re-equipped with small and agile Hanriot HD.1 single machine-gun fighters, which Coppens flew and liked. He flew during the winter of 1917–18 but failed to score a single victory.

In March 1918 three Belgian squadrons were combined to form a fighter group – the reasoning being that a large force could better take on the German Air Service. On March 18 Coppens attacked a German observation balloon, but his machine-gun did not have incendiary bullets and he failed to set the balloon on fire. The resourceful Coppens then obtained standard British .303in incendiary bullets and went on the attack against balloons, but without result.

On 25 April Coppens was flying his blue-painted Hanriot with his commanding officer on his wing, when he sighted a gaggle of enemy aircraft being pursued by other

The Chevalier Willy Coppens de Houthulst in full dress uniform in front of his aircraft.

Belgian aircraft. Coppens closed on the dogfight and came to close quarters with a German fighter. Seizing his chance, he poured a burst from his single machine-gun into the German, which turned over and went down, crashing to earth near the village of Ramscapelle. Coppens had scored his first victory.

May 1918 saw Coppens devise a method of ammunition loading whereby he inserted four incendiary bullets into the normal gun feed belt to his single machine-gun – he would then close to short range against a balloon for maximum effect. He scored a balloon victory with this method, then another over Houthulst Forest. Time after time he shot down German observation balloons in the forest zone, which was his favourite combat area. On one occasion he downed a balloon with but one incendiary bullet – an amazing feat.

On 14 October Coppens took off at dawn to attack balloons above Thourout and Praet Bosh. He shot down one balloon, but when attacking another he was hit by flak and received a wound to his leg. He managed to keep control of his Hanriot and crash-land: taken from the mangled wreckage by ground troops, he was rushed to La Panne hospital where his wounded leg had to be amputated.

The loss of a leg was the end of Coppens' war, although he stayed in the Air Arm until World War Two broke out, when he went to Switzerland after the Belgian surrender. He was knighted as a Chevalier of the Legion of Honour and awarded the British Distinguished Service Order, among many other decorations.

Fernard Jacquet (1888–1947) 7 victories

Jacquet was born at Petite Chappelle in 1888 and enrolled in the Brussels Military Academy in 1907, graduating as an officer on 25 June 1910. He was allocated to the 4th Regiment and then requested flying training. He was sent to flying school early in 1913: by the autumn he had graduated as a pilot and was posted to 2me Escadrille, equipped with Henri Farman aircraft.

By August 1914, when the war broke out, his squadron was stationed at Namur, but the Farman aircrafts' engines were underpowered and Jacquet was unable to fly. Eager to be at the throat of the enemy – the hallmark of the finest troops – Jacquet undertook ground attack in an 'armoured car' and accounted for a squadron of German cavalry.

Jacquet's squadron re-located to France and was re-equipped with Henri Farman 20s by the French. The German advance drove the Belgian Army back and by October Jacquet's squadron was near Dunkirk. The Compagnie des Aviateurs began to mount bombing raids using the Farmans, and Jacquet took part in a raid on a railway station.

In January 1915 Jacquet was posted to 1ère Escadrille and flew a Maurice Farman equipped with a Lewis machine-gun. It was not until 17 April that he brought the Lewis gun into action, when he shot down a German Aviatik over Beerst. This was his first victory, and also the first victory for the Belgian Air Arm. Jacquet's method of operating was to fly with his observer as a single aircraft intruding into German airspace. In this way he shot down several German aircraft, but as they were behind enemy lines, they could not be confirmed.

Commandant Fernand Jacquet, the first Belgian pilot to score a victory.

By February 1917 Jacquet was an 'ace', having shot down five enemy aircraft. By January 1918 he was in command of three Escadrilles and flying a SPAD S.11. By November 1918 he had shot down two more enemy aircraft making his official score seven – his unconfirmed score, however, was many more.

During World War Two he was an active member of the Resistance and was imprisoned by the Germans. Jacquet survived both wars and died in October 1947.

André de Meulemeester (dates unknown) 11 victories

Flemish-born de Meulemeester – 'The Eagle of Flanders' – volunteered for the embryo Belgian Air Arm and trained as a pilot at the Belgian flying school at Etampes.

Late in 1916 he was assigned to a top unit, the Nieuport-equipped 1st Escadrille whose squadron crest was a Scottish thistle and the Scottish national motto *Nemo me Impune Lacessit* ('no one injures me with impunity').

Andre de Meulemeester proved to be a natural pilot and opened his victory total on 30 April 1917, when he shot down a two-seater reconnaissance aircraft over the German front line at Lecke. He scored his second victory on 11 June over Beerst. On 14 June he shot down an Albatros in no man's land (the area between the opposing front lines). Five weeks later he downed another Albatros, but was wounded in the dogfight and hospitalised.

A month later he was back with the squadron and promoted to flight commander, which entitled him to a wingman: his was Willy Coppens, who was destined to be Belgium's leading ace. By October 1917 de Meulemeester was flying a new Hanriot HD.1 which he had painted a glaring yellow; he also began flying with two wingmen, who also had their aircraft painted yellow.

Sergeant André de Meulemeester, known as 'The Eagle of Flanders', wingman to Willy Coppens.

Lieutenant Jan Olieslagers posing in front of his aircraft.

On 2 November de Meulemeester shot down another Albatros over Dixmunde. On Sunday 4 November the trio were airborne in their yellow Hanriots when they came upon a dogfight between five German and four British aircraft. The Belgians joined the battle with gusto and de Meulemeester immediately shot down an Albatros that crashed in flames into the German front line.

It was not until 17 March 1918 that de Meulemeester increased his score, shooting down another Albatros over Houthulst whilst leading a 'finger-five' formation. On 3 May 1918 he downed another Albatros, and by the November Armistice his score stood at eleven.

Jan Olieslagers (1882–1942) 6 victories

Olieslagers was born in Antwerp in 1882. At seventeen years of age he became a motorcycle racing ace, gaining wealth and fame in the process. He bought his own Bleriot aircraft, taught himself how to fly it and took part in the first Belgian air display, in 1909. He then took his aircraft abroad to Algeria, Spain and Italy to give displays. He again became an ace – this time in the air.

When World War One broke out in August 1914 Olieslagers offered his aircraft and personnel in defence of his country. He joined the Belgian Air Arm as a corporal and a year later was made a 2nd lieutenant. By March 1915 he was flying Nieuport Scouts – his beloved Blériot was no match for the new German fighters. Like Jacquet, he preferred to fly deep into enemy territory and bring the fight to the enemy. In this way he shot down several German aircraft which were unconfirmed and not claimed.

Jan Olieslagers came through the war safely with six victories confirmed, his real score being much more. Postwar he lived in Antwerp where he died in 1942.

Edmund Thieffry (?–1929) 10 victories

Edmund Thieffry was conscripted into the 14th Regiment of the Belgian Army in 1912. Two years later he was back at Louvain University, studying to be a lawyer, but on 28

July 1914 he was back in the Army with the 10th Regiment at Liège, and soon in battle with the invading German.

He applied to join the new Belgian Air Arm and joined the Etampes flying school as a trainee pilot in July 1915. He gained his pilot's brevet in February 1916 and was sent to a reconnaissance squadron equipped with Voisin Canons and Farman F.20s. Unfortunately, Thieffry was prone to pilot-error accidents and was transferred to single-seat fighters – it was thought he was less of a risk if he flew alone!

Arriving at Houthem airstrip in December 1916, he joined 5me Escadrille equipped with Nieuport Bébé fighters. On 15 March 1917 he had his first victory, when he shot down a German reconnaissance biplane that was seen to crash behind German lines. On 23 March he clashed with a Fokker D V, bringing it down behind Belgian lines. Flying again the next day, he fought a duel with two enemy fighters but came off worst, crashing between the Belgian and German lines.

2nd Lieutenant Edmund Thieffry.

In May 1917 Thieffry's squadron was re-equipped with SPADs and on 12 May he shot down an Albatros, bringing his score to three. On 20 June he made it four when he shot down an Albatros in a dogfight; the next day Thieffry was himself shot down. but he walked away unharmed – he had an amazing record of crashes and emerging unscathed.

When acting as escort for slow observation aircraft on 3 July, and flying a powerful 220hp SPAD, Thieffry and his squadron clashed with the enemy over German lines. Within a few minutes he had shot down two Albatros aircraft: this feat brought him a commission from the Belgian king. On 16 August Thieffry fought two Albatros aircraft over Houthulst and sent one crashing earthwards. This was followed by a victory on the 22nd and another on 26 August; his score now stood at nine. He also shot down several enemy aircraft behind German lines which were not confirmed.

On 23 February 1918 Thieffry was again in action, but he was shot down himself and went missing, believed killed in action. Weeks later it was found that he had been wounded and made a POW, which he would stay until the November Armistice. He went into civil aviation after the war, but was killed on 10 April 1929 during a flight to the Congo.

BELGIAN PILOTS' VICTORIES 1914–18

37 kills 2nd Lieutenant W. Coppens
11 kills Adjutant A. de Meulemeester
10 kills 2nd Lieutenant E. Thieffry
7 kills Captain F. Jacquet
6 kills Lieutenant J. Olieslagers

4 kills Adjutant G. K. de Lettenhove
4 kills Lieutenant L. Robin
3 kills Sergeant E. Rage
2 kills
Lieutenant M. Benselin
Lieutenant P. Braun
2nd Lieutenant J. Goethals

Sous Officier L. Ledure
Adjutant C. Medaerts
Adjutant M. Medaerts
Sgt. Major C. Montigny
Adjutant R. Rondeau
27 other pilots scored one victory each.

Note
Adjutants C. Medaerts and M. Medaerts were twins and scored two victories each.
Adjutant G. K. de Lettenhove (4) and Sous Lieutenant C.K. de Lettenhove (1) were brothers.

6

RUSSIA

The World War One Russian Imperial Air Services comprised both Navy and Army Divisions – there was no independent air force as such. Before the war there were some 200 military airmen in the Air Services. In August 1914, when Russia went to war, the Air Services' strength was 224 aeroplanes, twelve airships and forty or so kite balloons. During the following three years aeroplane strength increased year on year to 1,039 in 1917.

Russia did have a small aircraft production capability, but mainly relied on foreign imports – mostly French and licence-built aircraft. Wartime production totalled only some 4,700 aircraft.

Staff Captain Peter Nikolaevich Nestorov, who scored just one victory but became a Hero of Russia by ramming the Austrian Baron von Rosenthal in action and saving the town of Sholkiv.

Staff Captain Peter Nikolaevich Nestorov scored but one victory but was regarded as a national hero. Flying an unarmed Morane-Saulnier Type M monoplane, he attacked three enemy aircraft and rammed the leading aircraft, killing himself in the process. A town was named after him.

Russian military records are somewhat sparse regarding their Air Services' pilots' victory totals, but the following list is reasonably accurate. Pilots shared in kills and had some unconfirmed, all of which distort true victory totals. The following is a selected roll of aces and distinguished airmen of the Imperial Russian Air Arms.

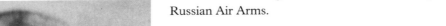

Pavel d'Argueff (1887–1922) 15 victories

Though d'Argueff was born in the Crimea in 1887, his family later moved to France: when World War One broke out he was still in France and enlisted in the 131st Infantry Regiment of the French Army.

Wounded in action, he left the infantry and enlisted in the air arm. In 1917 he was sent to Russia with Escadrille SPA124 and scored six victories, earning two Russian decorations, the Orders of St. George and St. Vladimir. During 1918 he returned to France and shot down nine German aircraft. During his French air service he gained seven mentions in despatches (Citations d'Armée). He died in France in 1922.

Viktor Georgiyich Fedorov (?–1922)
5 victories

Fedorov studied at Kharkov University where he became a Social Democrat and revolutionary. In August 1914, when World War One broke out, he was in France. He enlisted in the Russian Battalion, being wounded in February 1915.

During July 1915 he transferred to the French Air Arm and learnt to fly at Dijon. He was posted to SPA.3 in December 1915 and flew a Caudron G.IV with the rank of sergent. He flew with the same observer/mechanic, Pierre Lanero, for the duration of the war.

In the spring of 1916 Fedorov shot down three enemy aircraft over the Verdun battlefront in sixteen days and became known as 'The Russian Air Cossack of Verdun'. Promotion to lieutenant followed together with the award of the Croix de Guerre and Medaille Militaire.

On 2 April 1916 he was wounded in an air battle; when he recovered he was sent, with Lanero, to Rumania, then to Russia to teach Russians how to fly. Fedorov returned to France on 10 April 1918 and was soon in action, shooting down his fourth aircraft on 29 September 1918. His last victory was on October 9 1918 when he shot down an enemy fighter over Argonne.

He was wounded on 16 October 1918 and ended his service. He died in Paris in 1922.

Above: Lieutenant Victor Georgiyich Fedorov.

Below: Staff Captain Alexander Kazakov, the Russian Air Service's top-scoring pilot with 20 victories; his actual score was many more.

Alexander Alexandrovich Kazakov (1891–1919) 20 victories

Staff Captain Kazakov was the leading Russian air ace with 20 confirmed victories (he was unofficially credited with a total of 32 victories); he held 16 decorations including the British DSO. MC, and DFC, and the French Legion of Honour.

One of Kazakov's tactics was to use his aircraft's undercarriage to rip off the wing of his target in flight, causing it to crash. Kazakov then had to crash-land his Morane.

Over the next three years Kazakov increased his tally and was promoted to lead a group of four fighter squadrons. During 1916 he downed four Fokker monoplanes, an Albatros and a Brandenberg. 1917 saw him shoot down several more aircraft including an Albatros D I, a Rumpler and another Brandenberg, which was his last victory; his war ended with the Russian Revolution of 1917.

Kazakov joined the British Force in Russia with the rank of major and fought in command of the Slav-British Squadron. He died in an aircraft accident on 3 August 1919, aged 28.

Evgraph Nikolaevich Kruten (1890–1917) 7 victories

Kruten was born in the Ukraine in 1890 and was commissioned as a 2nd lieutenant in the Army in 1912. The following year he joined the XI Corps squadron as an artillery spotter and trained as a pilot. In September 1914 he began flying Voisins on night bombing missions.

Captain Evgraph Nikolaevich Kruten.

His first aerial victory came in May 1916 when he shot down a German Albatros. Three months later he forced an Albatros two-seater to land at Nesvish, where the crew were captured by Russian soldiers; on 14 August he shot down another Albatros over the same town. Kruten became a squadron commander and then commander of Fighter Group 2. His personal aircraft was blazoned with the head of a Russian medieval knight.

During the harsh Russian winter of 1916–17, Kruten was sent to France to learn British and French aerial battle tactics. He also became a successful author, writing seven small books on aerial fighting and bombing. Returning to operational combat flying in the summer of 1917, Kruten scored several more victories over the Galician front, bringing his confirmed victory total to seven. However, his true total is believed to be 15 enemy aircraft, but the other eight were not confirmed as they were downed behind enemy lines.

At the end of May 1917 Kruten was killed when his aircraft spun into the ground on landing approach.

Ivan Alexandrovich Orlov (?–1917) 5 victories

Details of Orlov's career are scanty, but it is known that he was Commanding Officer of 7 Fighter Detachment until the summer of 1916, when he was seconded to air arm duty in France.

On 12 June 1916 Ensign Orlov engaged an enemy aircraft at 7,500 feet over Podgaitsky and shot it down. A unique feat at the time; five more victories followed. Orlov returned to the air battle in Russia in 1917 and was shot down on 17 June.

He was awarded all four classes of the Cross of the Order of St. George. He also wrote a manual, Methods of Aerial Fighting.

Boris Sergievsky (1888–?) 2 victories

Sergievsky was born in 1888 and learned to fly in 1912. This earned him a captain's commission in the Imperial Air Service and command of No.2 Fighter Squadron. He shot down two enemy aircraft and was awarded ten medals and decorations, including the Cross of St. George.

Fleeing the Russian Revolution, he went to England and served with the RAF, then returned to White Russia in 1920. Two years later he emigrated to America, becoming an engineer and test pilot.

Alexander Nikolaevich Prokoffief de Seversky (1894–1974) 6 victories

Seversky was born in Tiflis in 1894 and was destined for a career in the Russian Imperial Navy. After graduating from the Imperial Naval Academy, he took a flying course at the Military School of Aeronautics and graduated as a pilot on a Farman 4 aircraft. He then obtained a commission as a 2nd lieutenant in the Russian Imperial Naval Air Service and was sent to the Baltic 2nd Bombing Squadron base at Oesel Island.

On 2 July 1915, whilst flying a two-seater seaplane on a night mission, his aircraft was shot down in the Gulf of Riga. His observer was killed and Seversky's right leg was blown off. Six months later, though, he was back in the air, shooting down thirteen German aircraft in 57 sorties.

31 July 1916 saw his last combat when he and another pilot, flying seaplanes, fought off seven German aircraft. During the two-hour combat Seversky – outnumbered seven to one, as his fellow pilot's machine-guns had jammed – took on the Germans single-handed, shot down two aircraft and drove the other five off. For this superb action he was awarded the exclusive Gold Sword of St. George.

In 1917 he went to America, became a test pilot and founded the Seversky Aero Corporation in 1922. He died in the USA in 1974.

Above: Russian ace Alexander Nikolaevich Prokoffiev de Seversky.

Below: Russian ace Lieutenant Ivan Vasilievich Smirnov, famous in later years as a designer.

Ivan Vassilievich Smirnov (1895–1956) 12 victories

Smirnov was born in Vladimir in 1895 and joined the 96th Infantry Regiment in 1914; he was awarded the Cross of St. George whilst with this regiment.

In 1915 Sergeant Smirnov moved to the XIX Corps Air Squadron, where during the next two years he shot down twelve enemy aircraft and was commissioned as a 1st lieutenant; further promotion to captain followed.

Due to the November 1917 revolution in Russia Smirnov left Russia and went to England, becoming a major in the RAF. In 1922 he joined the Dutch airline KLM, retiring from flying in 1949, he died in Majorca in 1956.

Grigori Eduardovich Suk (1896–1917) 9 victories

Suk was born in 1896 of Russo-Czech parents and trained at Moscow Flying School,

where he graduated in 1916. He was then posted to No.9 Fighter Squadron. The remainder of 1916 and part of 1917 saw Suk shoot down nine enemy aircraft, and he was decorated with all four classes of the Order of St. George.

On 15 November 1917 Grigori Suk was shot down in air combat over the Romanian Front.

Lieutenant-Commander Victor V. Utgoff (1889–?)

A much decorated pilot, Lieutenant-Commander Victor V. Utgoff was born on 14 July 1889 in Novoradomsk (in what is now Lodz, Poland). He became a naval cadet in the Imperial Russian Navy and served with the Black Sea Fleet.

In 1912 the Black Sea Fleet established an air arm and Utgoff was trained as a pilot, gaining his pilot's wings on July 1912. He was promoted to lieutenant on 12 December 1913 and awarded the Order of St. Stanislaus. He became the Russian Navy's first wartime pilot flying seaplanes with the Black Sea air arm.

In March 1915 Utgoff began flying offensive sorties against Turkey from a seaplane carrier. He was decorated with the Order of St. George, promoted to captain and made second in command of the air arm. In August 1916 Utgoff was flying M9 seaplanes and bombing the Bulgarian port of Varna to such good effect that he was awarded the Golden Sword of St. George.

The Russian Revolution began during 1917 and in the summer Utgoff and his family were sent to America. When the November revolution erupted Utgoff was still in America; he decided to stay there.

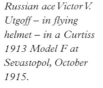

Russian ace Victor V. Utgoff – in flying helmet – in a Curtiss 1913 Model F at Sevastopol, October 1915.

Vasili Ivanovich Yanchenko (1894–?) 16 victories

Yanchenko was born on 4 January 1894 and joined the Imperial Russian Air Service on 22 November 1914. He learned to fly at Sevastapol and went solo on 4 September 1915.

Ensign Vasili Ivanovich Yanchenko, (left in flying helmet).

On 19 November that year he went to Moscow Air School to convert to Morane-Saulnier Type H fighters.

In March 1916 he joined 7th Fighter Detachment as a sergeant. He opened his score on 25 June, shooting down Austro-Hungarian Aviatik, No.33.30, whilst flying with Ensign Ivan Orlov. This earned him the Soldiers Cross of St. George, 2nd Class, and later the rank of warrant officer. On 21 August he was promoted ensign.

By 18 October he had scored three victories and further decorations. In early February 1917 he scored his fourth victory and on 13 April two more; by 5 October he had increased his total to fifteen. 14 October saw his last victory – an Albatros C.III over the front at Gorodok. A few days later the Air Arm fell under Bolshevik control and Yanchenko deserted, to join the Volunteer Army in 1918.

Yanchenko later moved to America and worked for the Sikorsky firm as an engineer.

Staff Captain Boris Victor Sergiesky, wearing full dress uniform and RAF pilot's wings.

RUSSIAN ACES 1914–17

20 kills Staff Captain A. A. Kazakov
16 kills Ensign V. I. Yanchenko
15 kills Captain Pavel. V. d'Argueff
12 kills Lieutenant I. V. Smirnov
9 kills Ensign G. E. Suk
8 kills Lieutenant Georges Marcel Lachman
8 kills Lieutenant Donat Adujovich Makeenok
7 kills Captain E. N. Kruten
7 kills Captain Vladimir

Ivan Strizhevsky
6 kills
Capitaine Louis Coudouret
Ivan Alexandrovich Loiko
Alexander Nikolaivich Prokoffief de Seversky
Kapitan Konstantin Konstantonovich Vakulovsky
5 kills
Lieutenant Viktor G. Fedorov
Juri Vladmirovich Gilsher
Captain Maurice Roch

Gond
Nikolai Kirillovich Kokorin
Ernst K. Leman
Ensign Ivan Alxandrovich Orlov
Lieutenant Edward Martynovich Pulpe
Lieutenant Alexander Mikhailovitch Pishvanov
Mikhail Ivanovich Safonov
Lieutenant Charles A. Revol Tissot

7

GERMANY

In order to understand the complexities of the various German kingdoms, principalities and states at this time and their unified approach to World War One, it may help to explain the way they developed and also kept, to a certain degree, their own identities.

The first German Reich followed the Franco-Prussian War of 1870–1, with the German states coming closer together to counterbalance the power of Russia, France and Austria-Hungary. The then King of Prussia became the first Kaiser (emperor), and the new German Empire was created and proclaimed, with a federal constitution, in the Hall of Mirrors at Versailles in 1871. For the first time since the middle ages, the majority of German-speaking people in Europe would be united in a single state.

The new German Empire was a confederation of 26 states: the Kingdoms of Prussia, Bavaria, Saxony and Württemburg; the principalities of Lippe, Ruess-Greiz, Ruess-Schleiz, Schaumburg Lippe, Schwarzburg-Rudolstadt, Schwarzburg-Sonderhausen and Waldeck; the Grand Duchies of Baden, Hesse, Mecklenberg, Scherwin, Mecklenberg-Strelitz, Saxe-Weimar and Oldenburg, the Duchies of Anhalt, Brunswick, Saxe-Alteberg, Saxe-Coburg-Gotha and Saxe-Meiningen; the territory of Alsace-Lorraine; and the cities of Bremen, Lübeck and Hamburg. By 1910 the population of Germany had risen to 65 million, with Prussia having over 40 million.

The first Kaiser, Wilhelm I, ruled over Germany from 1871 to 1888, being followed by Friedrich III during 1888 and Wilhelm II from 1888 until 1918. These three were members of the Prussian House of Hohenzollern, a dynasty descended from Frederick the Great.

Within the federal constitution some armies were under the control of the Prussian Army but the Royal Armies of Saxony and Württemburg retained their own war ministries, headquarters staff and establishments. The Royal Bavarian Army remained autonomous under the command of its king, with its own headquarters staff and headquarters establishment. The various military forces of the smaller states and provinces became integrated with the Prussian Army. At the outbreak of the war, however, the military forces of the Imperial German Empire came under unified command with only Bavaria maintaining a separate establishment.

Each of the German states had their own range of orders, decorations and medals, which they awarded to their subjects and to others whom they saw fit to reward.

During World War One the Pour le Mérite with Oak Leaves was Prussia's highest award for individual gallantry in action, but not one was awarded to any member of the German Army Air Service. Of the award Pour le Mérite, 81 were made to German aviation personnel during the war. The Order was discontinued after the defeat of Germany in 1918. It is believed by some that the slang name for the Pour le Mérite – 'Blue Max' was coined after the death of its first military aviation recipient, Max Immelmann.

The famous Iron Cross was instituted by Friedrich Wilhelm III, King of Prussia, in 1813 as an award for gallantry in combat. The 1st and 2nd Classes of the Iron Cross were reinstated for the Franco-German War of 1870–1 and continued to be awarded until the end of World War One. There were 219,300 awards made of the Iron Cross 1st Class and 5,500,000 of the Iron Cross 2nd Class from 1813 to 1918. The Cross consisted of a cross patèe in black iron edged with silver with a spray of oak leaves in the centre. The Imperial Crown and Royal Cypher were on the upper limb and the dates '1813', '1870', or '1914' respectively on the lower limb. The Iron Cross 1st Class was fixed to the uniform jacket like the Star of an Order, whereas the 2nd Class award was worn on the left breast from a black ribbon with white edges.

Until 1916 the Imperial German Aviation Service was regarded as part of the ground communications troops, although a separate command had been established in March 1915. Naval and military aviation remained separate. At first, aviation units were controlled by the individual armies to which they were attached. Politics and local pride created confusion: for example, Württemburg insisted that its aviation units be staffed only with its nationals. This confused situation reigned until 8 October 1916, when General Ernst von Hoeppner was appointed Officer Commanding of the Imperial German Aviation Service and immediately began to reorganise its structure, into fighter units of eighteen aircraft each, ground attack units of six to twelve aircraft each, bomber units with about twenty-four aircraft each and various reconnaissance and artillery units, and aircraft for home defence. The Imperial German Naval Aviation Service remained independent, operating flying boats from some thirty-two bases on the German and occupied coasts; they also operated land-based aircraft for coastal defence.

In Germany there was a certain social attitude towards flying aircraft in the early years. Prior to 1914, gentlemen of means employed chauffeurs to drive their cars and the task of piloting an aircraft was viewed in the same light. Consequently, the first pilots were drawn from the ranks of non-commissioned officers, while the commissioned officers – usually cavalrymen, some with the rank of Freiherr (baron) – acted as observers and sat in the rear cockpit. This sometimes caused great problems, as in the early years most of the 'cavalrymen' insisted on being properly dressed, and that included wearing swords. As the aircraft were made of wood and fabric, holes were frequently torn in the fuselage areas and the practice of carrying a sword was very soon dropped. However, it wasn't long before these frustrated cavalrymen were drawn into the excitement of the chase and quickly grasped the chance of knightly individual combat in the air, of flying out to offer symbolically – the tilting of the lance at their enemies, as the knights of medieval times had done.

The German Air Service had its beginnings in 1909 when the German Army used aircraft for the first time. The appointment of Hauptmann de la Roi of the Prussian War Ministry to head up an aviation test project, with a technical section under the control of a Major Hesse, established the basis of the German Air Service. The results were so encouraging that Generalleutnant Freiherr von Lyncker was put in charge of the Inspectorate of Transport Troops, under which umbrella the Imperial German Air Service flourished.

During the following years both civil and military pilots were licensed by the German Aviation Association and (military only) the Inspectorate of Military

Transport. The first pilot's certificates were issued to August Euler and Hans Grade on 1 February 1910. Euler – an engineer – went on to become an aircraft designer. During the spring of 1910 the first flying schools were set up. By December 1910, ten officers had completed their flying training and had been awarded their certificates.

The German War Department – encouraged by the results of military pilot training – allocated the sum of 110,000 Marks for the purchase of military aircraft. The future Imperial German Air Service was slowly coming into being and when World War One broke out on 4 August 1914, Germany had 228 aircraft on its strength, plus a small reserve. Aircrew strength stood at 600 officer pilots, 220 NCO pilots and 500 officer observers. They served with 41 Flieger Abteilungen (Flying Units) of which 33 were Feldflieger Abteilungen (Field Aviation Units). Eight Abteilungen were designated Fortress Flieger Abteilungen, whose role was to defend strategically important towns.

German army aircraft were placed under the control of the Army whilst their large fleet of airships was placed under the control of the Navy. At this time German thinking was that aircraft and airships were to be used for reconnaissance: aircraft for short-range missions, such as artillery spotting and photo reconnaissance, and airships for long-range reconnaissance.

The first long range bomber units, or Kampfgeschwader (KG), were formed in October 1914 and came under Army command. The first such unit was a clandestine one codenamed Brieftauben Abteilung Ostend (BAO), 'Ostend Carrier Pigeon Flight', under the command of Major Wilhelm Siegert.

The German High Command soon realised that their relatively slow reconnaissance and observation aircraft needed protection from faster enemy fighters. Early German fighters such as the Aviatik C I were two-seaters with the pilot and observer firing machine-guns sidewards and rearwards from their cockpits: firing forward through the propeller arc was impossible, as no means of preventing bullets from hitting the propeller blades had as yet been perfected. Some aircraft had machine-guns mounted on the upper wing to fire over the propeller, but this was not very successful.

It was not long before a reliable 'interrupter' mechanism that would allow a machine-gun to fire through the propeller arc without hitting the propeller blades was developed. The mechanism was said to have been invented by Anthony Fokker after seeing the French pilot Roland Garros's Morane Parasol after it had been shot down, though it is now accepted that it was probably the brainchild of Heinrich Luebbe, a member of Fokker's design team. On 23 May 1915 the Fokker Eindecker, equipped with a machine-gun firing through the propeller, came into front-line service with FA62 at Douai. Hauptmann Oswald Boelcke and Oberleutnant Max Immelmann, both already famous in Germany as pilots, immediately went into combat with the Eindecker. Boelcke shot down a Morane Parasol on 4 July and Immelmann a B.E.2c on 1 August. Both were soon to earn Prussia's highest decoration – the Pour le Mérite – on 12 January 1916. With the Eindeckers and their forward firing guns, the German Air Service kept air superiority over the Allies until the Allies produced their own aircraft with forward-firing machine-guns.

Shrewdly, the German War Ministry realised the propaganda value of casting their pilots and observers as national heroes, by awarding honours and decorations for the number of enemy aircraft shot down. At first four victories were needed to give 'ace' status (the Germans used the term Kanone, 'cannon'). Six kills were rewarded with the award of the Knight's Cross of the Hohenzollern House Order and eight with the award of the Pour le Mérite. The famous 'Aces of the Air' began to emerge: Boelcke, Immelmann, and Wintgens won the 'Blue Max' for their exploits and were immortalised on Sanke postcards. These postcards, many of them reproduced here, carried the portraits of the airmen in various heroic poses and were avidly bought and collected by an admiring German public.

During the winter of 1916 the tempo of aerial conflict increased and the number of victories required for high honours increased. To gain the Pour le Mérite, sixteen kills were now needed – this later rose to twenty and by the end of the war to 30. Strangely, some pilots with high scores – including Leutnant Paul Billik with 31 kills and Josef Mai with 31 – were never awarded it. Thirty-five other pilots scored between fourteen and 26 victories but were not decorated with the Pour le Mérite.

Nineteen known pilots were actually awarded the decoration but never received it for various reasons, including death: the decoration could only be awarded to a living officer. Non-commissioned ranks received the Golden Military Service Cross, of which there were eighty awards.

Winners of the Pour le Mérite – all named – taken from a Sanke card.

The new Albatros D I and D II scouts entered service in 1916 and could outfly most Allied aircraft, apart possibly from the British Sopwith Pup and the French Nieuport. By the end of 1916 the German Air Service had 24 operational Jastas and these took a heavy toll of Allied aircraft. Many fighter pilots rose to prominence including Hartmut Baldamus, Erwin Böhme, Otto Bernert, Albert Dossenbach, Wilhelm Frankl, Heinrich Gontermann, Max Muller, Hans Muller and Werner Voss. However, Oswald Boelcke died in combat with D.H.2s of 24 Squadron RFC on 28 October 1916 when his aircraft collided with that of Erwin Böhme, one of his former pupils.

Boelcke's death brought to the fore a pilot who was destined to become legendary, Freiherr Manfred von Richthofen. By the end of 1916 he had fifteen confirmed victories to his credit. In January 1917 von Richthofen took command of Jasta 11 and, under his inspired leadership, it became the second highest scoring Jasta in the German Air Service. During April 1917, known to the Allies as 'Bloody April', Jasta 11 shot down 89 enemy aircraft with their Albatros D IIIs. Richthofen had his Albatros painted bright red and gained the nickname 'Red Baron'. More and more fighter pilots rose to national fame, including Karl Almenroder, Lothar von Richthofen (brother of the Red Baron), Karl Schafer, Adolf von Tutschek and Kurt Wolf.

The German Air Service, though outnumbered, had air superiority over the Allies. To counteract their numerical inferiority, the Jastas were combined into groups called Jagdeschwader (JG). Jastas 4, 6, 10, and 11 were combined as JG I under the command of Manfred von Richthofen. JG I soon became known as the 'Flying Circus' from its ability to move quickly from battlefront to battlefront. By the summer of 1917, though, the RFC and French Air Service – aided by Sopwith Triplanes from the RNAS – had regained control of the air. New aircraft, such as the Bristol F.2b, Sopwith Camel and S.E.5, and the French SPAD S.VII and S.XIII were coming into front-line service to restore the balance.

The Allies' objective was to overwhelm the German Air Service in the air by numerical superiority, but the Allied pilots were, to a certain extent, not such skilled airmen as the Germans at this stage. The RFC were soon to change this and gain the edge. Tactical bombing by D.H.4 and then D.H.9 day bombers was increased. Fighting back, the German Air service took delivery of the Albatros D V and the Pfalz D VIII, but these fighters made little impact, in spite of the superior flying skills of the German pilots.

The Fokker Dr I Dreidecker (triplane) came into service in the autumn of 1917 but had to be withdrawn with wingroot problems: Heinrich Gontermann, destroyer of seventeen balloons, was killed when his triplane's top wing folded in flight. The Dr I re-entered service later and Kurt Wolf was killed in action flying one on 15 September. The high-scoring Werner Voss, also flying a triplane, fell in action against S.E.5s of the elite 56 Squadron RFC.

German aces continued to die in combat. Karl Schafer, Eduard Ritter von Dostler and Erwin Böhme fell, and the Red Baron himself was wounded and hospitalised. New aces such as Fritz Rumey and Otto Konnecke of Jasta 5 appeared to take up the challenge and many Allied aircraft fell beneath their guns.

1918 arrived and famous names continued to fall in aerial combat. Walter von Bulow died on 4 January and Max Ritter von Muller on the 9th: the brave Muller jumped to his death from his blazing aircraft, preferring a quick death to the agony of dying in the flames of his burning fighter.

January 1918 also saw the Fokker Triplane come into its own when von Richthofen discovered the agility of the machine in a dogfight. Again he had his aircraft painted in bright red. Some Jastas were equipped solely with the DR I, others partly. The triplanes of von Richthofen's 'Flying Circus' scored the most victories during March and April 1918. However, the Red Baron met his end on 21 April 1918, shot down by Australian ground forces on the Somme.

With the United States of America now in the war the German Government realised that they would have to increase their air arm to compete with America's industrial might. Forty new Jastas and two new Jagdeschwaders were created. Hauptmann Adolf von Tutschek commanded JG 2 and Oberleutnant Bruno Loerzer JG 3. Aircrew reinforcements became available from the now-defunct Russian front: these pilots and observers were battle-hardened from flying in Russia and provided a valuable pool of new blood.

Other pilots began to show their worth. Oberleutnant Ernst Udet of Jasta 11 ended the war with 62 victories and was the highest surviving ace; and Oberleutnant Hermann Wilhelm Göring – later to become Reichsmarschall of Nazi Germany – was appointed to command von Richthofen's JG 1, but only scored one kill with the unit, to bring his final total to 22 victories.

During April 1918 JG 1 began to receive the new Fokker D VII fighter. This machine went on to become the outstanding German fighter of the war.

By the end of May most of the Imperial German Air Service was battling against the French and United States Air Services on the Aisne front; the RFC had established air superiority over the British section of the front and was flying without opposition over and behind the German lines. The Allies' war of attrition was beginning to tell and the Germans were running out of experienced aircrew.

Germany was fighting on other fronts such as Palestine, Italy and the Dardanelles, where Hauptmann Hans Buddecke won the third Pour le Mérite of the war on 14 April 1916. In Italy the Germans had been assisting the Austro-Hungarians with three Jastas. With the big German offensives in France, these were withdrawn and the Austro-Hungarians fought on unaided.

The Imperial German Naval Air Service duelled with their British counterparts over the North Sea with seaplane fighters and land-based aircraft. Oberleutnant Friedrich Christiansen won his Pour le Mérite on 11 December 1917. His exploits included an air-to-surface battle against a British submarine – the C.25 – at the mouth of the River Thames. Two other naval fliers – Oberleutnant Gothard Sachsenberg and Leutnant Theo Osterkamp – scored many kills and both were awarded the Pour le Mérite. The German Naval Airship Division made many Zeppelin airship raids over England. Kapitanleutnant Horst Treusch Freiherr von Buttlar-Brandenfels won his Pour le Mérite for flying nineteen missions against England and Fregattenkapitan Peter Strasser won the supreme award in 1917, but lost his life in Zeppelin L70 when leading a mass Zeppelin attack against England

The last three months of the war saw the German Air Service still hard at battle. On 8 August 1918 the RAF suffered its highest casualty total of World War One, its pilots going down to aces such as Otto Konnecke, Erich Lowenhardt, Lothar von Richthofen, Ernst Udet and Arthur Laumann.

Though the ground war was going badly for the Germans, their Air Service was – though hard pressed and outnumbered three to one – still an effective fighting force. During September 1918 they inflicted the most aerial casualties sustained by the Allies since April 1917. However, at 11am on 11 November World War One ended and the Germans capitulated. The German Air Service was bruised, battered and bloodied, but unbowed. They had fought a good fight, largely with honour, but had succumbed to the overwhelming material power and resources of the Allies. Some – but not many – of the German aces survived World War One. Some would die between the wars by murder, revolution and accident, and some would serve again in World War Two.

Outstanding aircraft flown by German Air Services during World War One included the following:

Fokker E III Eindecker. The third of the 'E' series manufactured by Fokker Flugzeug-werke. 300 were built but its pilots shot down 1,000 Allied aircraft. Powered by a 100hp Oberursel 9-cylinder rotary engine, it was armed with one Spandau 7.92mm machine-gun firing through the propeller arc via interrupter gear and had a maximum speed of 140kph.

Fokker Dr I. Fokker designed his triplane after seeing the Sopwith Triplane in April 1917, and the F.102/17 and F.103/17 pre-production aircraft were delivered to Courtrai in August 1917. Werner Voss flew 103/17 with Jasta 10 and scored ten victories with it; Manfred von Richthofen flew 102/17 and later Dr I 427/17 in which he was killed 21 April 1918. Powered by a Le Rhône or Oberursel 110hp engine, it attained a maximum speed of 165kph and was armed with twin Spandau 7.92mm machine-guns.

Fokker D I, D II and D III. The best was the D III flown by Boelcke, Richthofen, Udet and Kissenberth., and powered by a 160hp Oberursel UIII 14-cylinder engine giving a maximum speed of 160kph. These aircraft were armed with one or two Spandau 7.92mm machine-guns.

Albatros D I, D.II, D.III, D.V and D.Va. Manufactured by Albatros Werke and subcontractors. Late in 1916 the D.I and D.II. achieved air supremacy for a time; an all-red D.III was flown by Manfred von Richthofen, in which he scored 35 of his victories. They were powered by a 160hp Mercedes D.IIIa 6-cylinder in-line engine which gave a maximum speed of 165kph. Armament was two Spandau 7.92mm machine-guns.

Pfalz D III and D IIIa. Manufactured by Pfalz Flugzeugwerke under licence from LFG Roland. The D III, powered by a 160hp Mercedes engine, had a splendid, stream-lined fuselage but its performance did not match its appearance. A few D IIIs were fitted with three machine-guns for use against Allied balloons. The D III was replaced by the D IIIa with a 180hp Mercedes engine. Five other unsuccessful Pfalz designs followed, but no production orders. Pfalz also produced the Pfalz Dr I triplane design of which ten were built. They also produced the Pfalz E-series which were similiar to the Fokker E-series, but only a few reached service use.

Halberstadt Cl II, Cl IIa and Cl IV. Built by Halberstadt Werke principally for attacking enemy trenches, these aircraft could carry three heavy machine-guns and gave a good account of themselves against the British infantry at Cambrai in November 1917. Halberstadt also produced 85 of their D I to D V scouts.

Hansa Brandenburg W.12 and W.19. These two-seater seaplanes were designed by Ernst Heinkel in 1916 and came into service in February 1917. Powered at first by 160hp Mercedes engines, the twin floatplane was armed with a Spandau and a Parabellum machine-gun. Oberleutnant F. Christiansen flew W.12s to great advantage out of Zeebrugge against the RNAS. The W.19 came into use in late 1917 powered by a 240hp Maybach engine; one seaplane carried a 20mm Becker cannon. The company also produced 58 KDW single-seat seaplanes, and late in 1917 the W.29 and W.33 seaplanes with 195hp Benz engines and heavily armed with twin Spandau machine-guns on each side of the cockpit and a Parabellum machine-gun for the observer.

GLOSSARY

AFP (Army Flug Park)	Supply depot
Bogohl (Bombengeschwader)	Bombing unit
FA (Flieger Abteilung)	Flying section
FA(A) (Flieger Abteilung Artillerie)	Artillery flying section
FEA (Flieger Ersatz Abteilung)	Pilot training unit
FFA (Feldflieger Abteilung)	Field aviation unit
Fr.v (Freiherr von)	Baron of (noble family title granted by royal decree)
Jasta (Jagdstaffel)	Fighting squadron
JaSch (Jastaschule)	Fighter pilot school
JG (Jagdeschwader)	Jasta group (permanent)
Jgr (Jagdgruppe)	Jasta group (temporary)
Kanone	Ace (pilot with ten or more aerial victories)
Kagohl (Kampfgeschwader der Obsten Heeresleitung)	Combat squadrons of the supreme commander
Kasta (Kampfstaffel)	Fighting unit or section
Kek (Kampfeinsitzerkommando)	Fighter group
Kest (Kampfeinsitzer Staffeln)	Home defence squadron
KG (Kampfgeschwader)	Bombing squadron
KOFL (Kommandeur der Flieger)	Commanding officer (army) aviation
Kogenluft. (Kommandierender General der Luftstreitkrafte)	GOC German aviation
MFJ (Marine Feld Jasta)	Marine fighting squadron
Ritter von	Knight of – title awarded by royal decree
SFA (Seefrontstaffel)	Marine unit
SF1S (Seeflug Station)	Naval base air
SST (Schutzstaffel)	Ground support unit
Schusta (Schlachstaffel)	Ground support unit

CLASSIFICATION OF GERMAN AIRCRAFT

A	Unarmed monoplanes
B	Unarmed biplanes for observation and training.
C	Armed biplanes for reconnaissance and bombing
CL	Light C-plane
CLS Schlachtflieger	C plane for ground attack
D	Single-seater armed biplane fighter
DJ	Single-seater ground attack
Dr	Single-seater armed triplane
J	Two-seater ground attack infantry support aircraft
E	Single-seater armed monoplanes
F	The first Fokker Dr Is
G Grossflugzeug	Twin-engined biplane bombers

R   Riesenflugzeug   Multi-engined armed biplane long-range bombers
S   Schlachtflugzeug   Ground attack aircraft

GERMAN AIRCRAFT SERIAL NUMBERS

The aircraft serial number on the sides of the fuselage or fin(s) showed the maker, type, serial number and year of production, e.g. Fokker DVII 4253/18 (used by Ernst Udet).

AUSTRO-HUNGARIAN AIRCRAFT DESIGNATIONS

A   Monoplane
B   Older biplane of up to 150hp
C   Biplane two-seater of 150hp to 250hp
D   Single-seater fighter
F   Single-engined biplane of 350hp upwards
G   Twin-engined bomber
R   Giant bomber

These aircraft also bore a manufacturer's number code, each manufacturer being allocated an identifying letter and number abbreviation.

COMPARATIVE RANKS

German	British	German	British
		Wachtmeister	Sergeant-Major
German Army		Feldwebel	Sergeant
General Oberst	None	Unteroffizier	Corporal
General Kavallerie	General	Gefreiter	Lance Corporal
General Leutnant	Lieutenant-General	Flieger	Private
General Major	General	**German Navy**	
Oberst	Colonel	Kapitainleutnant	Captain
Major	Major	Leutnant zur See	Lieutenant
Rittmeister	Cavalry Captain	Oberflugmeister	Naval Aviation Senior NCO
Hauptmann	Army Captain		
Oberleutnant	Lieutenant	Vizeflugmeister	Naval Aviation Junior NCO
Leutnant	2nd Lieutenant		
Fahnrich	Officer Cadet	Flugmeister Naval	Aviation Airman
Offizierstellvertreter	Warrant Officer		
Vizefeldwebel/	or Acting Officer		

Leutnant Karl Allmenroder (1896–1917) 30 victories

Karl Allmenroder was born on 3 May 1896 in the small town of Wald, near Solingen. He joined the German Army's Field Regiment 62 and after training was posted to the 20th Field Regiment. He saw active service in Poland and was awarded the Iron Cross 2nd Class in March 1915, and a commission on 30 March. In August 1915 he was awarded the Friedrich August Cross 1st Class.

His brother Willi had enlisted in the German Army, and together they applied for, and were accepted into, the German Army Air Service on 29 March 1916. On completion of their training at Flying School Halberstadt, they were both posted to FA 227 and in November 1916 to Jasta 11 (Royal Prussian). Jasta 11 was led by the legendary Manfred von Richthofen.

Allmenroder scored his first victory on 16 February 1917 when he shot down a B.E.2c of 16 Squadron RFC. By the end of March he had raised his score to five and was awarded the Iron Cross 1st Class. April saw a victory over a B.E.2 of 13 Squadron RFC over Lens. On the 25th, 26th and 27th he shot down three aircraft on consecutive days, bringing his score to nine.

Thirteen victories in May brought Allmenroder's score to 22, and June saw his score rise to 26. On 6 June he was awarded the Knight's Cross of the House of Hohenzollern Order and the following day the coveted Pour le Mérite. On the 18th, 24th, 25th and 26th four more British aircraft fell to his guns, bringing his score to 30.

On 27 June his patrol was attacked by British fighters over Zillebeke and Allmenroder's aircraft was shot up: he died in the ensuing crash. He was posthumously awarded the Oldenburg Friedrich August Cross 1st and 2nd Class and the Bayern Militär Kronen Order 4th Class on 20 July 1917. He was 21 years old.

Leutnant Karl Allmenroder.

Leutnant Paul Baümer (1896–1927) 38 victories

Paul Baümer was born on 11 May 1896 at Duisberg and spent most of his childhood fascinated by the giant Zeppelin airships that operated from Friedrichshafen, near his home. He learned to fly at his own expense and gained a pilot's licence.

When war broke out Baümer tried to enlist as a naval airman, but was turned down. He then volunteered for the 70th Infantry Regiment at Saarbrucken and after training saw combat at St. Quentin in France. In the early part of 1915 he was posted to the XXI Army Corps on the Russian Front, where he was badly wounded in the left arm.

Whilst recovering in hospital he applied for transfer to the German Air Service but was refused. He then saw vacancies in the German Air Service for technicians and, using his experience as a dental assistant, persuaded the authorities to accept his transfer. At the beginning of 1916, he was accepted for 'general duties' in the German Air Service and posted to Döberitz. Within a few months he had asked his commanding officer to look at his previous flying experience and put his name forward for flying training, and spring 1916 saw Baümer at flying school. After qualifying he was posted in October to Armee Flugpark No.1 as a ferry pilot and flight instructor. He was promoted on 19 February 1917 to the rank of gefreiter and posted to FA 7 on 26 March. Three days later he was promoted to unteroffizier.

On 15 May Baümer was awarded the Iron Cross 2nd Class and two days later was sent for fighter pilot training. On completion of training he was posted to Jasta 2

(Boelcke) on 28 June for two days, then to Jasta 5. On the 12th, 13th and 15th of July he scored his first three victories when he shot down three reconnaissance balloons: for these victories he was awarded the Iron Cross 1st Class. Baümer was posted back to Jasta 2 in August and by the end of the year his score had risen to eighteen.

On 12 February 1918 he was awarded the Gold Military Service Cross. His 19th victory, a Sopwith Camel shot down whilst on patrol over Zonnebeke on 9 March, was recognised by granting him a commission to the rank of leutnant in April. The 200th victory of Jasta 2 (Boelcke) on 23 March, was Baümer's 20th and was made even more remarkable by him shooting down two R.E.8 aircraft and one Camel in under three hours. Nine days later, whilst trying to land a badly shot-up Pfalz D VIII, Baümer was injured in the crash-landing, breaking his jaw amongst other injuries.

He returned to Jasta 2 in the September and was immediately given the nickname of 'Der Eiserne Adler' (The Iron Eagle) after being awarded the Silver Wound Badge. By the end of September he had increased his score to 38, shooting down eight Allied aircraft in less than a week during one period. His 30th victory brought the nation's highest award, the Pour le Mérite awarded on 2 November. This award made him one of only five recipients of both the Pour le Mérite and the Golden Military Service Cross.

When the war ended, Paul Baümer had taken his tally to 43 victories. He went to work for Blohm and Voss, the ship and aeroplane builders, at their factory in Hamburg, but he could not settle and returned to his studies to become a professional dentist. Baümer continued his interest in flying by taking part in aerobatic competitions, before starting his own aircraft company – Baümer Aero GmbH – in Hamburg. His designers were the Guether Brothers who later became famous working with the Ernst Heinkel design team. During an aerobatic display in Copenhagen, whilst he was testing the Rohrbach Rofix fighter, an all metal cantilever monoplane, the aircraft stalled at 2,000 feet and spun into the waters of the Oere Sound. His body was later recovered and interred at Ohesdorf, near Hamburg.

Leutnant Oliver Freiherr von Beaulieu-Marconnay (1898–1918) 25 victories

The son of an aristocratic Prussian army officer, Oliver Beaulieu-Marconnay was born in Berlin on 14 September 1898. At seventeen he joined up as a cadet, one year after the beginning of the war. He enlisted in his father's old regiment, the 4th Prussian Dragoon Regiment, and was almost immediately in combat. By July 1916, after battles in the Rokitno Swamps, he was awarded the Iron Cross 1st Class and promoted to the rank of leutnant.

He applied to be transferred to the Air Service. Early in spring 1917 he was accepted and sent to flying training school, graduating in November. On 1 December he was posted first to Jasta 18 (Royal Prussian), then a few months later to Jasta 15 (Royal Prussian), commanded by Leutnant Josef Veltjens.

Under Veltjens he progressed rapidly and on 28 May 1918 'Bauli', as he became known, scored his first victory, an AR2 over Soissons. This was followed on 6 June by two victories, a D.H.4 from 27 Squadron RFC and an S.E.5a from 32 Squadron. By the end of June he had raised his score to eight, shooting down three Sopwith Camels, an S.E.5a and a D.H.4. 9 August saw him increase his score to ten in the space of 15 minutes, when he shot down a Sopwith Camel and a SPAD II. On 2 September he was given command of Jasta 19 (Royal Prussian), aged nineteen. By the end of September he had increased his score to 21.

Beaulieu-Marconnay continued to fly combat missions. In the first two weeks of October he raised his score to 25. Then, on 10 October 1918, whilst flying his favourite aircraft, a Fokker DVII with his personal insignia '4D' (the 4th Dragoons) painted on the side of the blue fuselage, his Jasta was attacked by Allied aircraft. Marconnay's aircraft was caught in crossfire from his own Jasta which badly wounded him. He managed to land his aircraft and was rushed to hospital. As he lay dying he was informed that he had been awarded the Pour le Mérite – the youngest recipient of the 'Blue Max' in the war at the age of twenty. He died on 26 October 1918.

Oberleutnant Fritz Otto Bernert (1893–1918) 27 victories

The son of the Burghermeister of Ratibor in Upper Silesia, Bernert was born on 6 March 1893. He joined the 173rd Infantry Regiment, being commissioned as a leutnant just after the outbreak of the war. Bernert was wounded in November and awarded the Iron Cross 2nd Class. By the end of 1914 he had been wounded again, none of the wounds proved serious. In December 1914, during close-quarter hand-to-hand fighting, he received a bayonet wound in his left arm that severed a main nerve. He was deemed unfit for further military ground duties and applied to join the German Army Air Service as an observer.

Bernert passed a medical examination for the Air Service and in February 1915 was sent for training. After graduating he was posted to FFA 27 and for six months carried out reconnaissance and scouting missions.

In July 1915, Bernert was posted to FFA 71 and applied for pilot training. In November his application was accepted and he was posted to Jastaschule for training.

Oberleutnant Fritz Bernert.

He was able to conceal the fact that one of his arms had only limited mobility. Also, he was only one of three Jasta pilots in the German Air Arm Service who were known to wear glasses. On graduating in March 1916, Bernert was assigned to Kek Vaux where, on 17 April, he opened his score by shooting down a Nieuport fighter.

During the summer months of 1916, there was a lull in the action in Bernert's sector and in late August he was posted to Jasta 4. On 6 September he scored his second victory, over a Caudron whilst on patrol over Dompierre, and on the 11th shot down a Nieuport fighter over Allenes. By the end of November Bernert had raised his score to seven, the last three all on 9 November – two D.H.2s and an F.E.8. In February 1917 Bernert was posted to Jasta 2 and awarded the Iron Cross 1st Class, the Saxon Albert Order, the Knight 2nd Class with Swords and Knight's Cross with Swords of the Hohenzollern House Order.

Bernert opened his score with Jasta 4 by shooting down a Sopwith Camel whilst on patrol over Ecourt-Mory; a B.E.2d followed at the end of March. On consecutive days starting on 1 April Bernert scored four victories. He continued to score almost daily and on 23 April he was awarded Prussia's highest decoration, the Pour le Mérite. The very next day, Bernert claimed five victories in one day: three B.E.2es (all from No.9 Squadron RFC), a D.H.4 and a Sopwith 1½ Strutter.

On 1 May Bernert was appointed commander of Jasta 6 with his score standing at 24. Bernert added three more victories by the end of May, before taking command of Jasta 2 (Boelcke) on 9 June.

He continued to fly, though he scored no more victories, and on 18 August was wounded. On his release from hospital in November he was deemed to be unfit for flying duties and promoted to oberleutnant. The following September Bernert contracted influenza and died in hospital, on 18 October 1918.

Oberleutnant Hans Berr (1890–1917) 10 victories

Hans Berr was born on 20 May 1890 in Braunschweig, Bavaria. By the time he was eighteen years of age he had been commissioned as a leutnant in the infantry.

When World War One broke out in 1914, Berr was serving with the 7th Light Infantry (Reserve) Regiment, and saw action on the Western Front. He was wounded on 6 September 1914, awarded the Iron Cross 2nd Class, and promoted oberleutnant on 27 January 1915. He joined the German Army Air Service on 3 March 1915 and trained as an observer. After several months flying observation missions on the Western Front Berr applied for pilot training and was posted to the Jastaschule at Metz, where he trained to fly single-seater fighters. On graduation he was posted to Kek Avillers, flying Fokker Eindeckers. This unit later became Jasta 5.

On 8 March 1916 he opened his score when he shot down a Nieuport of Escadrille MS3 over the Verdun sector of the Front. A week later he downed a Caudron over Verdun. With two victories to his credit he was appointed to command of Jasta 5 (Royal Prussian) on 21 August, based at Bechamp near Verdun. With the appointment came awards of the Bavarian Military Merit Order 4th Class with Swords and the Brunswick War Merit Cross.

On 7 October 1916, he shot down a Caudron over Combles, then a B.E.2b of 34 Squadron, also over Combles. Between 20–26 October he added two F.E.2bs, a Morane Parasol and a balloon; his total now stood at eight.

By the time he had scored his tenth and final victory on 3 November 1916 he had been awarded the Iron Cross 1st Class, the Knight's Cross with Swords of the Hohenzollern House Order, the Bavarian Military Merit Order 4th Class with Swords, the Brunswick War Merit Cross, the Ruess War Merit Cross and Honour Cross 3rd Class with Swords, and the Hamburg Hanseatic Cross. On 4 December 1916 he was awarded the Pour le Mérite this was before the German High Command had altered the requirement for the 'Blue Max' to sixteen confirmed victories.

Berr continued to fly in combat but did not add to his victories. On Good Friday, 6 April 1917, Jasta 5 engaged in aerial combat with 57 Squadron RFC; in the heat of battle Vizefeldwebel Paul Hoppe moved in behind a Vickers Gunbus when Berr came swooping in from the right hand side and crashed into Hoppe. The two aircraft fell to the ground, killing both pilots.

Hauptmann Rudolf Berthold
(1891–1920) 44 victories

Rudolf Berthold was born at Ditterswind, near Bamberg in northern Bavaria on 24 March 1891. At the age of 19 he joined the Army and was assigned to Brandenburg Infantry Regiment No.20.

Berthold decided to learn to fly at a private flying club; after gaining his licence, No.538, on 26 September 1913, he applied for transfer to the newly formed German Army Air Service. At the outbreak of the war, Berthold was posted for flying training as an observer on Halberstadt two-seaters with FFA 23. By the end of 1914 he had been awarded the Iron Cross 2nd Class for a number of reconnaissance flights and promoted to feldwebel.

In 1915 Berthold transferred to DFW aircraft and carried out a large number of observation flights over enemy lines. He was awarded the Iron Cross 1st Class in autumn 1915 and applied for transfer to a fighter unit.

Hauptmann Rudolph Berthold.

He went to Jastaschule in December 1915 and on graduating was posted to Kek Vaux, flying single-seater Fokkers. On 2 February 1916 he opened his score by shooting down a Voisin whilst on patrol over Chaulnes. By the end of April his score stood at five and he had been awarded the Bayerisch Kriegsverdeinst-Orden 4th Class, the Knight's Cross of the St. Heinrichs Order and the Saxon Knight's Cross of the Military St. Henry Order.

Returning from a mission on 25 April, Berthold suffered severe injuries during a seriously misjudged crash-landing in a Pfalz E.IV. Berthold returned to his unit before his wounds had properly healed and was commissioned leutnant.

In August 1916, Berthold was given command of Jasta 4 after it formed from Kek Vaux. On 27 August came another award, the prestigious Knight's Cross with Swords of the Royal Hohenzollern House Order.

On 14 October he handed Jasta 4 over to Hans Buddecke and took command of Jasta 14. On 24 March 1917 he increased his score by shooting down a Farman of Escadrille F.7. In May, however, he was shot down by a British fighter: his aircraft crashed within German lines and he was pulled from the wreckage, having sustained a fractured skull, a broken nose, pelvis and thigh. After two months in hospital, Berthold again discharged himself and returned to Jasta 14.

On 12 August he was given command of Jasta 18 and promotion to oberleutnant. He shot down a SPAD on 21 August, raising his score to 13; during September he scored 14 more victories. On 2 October he scored his 28th victory, shooting down a D.H.4 of 57 Squadron RFC. On 10 October 1917, during a dogfight with a British patrol, his right upper arm was smashed by a bullet. Whilst in hospital he received Prussia's highest award, the Pour le Mérite and ten days later, promotion to hauptmann. Once again he discharged himself early and returned to his Jasta.

Berthold was given command of Jagdgeschwader II in March 1918, and took with him nearly all the best pilots of Jasta 14, exchanging them with pilots of Jasta 15. His aircraft, with its distinctive livery of a red and blue fuselage (red from the nose to the cockpit, then blue to the tail) and its winged sword painted on the fuselage, was well known to the Allies.

On 10 August Berthold's patrol became involved with a patrol of D.H.4s and during the ensuing dogfight Berthold shot down two aircraft, but collided with one of his victims. His Fokker D VII was badly damaged: Berthold struggled to keep control but crashed into a house. He survived the crash but it effectively ended his combat career.

On his release from hospital the war was over. In 1919 he joined the Eisern Schar (Iron Horde) of the Freikorps and fought during the post-war German revolution. On 15 March 1920, Berthold was in Harburg when he was attacked by rioters and it is said that he was beaten, then strangled with the ribbon of his Pour le Mérite.

Leutnant Walter Blume (1896–1964) 28 victories

Walter Blume was born on 10 January 1896 in Hirschberg. On the outbreak of war he enlisted in the Silesian Jäger Battalion No. 5 and was posted to East Prussia. During heavy fighting near Lyck, Blume was severely wounded and decided to apply for transfer to the German Army Air Service.

On 30 June Blume reported to the Flying Reserve Unit at Grossenhaim and was posted to the flying school at Leipzig-Mockau. On graduating and receiving his pilot's badge, Blume was assigned to the Research and Exercise Field West Unit near St. Quentin on the Western Front. After two months he was assigned to the Army Aeroplane Park A at Strassburg. On 18 June 1916, Blume was assigned to FA 65 as a reconnaissance pilot, then one month later to FA(A) 280. He quickly distinguished himself and was awarded the Iron Cross 2nd Class on 24 July and promoted to vizefeldwebel on 23 August. He was promoted leutnant der reserve on 31 January 1917.

At the beginning of March 1917, Blume was selected by Bruno Loerzer and Hermann Göring to be one of the pilots to form the nucleus of Jasta 26, a fighter unit. One month later, after conversion and tactical training, the squadron was ready and was assigned to the St. Quentin area. Within days of arriving the Jasta was in heavy aerial fighting, and on 10 May, Blume opened his score, shooting down a D.H.4 of 55 Squadron RFC over Gouzencourt. He continued to score steadily and by the end of November had raised his score to six and been awarded the Iron Cross 1st Class. On 29 November his flight encountered Bristol Fighters from 48 Squadron RFC. During the action Blume was hit in the chest but managed to keep control of his badly damaged aircraft: fighting unconsciousness, Blume managed to nurse his crippled aircraft back to base.

On 5 March 1918 Blume returned to the front in command of Jasta 9 and was assigned to the Champagne Front. On 21 April he shot down a SPAD over Chiry-Ourscamp, taking his score to seven.

ollowing three months Blume accounted for ten more Allied aircraft; the
>wn of a SPAD over Bazoches on 6 August brought the award of the Knight's
Swords of the Hohenzollern House Order. By the end of September Blume
had raised his score to 26: this was followed on 2 October by his 27th victory and the
Jasta's 100th.

On landing Blume was ceremoniously awarded Prussia's highest award, the Pour le
Mérite. Blume scored his final victory on 28 October, a Sopwith Camel of 209
Squadron over Remaucourt.

Blume returned home to complete his engineering studies and earned a degree. He
became a designer with the Arado and Albatros aviation companies, and contributed to
many of the aircraft designs used in the Second World War. Walter Blume died on 27
May 1964.

Hauptmann Oswald Boelcke (1891–1916) 40 victories

Hauptmann Oswald Boelcke.

One of six children, Oswald Boelcke was born in Giebichenstein, near Halle in Saxony
on 19 May 1891. After leaving school he
decided on a military career and in March
1911 he joined the Prussian Cadet Corps,
being posted to No.3 Telegrapher
Battalion at Koblenz. After completing his
initial training, he was posted to the War
School at Metz to complete his officer
training.

After graduating Boelcke applied for
transfer to the German Army Air Service
for training as a pilot and was accepted.
He was posted to the flying school in
Halberstadt, completing his flying
training in October 1914. Boelcke was
assigned to Trier and two weeks later
posted to FA 13 near Montmédy, where
his older brother Wilhelm was an
observer. The two brothers became a
team, flying observation missions over the
Argonne region.

In October 1914, Boelcke received the
Iron Cross 2nd Class for his work flying
reconnaissance missions. He continued
flying reconnaissance missions into the
first quarter of 1915 and received the Iron
Cross 1st Class on 4February. At the
beginning of May, Boelcke was
transferred to FA 62, equipped with LVG
C.Is. On 4 July 1915, together with his
observer, Leutnant Heinz von Wuhlisch,

Boelcke went on patrol over Valenciennes and encountered a Morane Parasol. After a short action the Morane was shot down: Boelcke's first kill. His enthusiasm for engaging enemy aircraft prompted his squadron commander to transfer him to single-seater fighters – single-seater Fokker Eindeckers had been allocated to the squadron for scouting and protection of the reconnaissance aircraft.

Early in July, Boelcke saved the life of a 14 year old French boy, and was awarded a life-saving medal. On 19 August, flying in an Eindecker from Douai, Boelcke shot down a Bristol biplane over the front. It was also whilst at Douai that he met Max Immelmann, both learning tactics from each other. By the end of the year, Boelcke had raised his score to six and had been awarded the Knight's Cross with Swords of the Hohenzollern House Order.

In the first two weeks of January 1916, Boelcke shot down three more Allied aircraft, bringing Prussia's highest award, the Pour le Mérite – Boelcke was the first fighter pilot to receive it. Every month communiques to the German High Command mentioned Boelcke as he steadily increased his score. By the end of June 1916 his score was 19 and he had become a household name in Germany.

When Max Immelmann died in June, the German High Command decided to send Boelcke on an inspection and public relations tour of Vienna, Budapest, Belgrade and Turkey. This gave him the chance to study the way air fighting was developing, and he wrote a thesis, *Air Fighting Tactics*, which he submitted to the German High Command. It was to become the 'bible' of German fighter pilots.

In July, Boelcke was recalled from his PR tour and given command of Jasta 2 with promotion to hauptmann. Among those he chose to join the Jasta were Manfred von Richthofen, Max Muller and Erwin Böhme. On 2 September Boelcke scored his 20th victory when he shot down a D.H.2 of 37 Squadron RFC. By the end of September he had shot down nine more, and by 26 October he had shot down a further eleven aircraft, bringing his total to 40.

On 28 October, whilst on patrol with von Richthofen and Böhme, Boelcke attacked a flight of seven Allied aircraft. Boelcke and Böhme chased a British fighter, but just as they closed on it another British fighter, chased by von Richthofen, cut across in front of them. Böhme rolled out of the way at the same time as Boelcke, and the two aircraft collided. Böhme kept control of his aircraft, but Boelcke's Albatros D II spun into the ground, killing Boelcke.

Oberleutnant Oskar Freiherr von Boenigk (1893–1946)

26 victories

The son of an army officer, Oskar von Boenigk was born in Siegersdorf, near Bunzlau, Silesia on 25 August 1893. He was commissioned into the König Friedrich III Grenadier Regiment on 22 March 1912. By the time war broke out, Boenigk was a platoon leader with his regiment, and he was soon in action. In October 1914 he was badly wounded and spent many months in hospital; for this he was awarded the Iron Cross 2nd Class. On his return to his unit in 1915 he was wounded again. He returned after recuperating and fought at Loretto Heights and Arras.

He applied for transfer to the Air Service and was accepted. He was posted to observer school FEA 7 in December 1915 and after training, was posted to

Kampfstaffel 19 of KG 4, in March 1916. At the beginning of January 1917 he applied for training as a pilot and on graduating from Jastaschule was posted to Jasta 4, on 24 June 1917.

Boenigk opened his score on 20 July when he shot down a Sopwith Camel over Tenbrielen. One week later he shot down another Camel, of No.70 Squadron RFC over Moorslede. By the end of September he had taken his score to five and was awarded the Iron Cross 1st Class and, on 21 October, command of Jasta 21. By the end of the year he had raised his score to six.

During early 1918 Boenigk claimed six more victories: two SPADs, one Bréguet XIV and three balloons. By the end of August he had increased his score to 19 and been awarded the Knight's Cross with Swords of the Hohenzollern House Order. He was given command of JG 2 on 31 August and promoted to oberleutnant. The Geschwader was moved to the St. Mihiel Front in September to oppose the American forces that were massing there, and by the end of the month Boenigk had raised his score to 26.

At the beginning of October Boenigk received the Saxon Albert Order 2nd Class with Swords, the Sax-Ernestine House Order, Knight 2nd Class with Swords and the Prussian Order of St. John, Knight of Honour. It was this last award that entitled him to use the title Freiherr von. On 25 October von Boenigk was awarded Prussia's highest honour, the Pour le Mérite

Oberleutnant Oskar Freiherr von Boenigk.

During the Second World War, Boenigk served in the Luftwaffe as commander of various airfields, then as an area commander, attaining the rank of major-general. He was captured by the Russians in May 1945 and died in a prison camp the following year.

Leutnant der Reserve Erwin Böhme (1879–1917) 24 victories

Erwin Böhme was born in Holzminden, on the Weser, on 29 July 1879. He learned to fly whilst working in Africa, but returned to Germany when the war broke out and joined a Jäger Regiment. In spring 1915 he volunteered for the German Army Air

Leutnant Erwin Böhme.

Service and, because of his experience as a pilot, was accepted as an instructor.

In June 1916 Böhme applied for a posting to a front-line unit and was posted at the end of July to Kasta 10, a unit within Kagohl 2 that was commanded by Hauptmann Wilhelm Boelcke, brother of Oswald Boelcke.

Böhme opened his score on 2 August by shooting down a Nieuport 12 over Radzyse. Later that month he was introduced to Oswalde Boelcke, who asked for Böhme to be assigned to the new Jasta 2 which by the beginning of September was ready for action. On 17 September Böhme scored his second victory, a Sopwith 1½ Strutter of No.70 Squadron RFC, over Hervilly, and was awarded the Iron Cross 2nd Class.

On 28 October tragedy struck for Böhme. With his score now standing at five, he was on patrol with Boelcke and Manfred von Richthofen, when they joined in a dogfight with D.H.2s of No.24 Squadron RFC. Böhme and Boelcke dived in tandem on one of the British fighters, when another British fighter, hotly pursued by Richthofen suddenly cut across their path. Böhme banked sharply, as did Boelcke, but their aircraft touched and Boelcke's wing was badly damaged. Böhme managed to keep control of his aircraft, but Boelcke's aircraft plunged to the ground, killing him. Böhme was devastated and blamed himself, but a board of enquiry cleared him of all blame.

By the end of the year he had raised his score to eight. On 7 January 1917 he opened the new year by shooting down a D.H.2 of No.32 Squadron RFC over Beugny. Two more victories on 4 February, another D.H.2 of No.32 Squadron and a B.E.2c of No.15 Squadron brought his score to 11. Then on 11 February he was wounded in a dogfight with a Sopwith 1½ Strutter and was hospitalised for a month. He was awarded the Iron Cross 1st Class, this being followed on 12 March by the award of the Knight's Cross with Swords of the Hohenzollern House Order.

On being released from hospital at the end of March, Böhme was given an instructing post as part of his recuperation. On 2 July he was posted to Jasta 29 as commander, but only managed to claim one more victory before being posted back to Jasta 2 as its commander. He was wounded again on 10 August, when his aircraft was shot up by a Sopwith Camel whilst he was in the process of attacking a two-seater bomber. The wound was to his hand and kept him behind the desk at Jasta 2 for a month. Two more kills in September and six in October brought his score to 21. On 6 November he shot down a Camel from No.65 Squadron, followed by a Nieuport Scout from No.1 Belgian Escadrille.

On 24 November he was awarded Prussia's highest award, the Pour le Mérite. On 29 November, over Zonnebeke, his flight was attacked by a patrol of No.10 Squadron RFC. During the action Böhme shot down a Camel but failed to see an F.K.8 behind him. Seconds later he was dead, and his plane crashed over British lines.

Two days later he was buried by the British with full military honours at Keerselaarhook; his remains were reinterred at Hinter den Linden after the war.

Rittmeister Karl Bolle (1893–1955)

36 victories

Karl Bolle was born in Berlin on 20 June 1893, the son of an academic. Just before the outbreak of the war he joined the 7th von Seydlitz Kurassier Regiment with the rank of leutnant and almost immediately was in France, fighting on the Western Front. At the beginning of 1915 the regiment was moved to the Eastern Front, and fought in Poland and Courland. At the end of 1915, after receiving the Iron Cross 2nd Class, Bolle decided to apply for transfer to the German Army Air Service. His application was accepted and in February 1916 he was posted to Valenciennes for flying training.

On completion of his training in July 1915, he was awarded his pilot's badge and posted to KG.4

Leutnant Karl Bolle.

as a reconnaissance pilot. After spending several months carrying out scouting and reconnaissance missions, Bolle was posted to Kampstaffel 23 at the end of 1915 and was awarded the Württemburg Friedrich Order and the Knight's Cross 2nd Class with Swords. It was at Kampfstaffel 23 that he met his new observer, Lothar von Richthofen. In October 1916, Bolle was badly wounded; recovering from his wound, he applied to transfer to single-seat fighters.

After training in July 1917, he was posted to Jasta 28. On 8 August he opened his score by shooting down a D.H.4 of 57 Squadron RFC over Kachtem. His second, a Martinsyde G100 bomber of 27 Squadron, was shot down over Seclin on 21 August. On 18 December he scored his next victory, a Sopwith Camel of 65 Squadron. On 29 January 1918, Bolle scored his fourth victory when he shot down another 65 Squadron Camel. The following day he shot down a D.H.4 of 5 Squadron RNAS. Bolle was given command of Jasta 2 on 20 February 1918 and promoted to oberleutnant. On 3 April he shot down a D.H.9 bomber over Frezenberg and on 25 April a Sopwith Camel, raising his score to seven.

The Allies started making their big push and the skies were filled with aircraft. By the end of July, Bolle had shot down a further 21 Allied aircraft, bringing his score to 28, but at a great cost to his squadrons. He was promoted to rittmeister at the beginning of August and awarded the Order of Max Joseph, the Mecklenburg Military Cross of Merit with Swords and the Knight's Cross with Swords of the Hohenzollern House Order. On 28 August 1918. he received the Pour le Mérite, Prussia's highest award; by the end of the war he had raised his score to 36.

Bolle became an instructor and in the early 1920s was appointed Director of the German Transportation Flying School, in charge of pilot training. During World War Two he became special advisor to the Luftwaffe, a post he held throughout the war. Karl Bolle died in Berlin on 9 October 1955.

Leutnant der Reserve Heinrich Bongartz (1892–1946) 33 victories

The son of a schoolteacher, Heinrich Bongartz was born in Gelsenkirchen, Westphalia on 31 January 1892. In August 1914 he volunteered for the Army and joined Infantry Regiment No.3, then later Reserve Infantry Regiment No.13 with the rank of sturmoffizier. The regiment was stationed on the Western Front near Verdun, and throughout 1915 Bongartz saw some of the heaviest fighting of the war. In March 1916 his bravery and leadership qualities earned him a commission to leutnant and the award of the Iron Cross 2nd Class.

He applied for transfer to the German Army Air Service, was accepted and posted for training as a pilot to FA.5 in autumn 1916. On completion of his training in October he was posted to Kaghol 5 as a reconnaissance and scouting pilot. In April 1917 he was posted to Jasta 36.

Bongartz had opened his tally when he shot down a SPAD VII from SPA31 over Viry. By the end of the month he had increased his score to four. He continued to score steadily until 13 July when – with his score standing at 11 – he was wounded in battle with Allied fighters. The wound put him out of action for two months. On 26 September he shot down a Sopwith Triplane over Houthulst Forest, and at the en September he was made commanding officer of the following two months Bongartz scored victories, bringing his total to 25 and with it the av Knight's Cross with Swords of the Hohenzollern Hous Bongartz finished the year by shooting down another two Allied i

Leutnant Heinrich Bongartz.

raising his score to 27. On 23 December 1917, he was awarded Prussia's h honour, the Pour le Mérite.

On 29 January Bongartz shot down a Sopwith Camel over Poelcapelle; two mo victories in February and three in March took his score to 33, but on 29 March he wa wounded in action.

On 25 April he was slightly injured but then on the 29th he was seriously wounded when, on patrol over Kemmel Hill, he clashed with fighters of No.74 Squadron RFC and was wounded in the head. The bullet passed right through his left temple, left eye and nose. His aircraft crashed near Kemmel Hill and he was taken unconscious to hospital. He lost his left eye, which finished his wartime career. He later took over as Director of the Aeroplane Inspectorate at Aldersdorf, where he stayed until the end of the war and helped to deactivate the German Army Flying Corps.

During the post-war revolution Bongartz fought against the Spartacists, a group of German left-wingers who formed the nucleus of the German Communist Party. But again he was seriously wounded, this time in the leg. His military career was finally finished and he was invalided out. He became Director of German Air Trade, a department that was using airships for trade and transport. In January 1921 he was involved in a crash, was severely injured but recovered. Heinrich Bongartz died of a heart attack on 23 January 1946.

Leutnant Franz Büchner (1898–1920) 40 victories

Franz Büchner was born on 2 January 1898 in Leipzig. At the onset of war in 1914 he was only 16 but he joined the 106th Saxon Infantry Regiment. The regiment moved to the Russian Front in March 1915 and in August Büchner was commissioned. Moving back to France in September with his regiment, he was awarded the Iron Cross 2nd Class after being involved in a number of actions. On 3 April 1916 he was wounded.

He decided to apply for a transfer to the German Army Air Service, was accepted and posted to FFA 270 for training as a pilot. On graduating in July 1916, he was posted to Jasta 9, flying single-seater aircraft, and shot down a Nieuport fighter on 17 August over Chappy.

In October Büchner was posted to Jasta 13. On 10–11 June 1918 he increased his score by shooting down two SPADs over Vauxaillion. Büchner was appointed staffelführer on 15 June, despite only having scored four victories, such was the high regard in which he was held, and by the end of July his score had risen to twelve. Büchner was awarded the Iron Cross 1st Class in August, followed by the Knight's Cross with Swords of the Hohenzollern House Order and the Saxon Merit Order 2nd Class with Swords. He shot down another eight Allied aircraft, bringing his score to twenty by the end of August.

On 12 September 1918, Büchner shot down a D.H.4 of 8th Aero Squadron USAS whilst on patrol over Hattonville; this was one of the first contacts the Germans had with Americans. The same day he shot down another D.H.4 and a Bréguet XIV bomber. By the end of September Büchner had shot down eighteen USAS aircraft, bringing his total score to 37. For this achievement he was awarded the Military St. Heinrich's Order (Saxony's highest award) and the Saxon Albert Order 2nd Class with Swords.

Büchner then shot down a Salmson 2A2 bomber, but on 10 October a collision with one of his fellow pilots nearly ended his life. Both aircraft had attacked an Allied bomber when they collided in mid-air: the pilots took to their parachutes and fortunately for them both, the parachutes opened – not always a certainty in those early days – taking them safely to the ground.

Büchner managed to add another two kills to his score before the war ended. On 25 October, at the age of twenty, he was awarded Prussia's premier decoration, the Pour le Mérite.

The war in Europe may have ended for the Allies, but it still continued within Germany as the post-war revolutionaries attempted to take over. Büchner continued to fight on with the Reichswehr, but on 18 March 1920 he was shot down and killed whilst on a reconnaissance flight near his hometown of Leipzig. Like Rudolf Berthold, he was killed by his own countrymen.

Leutnant der Reserve Julius Buckler (1894–1960) 36 victories

Julius Buckler was born in Mainz on 28 March 1894. In 1913 he joined Infantry Line Regiment No.117, and within days of the outbreak of war, was in action on the Western Front; within a few weeks he received the Iron Cross 2nd Class. In August he was badly wounded, and after being released from hospital in October 1914 was deemed to be unfit for Army service.

In November 1914, he volunteered for flying duties and was accepted for training as an observer. He joined FEA 6 two weeks later and after only four weeks' instruction passed his flight exams. Such was the natural aptitude and ability of Buckler, that he remained at FEA 6 as an instructor. After spending over six months at FEA 6 he was posted to FA(A) 209 as an observer, where he spent nearly a year and was awarded the Iron Cross 1st Class. In spring 1916 he requested pilot training, was accepted and on completion of his training in November was posted to Jasta 17 with the rank of vizefeld-webel, and was soon in action over Verdun. On 17 December he opened his score by shooting down a twin-engined Caudron over Bras.

Two more Caudrons on 14 and 15 February brought his score to three, and by the end of April he had raised his score to six. On 17 July 1917 his patrol ran into a patrol of Sopwith Camels and Pups over Keyem. After shooting down one Pup, Buckler was badly wounded in a fight with another. He managed to break away and return to his field. On 12 August, with his score now standing at thirteen, he was again shot and wounded in a dogfight with a Camel, but again he managed to break away and return to his field. On 12 November, after his 25th victory, he was promoted to leutnant and awarded the Golden Military Service Cross. He shot down an R.E.8 of No.21 Squadron RFC on 15 November, followed by two balloons and an R.E.8 on 18 November.

Buckler crashed on 30 November after being attacked by Allied fighters, his aircraft surviving a plunge to the ground from 800 metres. Considering the fall, his injuries were extremely light: two broken arms and numerous bruises. His score at this time stood at 30 and on 4 December, whilst he was in hospital, he was awarded Prussia's highest award, the Pour le Mérite. The award made him one of only five airmen to be awarded the Pour le Mérite and the Golden Military Service Cross.

Buckler returned to Jasta 17 at the beginning of April 1918 and was soon back in action. On 16 April he shot down a Bréguet XIV over Vaux and on the 21st another over Mareuil. Buckler was wounded again on 6 May, this time in the ankle. It was a wound that was to put him in hospital for nearly eight weeks and was to win him the award of a Golden Wound Badge, this being his fifth wound.

He returned to Jasta 17 at the beginning of July. On 22 September 1918 he was made staffelführer, a post he held until the end of the war. His tally at the end of hostilities stood at 36.

During the Second World War, Julius Buckler served with training squadrons of the Luftwaffe. He died in Berlin on 23 May 1960.

Hauptmann Hans-Joachim Buddecke (1890–1918) 13 victories

The son of an Army General Staff Officer Hans-Joachim Buddecke was born in Berlin on 22 August 1890. He learned to fly at his own expense and bought his own second-hand aircraft. At the beginning of June 1915, Buddecke joined the Imperial German Air Service with the rank of leutnant. After a brief period at Jastaschule, he was posted to FA 23 as a scout and reconnaissance pilot, flying Fokkers.

On patrol with Berthold over St. Quentin, they sighted a patrol of British aircraft of No.8 Squadron RFC. As the two patrols closed on each other, Berthold came under attack from a B.E.2c. Quickly Buddecke closed on the British aircraft and shot it down. Buddecke shot down a second B.E.2c on 23 October and a third on 11 November, bringing the award of the Iron Cross 2nd Class. At the end of December Buddecke was posted to Gallipoli with Ottoman FA 6 flying Halberstadt D IIs, D Vs, and Fokker E IIIs as a scout and reconnaissance pilot, with promotion to oberleutnant.

On 6 January Buddecke scored his fourth victory a Maurice Farman of No.2 Squadron RNAS – over Cape Narors. By the end of the month he had raised his total to seven and was awarded the Silver Liaket Medal and the Iron Cross 1st Class. At the end of April 1916 he was awarded the Pour le Mérite, the Golden Liaket Medal, the Saxon Military St. Henry Order 4th Class and the Knight's Cross with Swords of the Hohenzollern House Order. The Turks nicknamed him 'The Shooting Hawk' and the 'Hunting Hawk'.

Buddecke was posted back to France at the beginning of August and appointed staffelführer of Jasta 4 on 28 August 1916 with promotion to hauptmann.

He increased his score to ten during September, then returned to Turkey in the middle of December to join Ottoman FA 5. On 30 March 1917, whilst on patrol over Smyrna, he came across a patrol of British reconnaissance fighter-bombers. After a short action, Buddecke shot down a Farman F.27 and a Nieuport 12 of No.2 Squadron RNAS, raising his score to twelve. For the rest of the year he flew reconnaissance and scouting missions.

At the beginning of 1918, he received a message from Rudolf Berthold, who was now commander of Jasta 18, asking him to join him as his deputy. Buddecke returned to France at the beginning of February, going first to Jasta 30 then on to Jasta 18. On 19 February 1918, over Neuve Chapelle, he shot down a Sopwith Camel of No.80 Squadron RFC.

On 10 March, whilst on patrol with Berthold over Harmes they ran into a patrol of Sopwith Camels of No.3 Squadron RNAS. Berthold was attacked and Buddecke went to his aid, but was caught by another Camel and shot down. He was buried in Berlin with full military honours on 22 March 1918.

Leutnant Walter von Bülow-Bothkamp (1894–1918) 28 victories

Walter von Bülow-Bothkamp was born on 24 April 1894 at Borby, near Eckemforde in Holstein. At the outbreak of war he joined the famous Saxon Hussar Regiment No.17, the 'Death's Head' Hussars, whose commander was the legendary Field Marshal August von Mackensen. The Hussars were soon in action and early in 1915 they saw heavy fighting in Alsace. Walter von Bülow stood out from the rest of the men and, after a series of skirmishes in which he distinguished himself, was given a field commission to leutnant and was awarded the Iron Cross 2nd Class.

In spring 1915, von Bülow applied for transfer to the German Army Air Service and was accepted. He was posted to Valenciennes for pilot training in June, and on graduating was assigned to FA 22, flying reconnaissance missions in twin-engined AEG G.II biplanes. On 10 October 1915, von Bülow opened his score when he shot down a Voisin whilst on a reconnaissance mission over Metz. The next day he scored another victory, a Maurice Farman over the Champagne region. For these two victories he was awarded the Iron Cross 1st Class.

In January 1916 von Bülow was posted to FA 300 in Palestine. It was a welcome relief as far as the weather was concerned, but there was comparatively little action. It wasn't until 8 August that von Bülow scored his next victory, an EA over El Arish, Suez. On 17 September he shot down two Sopwith Babys – the first one from the seaplane carrier *Ben-my-Chree* – again over El Arish.

After several applications von Bülow was posted back to the Western Front to join Jasta 18 in December 1916. He took his score to six on 23 January 1917, when he shot down a Sopwith 1½ Strutter of 45 Squadron RFC and an F.E.8 of 41 Squadron, over Gheluvelt in his Albatros D V. By the end of April he had increased his score to twelve and had been awarded the Knight's Cross with Swords of the Hohenzollern House Order and the Saxon Military St. Henry Order. On 10 May he was appointed commander of Jasta 36.

Von Bülow continued to score regularly and by the beginning of October 1917, had raised his score to 21. On 8 October he was awarded Prussia's highest honour, the Pour le Mérite. On 13 December he was made commander of Jasta 2 'Boelcke', with his score at 28.

Whilst on patrol in his Albatros D V over Ypres on 6 January 1918, east of Passchendaele, his patrol was jumped by British fighters of 23 and 70 Squadrons RFC. After a brief fight, von Bülow's aircraft was seen to spin out of control and crash into front-line trenches. His body was recovered and buried with full military honours. He was aged 24.

Kapitänleutnant Horst Freiherr Treusch von Buttlar-Brandenfels (1888–1943)

Horst Treusch von Buttlar-Brandenfels was born on 14 June 1888 in Hannau, Darmstadt. After finishing high school in Darmstadt, he followed the family tradition and joined the Imperial German Navy in 1903 as a sea cadet. On completion of his initial training, Buttlar-Brandenfels was commissioned to the rank of leutnant zur see and sent on a radio-telephony course. Upon graduating he was posted as RT officer to the staff of the Commander of Reconnaissance Ships.

Zeppelins at this time were beginning to show their worth and flight trials were begun in 1910, with the intention of using the Zeppelin as an aerial scouting ship for the navy. The first air-to-ship radio test flight was with the airship L.2, but because of the extra equipment aboard some of the crew, including Buttlar-Brandenfels, were scratched from the flight. During trials the airship crashed, killing all on board. Buttlar-

Brandenfels applied to become an airship pilot and was accepted, and at the age of 26 was in command of airship L.6.

His first contact with the enemy was on Christmas Day 1914, when, whilst on patrol off Heligoland, he sighted three mine-layers accompanied by two cruisers and eight destroyers. Buttlar-Brandenfels attempted to send a radio message, but his equipment was out of order. He decided to attack and from a height of over 4,000ft dropped three 110lb bombs. The bombs did no damage and L.6 came under heavy and accurate fire from the cruisers. Buttlar-Brandenfels withdrew L.6 into cloud cover, then came in low, strafing the enemy ships with machine-gun fire from the two gondolas and the upper gun platform. The ships returned fire and punctured the L.6 repeatedly. Buttlar-Brandenfels abandoned his attack and turned for base. He received the Iron Cross 2nd Class for the mission, and promotion to kommander.

On 19 January 1915 Buttlar-Brandenfels, with L.6, awaited orders to carry out the first attack on Britain. On 17 August he was to carry out his first successful raid, in the L.11. Before the end of the war, Buttlar-Brandenfels was to fly more than nineteen missions against England. He was awarded the Iron Cross 1st Class and promotion to kapitänleutnant. After his fifteenth mission he was awarded Prussia's highest award, the Pour le Mérite. His airship crew each received the Iron Cross 1st Class.

At the end of the war, Buttlar-Brandenfels was one of those responsible for destroying the entire airship fleet at Nordholz in defiance of the Versailles Treaty. During the Second World War, he served with the Luftwaffe, and was killed in action in 1943.

Airship Commander Kapitänleutnant Horst Freiherr Treusch von Buttlar-Brandenfels.

Kapitänleutnant zur See Friedrich Christiansen (1879–1972)

13 victories

The son of a sea captain, Friedrich Christiansen was born at Wyk-on-Fohr on 12 December 1879. In 1913 he decided to learn to fly. After graduating and gaining licence No.707 he became an instructor at a civilian flying school.

In August 1914 Christiansen was called up and was posted to Zeebrugge as a naval aviator. For a year he was flying Brandenburg W12 seaplanes on missions over the North Sea and Britain. He even carried out a bombing mission on Dover and Ramsgate, for which he was awarded the Iron Cross 2nd Class. On 27 April 1916 as leutnant der matrosen artillerie (lieutenant of naval artillery), Friedrich Christiansen was awarded the Iron Cross 1st Class and the Knight's Cross with Swords of the Hohenzollern House Order.

Oberleutnant Friedrich Christiansen.

Christiansen claimed his first victory on 15 May 1917, when he shot down a Sopwith Pup off Dover. On 1 September 1917 he took command of the Naval Air Station at Zeebrugge and was promoted to oberleutnant; the same day he shot down a Porte FB2 Baby, off Felixstowe.

Christiansen continued to carry out reconnaissance, rescue and bombing missions, and by December 1917 had completed 440 missions, including the shooting down of Airship C.27. At the end of December he was awarded Prussia's highest award, the Pour le Mérite

Christiansen increased his tally on 15 February when he shot down a Curtiss H12B flying boat from Felixstowe. This was followed by two more Curtiss H12Bs on 24–25 April. In June and July he claimed three more flying boats, all Felixstowe F.2as. On 6 July, Christiansen was on patrol in the Thames Estuary, when he surprised the British submarine C-25 cruising on the surface. He attacked the submarine, killing the captain and five crewmen. Christiansen thought he had sunk the submarine, but in fact she managed, with difficulty, to limp back to harbour.

By the end of the war, Christiansen had raised his personal tally to thirteen, but this is speculative because there are possibly shared victories. Christiansen returned to the merchant marine for a while before taking a post as a pilot for the Dornier company. It was whilst with Dornier that he flew the largest seaplane in the world at that time, the Dornier Do.X, flying it on its maiden Atlantic flight to New York in 1930.

In 1933 Christiansen joined the German Aviation Ministry as it attempted to rebuild its air force. He was appointed Korpsführer of the National Socialist Flying Korps (NSFK) at its conception in 1937. Two years later, when war was declared and the German Army occupied Holland, Christiansen was appointed officer commanding occupied Holland, a post he held until the end of the war when he was imprisoned by the Allies. On his release from prison he retired to West Germany, and died at Innien in December 1972 at the age of 93.

Leutnant Carl Degelow (1891–1970) 30 victories

Carl Degelow was born on 5 January 1891 in Munsterdorf, Germany. At the onset of war he joined the Nassauischen Infantrie Regiment No.88 and was sent to the Western Front. His regiment was in action immediately, and Degelow showed his leadership qualities. Within three months he had been promoted from gefreiter to unteroffizier and had been awarded the Iron Cross 2nd Class. At the beginning of 1915 the regiment was posted to the Russian Front: once again Degelow showed his leadership qualities by leading a succession of offensives against the Russians, for which he was promoted to vizefeldwebel and awarded the Iron Cross 1st Class. It was on one of these offensives that he was badly wounded in the arm; on 31 July, whilst in hospital, he was awarded a commission to leutnant and decided to apply for a transfer to the German Army Air Service.

In April 1916 his transfer came through and he was posted to flying school in Germany. After graduating at the beginning of 1917, he was posted to FA(A) 216 on the Somme, as a reconnaissance pilot. Together with his observer, Leutnant Kurten, he flew artillery support and reconnaissance missions in an Albatros C. V. Whilst on an artillery support flight over Braye on 22 May 1917, they were attacked by a Caudron G. IV. They managed to shoot it down, though the kill was unconfirmed. Three days later, on a reconnaissance mission over Bailly Braye, they were attacked by another Caudron G. IV. Degelow and his observer shot it down, and it was confirmed as his first victory.

Degelow applied for transfer to single-seater fighters and was posted to Jasta 36 for training; but within days he had been returned to his unit after accidentally shooting an airman whilst carrying out gunnery practice on the ground. On 17 August he was posted to Jasta 7 where he scored two victories, but they were unconfirmed. On 25 January 1918 he shot down a Bristol F.2b of 20 Squadron, followed by a Sopwith Camel of 54 Squadron on 21 April, and then on 16 May an R.E.8, raising his score to four.

Degelow was posted to Jasta 40 on 16 May 1918, taking command on 11 July. As commander Degelow shot down six more aircraft in July, bringing his score to thirteen.

He was awarded the Knight's Cross with Swords of the Hohenzollern House Order on 9 August, and shot down another six Allied aircraft in September. By the end of October he had shot down another ten Allied aircraft, raising his total to 29. He made it 30 on 4 November 1918 when he shot down a D.H.9 near the Dutch border. On 9 November he was awarded Prussia's highest award, the Pour le Mérite, the last member of the German Army Air Service to receive the award.

After the war Degelow created the Hamburg Zeitfreiwillingen Korps and fought against the communists in the post-war revolution. At the beginning of the World War Two, he joined the Luftwaffe, becoming a major. After surviving the war, Degelow died in Hamburg on 9 November 1970.

Leutnant der Reserve Albert Dossenbach (1891–1917) 15 victories

The son of a hotel owner, Albert Dossenbach was born in St. Blasien in the southern part of the Black Forest on 5 June 1891. When war was declared he enlisted in the Army and was promoted to unteroffizier within weeks; a month later he was awarded the Iron Cross 2nd Class for carrying his wounded commanding officer away from the front line to safety. Within four months he had been awarded the Iron Cross 1st Class and the Military Merit Cross, and had been promoted to feldwebel.

He was commissioned leutnant on 27 January 1915 then applied for transfer to the German Army Air Service. In spring 1916 he was posted to Jastaschule, graduating in June 1916. Posted to FA 22, he joined up with observer Hans Schilling, flying an Albatros C. II. Within three months Dossenbach and his observer had been credited with shooting down eight Allied aircraft. Dossenbach was awarded the Knight's Cross

Leutnant Albert Dossenbach.

2nd Class with Swords to the Order of the Zahringer Lion. On 21 October 1917 he was awarded the Knight's Cross of the Hohenzollern House Order. The same day he and his observer shot down an F.E.2b of 25 Squadron over Tourmignies.

On 11 November 1916 Dossenbach was awarded Prussia's highest honour, the Pour le Mérite, the first two-seater pilot to receive this award. A further award was made on 9 December, when he was decorated with the Knight's Cross of the Karl Friedrich Military Merit Order.

Dossenbach applied for single-seater training. After graduating he took command of Jasta 36 on 22 February 1917 and set the standard by scoring the unit's first victory – a French Caudron from Escadrille SPA12 on 5 April. By the end of the month Dossenbach had raised his personal score to fourteen.

A bombing attack on his airfield on 2 May left Dossenbach badly wounded from bomb splinters and put him in hospital for a month. On release from hospital he was given command of Jasta 10, taking up the post on 21 June. He opened his score with the Jasta on 27 June by shooting down an observation balloon over Ypres. On 3 July 1917 his patrol was jumped by British fighters of 57 Squadron RFC over Frenzenberg. Heavily outnumbered, Dossenbach was attacked by four fighters and during the ensuing action his aircraft caught fire. It is not certain whether he jumped or fell to his death from his blazing aircraft.

His remains were returned to German forces who buried him with full military honours at Freiburg.

Oberleutnant Eduard Ritter von Dostler (1892–1917) 26 victories

Eduard Dostler was born on 3 February 1892 at Pottenstein in Swiss Franconia, the son of a surveyor. After leaving school he joined the 2nd Pioneer Battalion as a cadet, graduating on 28 October 1912. He was commissioned leutnant and assigned to the 4th Pioneer Battalion. In 1913, during a military exercise which involved crossing the heavily flooded Danube River, Dostler saved the life of a fellow officer; for this extreme act of bravery, he was awarded the Bavarian Life Saving Medal.

At the outbreak of war in August 1914, Dostler's engineering unit was sent into the thick of the fighting and he was awarded the Iron Cross 2nd Class in November. In March 1915, he was awarded the Iron Cross 1st Class and the Bavarian Military Service Order 4th Class with Swords. He continued to fight with his battalion until November when he heard that his brother, a pilot, had been killed in action.

Dostler applied to be transferred to the German Army Air Service and in February 1916 was posted to Schutzstaffel 27. On graduating on 15 June he was posted to

Kampfstaffel 36, flying Roland C IIs. With his observer, Leutnant Boes, Dostler carried out reconnaissance missions throughout the rest of 1916. On 17 December he opened his tally when he shot down a Nieuport Scout over Verdun.

Ten days later both Dostler and his observer were posted to Jasta 13, where they increased their score by shooting down a Caudron over Nixeville on 22 January. Early in February they were posted to Jasta 34 where they stayed until the beginning of June, by which time their score had risen to eight.

On 10 June, Dostler was given command of Jasta 6. By the end of July his score had risen to 21 and he was awarded the Knight's Cross with Swords of the Hohenzollern House Order. This was followed by the award of Prussia's highest award, the Pour le Mérite.

Dostler's score continued to mount and by 18 August had reached 26. On 21 August over the Roulers area his patrol was attacked by R.E.8 fighters of 7 Squadron RFC. During the action Dostler's aircraft was hit several times and he was killed.

He was posthumously awarded the Bavarian Military Max Joseph Order, making him a Ritter (Knight); the award was backdated to 18 August.

Leutnant der Reserve Wilhelm Frankl (1893–1917) 20 victories

The son of a Jewish salesman, Wilhelm Frankl was born on 20 December 1893 in Hamburg. Even at this early time resentment against Jews was festering in Germany and Wilhelm Frankl was to find that obtaining promotion was not easy. On 20 July 1913 Frankl learned to fly at the local flying school, and gained his licence.

At the outbreak of war he applied to join the German Army Air Service and was accepted. Even though he was a qualified pilot he was trained as an observer and posted to FA

Oberleutnant Eduard Dostler.

40 in Flanders. He carried out a number of reconnaissance missions during 1914 and was awarded the Iron Cross 2nd Class. During the early part of 1915 there were more reconnaissance missions, and on 10 May 1915 he scored his first victory by shooting down a Voisin with a carbine. For this incident, he was awarded the Iron Cross 1st Class and was promoted to vizefeldwebel.

In autumn 1915 Frankl applied for training as a fighter pilot and was sent to Jastaschule that November. He graduated in December and was posted to Kek Vaux at the beginning of January 1916, flying Fokker Eindeckers.

He scored his second victory, another Voisin, over Woumen; nine days later he added a third to his tally. At the end of May he had taken his score to six and been promoted to leutnant. He was awarded the Knight's Cross of the Hohenzollern House Order and the Hanseatic Cross. On 10 July Frankl took his score to eight and two days later was awarded Prussia's highest decoration, the Pour le Mérite.

Frankl was posted to Jasta 4 on 1 September and by the end of the year had added five more victories to his score. On 6 April 1917 he claimed four more victims – one at night and the others later that same morning all within a space of an hour. He scored one more on 7 April, bringing his total to twenty.

On the afternoon of 8 April 1917 Wilhelm Frankl took off and flew into a patrol of British fighters of 48 Squadron. He was outnumbered, and his Albatros took heavy machine-gun fire and was seen to break up in the air, the remains of the aircraft and Frankl's body falling to the ground near Vitry-Sailly.

Frankl's body was sent back to Germany and was buried with full military honours in Berlin-Charlottenburg. In the 1930s the Nazi party removed his name from the list of air heroes of World War One, because he was Jewish: it wasn't until 1973 that his name was revived and Luftwaffe Squadron No.74 was named after him.

Oberleutnant Hermann Fricke (1890–?)

Hermann Fricke was born on 16 June 1890 at Münster, Westphalia. When he was 22 he applied to join the German Air Service, was accepted and was assigned to FA 2. Two years later, on 1 July 1914, he realised his wish to fly as a pilot and entered the German Flying School at Johannisthal for pilot training. In August 1914 he was awarded his pilot's certificate, and he rejoined his unit in September as a reconnaissance pilot.

With World War One now in progress he was posted with his unit to the Western Front and began flying reconnaissance and artillery spotting sorties. Having an interest in photography he began to apply this knowledge to taking aerial photographs of Allied positions. His efforts met with considerable success, which was recognised by the German High Command with the award of the Iron Cross 2nd Class and the Knight's Cross of the Hohenzollern Order.

Wishing to experience what the German infantry was going through on the ground, he asked to be allowed to command an infantry company for a short time. His unusual request was granted and he took a front-line ground command for several weeks. Rejoining his unit, he was better able to understand the problems of the German infantry soldier.

During the battles of the Somme, Arras and Flanders Fricke flew sortie after sortie, taking aerial photographs of the ground struggle beneath his reconnaissance aircraft. During the harsh, muddy winter of 1916–17 the German High Command instructed the now Oberleutnant Fricke to establish a War Photography Office at Headquarters. Fricke was appointed to command a new unit, Group 2 Series Photography Unit. He equipped his unit's aircraft with Reihenbildner built-in cameras; these cameras were capable of photographing a mile-long strip of the ground below, the strips being joined together to form an invaluable aerial view of Allied positions. Fricke's aerial photographic maps provided the German High Command with the means to deploy and direct their forces on the ground to good effect.

Fricke had by now flown well over 160 combat sorties and his unit had photographed some 3,700 square miles of Allied positions with their aerial cameras. His innovative aerial photographs gained him the award of the Pour le Mérite on 23 December 1917, for outstanding combat service as an observer with FA 2.

Oberleutnant Herman Fricke continued to fly to the end of World War One and flew again in World War Two in the Luftwaffe.

Leutnant der Reserve Heinrich Gontermann (1896–1917) 39 victories

Leutnant Heinrich Gontermann.

Heinrich Gontermann, the son of a cavalry officer, was born on the 25 February 1896 in Siegen, southern Westphalia. In August 1914 he joined the 6th Uhlan Cavalry Regiment in Hanau and after initial training was sent to the front. The following months were hard, but Gontermann's leadership qualities started to show themselves. He was slightly wounded in September, and promoted to feldwebel. In spring 1915 because of his leadership qualities he was given a field commission to leutnant and awarded the Iron Cross 2nd Class.

He applied for transfer to the Imperial German Air Service and was accepted for pilot and observer training. On graduation, early in 1916, he was posted to Kampfstaffel Tergnier as a reconnaissance pilot flying the Roland C II. In the spring he was posted again, this time to FA 25 where he flew both as a pilot and as an observer on AGO C.Is. After nearly a year of flying reconnaissance missions, Gontermann applied for Jastaschule and the transfer to a fighter unit. He was accepted and after graduating on 11 November 1916, was posted to Jasta 5. Within three days he had opened his score by shooting down an F.E.2b over Morval.

In March 1917 Gontermann scored another victory and on 5 March was awarded the Iron Cross 1st Class. On 6 March he shot down an F.E.2b of 57 Squadron RFC and by the end of the month had raised his score to six. One month later he had raised it to seventeen and was made commander of Jasta 15. On 6 May he was awarded the Knight's Cross with Swords of the Hohenzollern House Order. Another victory followed on 10 May when he shot down a SPAD and a Caudron R4; the following day he shot down another SPAD and received the Bavarian Order of Max Josef. On 14 May he was awarded the final decoration, the Pour le Mérite, with his score standing at 21.

From June until the end of September Gontermann added 17 more victories bringing his total to 38. Eleven of the 17 victories were observation balloons, four of which were shot down on the evening of 19 August within a space of three minutes. On 2 October 1917, he shot down a SPAD whilst on patrol over Laon.

On 30 October Gontermann was air testing the latest Fokker triplane that had just been delivered to the Jasta. Minutes into the air test above the airfield the upper wing of the Fokker suffered structural failure and the aircraft spun out of control into the ground. Gontermann was pulled from the wreckage still alive, but died from his injuries some hours later. He was just 21 years old.

Oberleutnant Hermann Wilhelm Göring (1893–1946) 22 victories

Next to Manfred von Richthofen, Hermann Göring was probably the most famous – or infamous – German pilot to come out of World War One. It was not for his actions during this war that his infamy spread, though, but for his part in World War Two.

Hermann Göring was born on 12 January 1893 in Rosenheim, Upper Bavaria. He was the son of Heinrich Göring, a very high-ranking army officer who had also been a Governor of German South-West Africa. In 1912 Hermann Göring graduated from the Lichterfelde cadet school with brilliant results and was commissioned into the Prinz Wilhelm Regiment No.112 and posted to its headquarters at Mülhausen. It was here that Göring contracted rheumatic fever and was hospitalised. In hospital Göring was visited by his friend Bruno Loerzer who had served with him in his regiment but had transferred to the German Army Air Service and become a pilot. Göring applied to the commanding officer requesting a place at Freiburg flying school. After waiting over two weeks and receiving no reply, Göring obtained the papers and signed them himself, including a transfer paper to the flying school. During this two-week period he had been flying with Loerzer at every opportunity, getting in all the training he could. His transfer was refused and he was ordered to return to his unit, which was something Göring had no intention of doing. Now this situation posed a very serious problem for Göring, as he was open to a charge of desertion and forging papers. He immediately telegraphed his godfather, Ritter von Epstein, who moved in extremely high circles; suddenly the Crown Prince Friedrich Wilhelm intervened and asked that Göring be posted to the German Fifth Army field air detachment. The charges were suddenly reduced to one of lateness and he was given a medical certificate saying that he was not fit for duty on the front line.

In autumn 1914 Göring completed his training with FEA 3 as an observer then joined Loerzer at FEA 25. They soon acquired a name for carrying out the most dangerous of missions and in March 1915 they received the Iron Cross 2nd Class. In May they carried out one of their most dangerous missions: they had to carry out a reconnaissance of the fortresses in the Verdun area that were held by the French, and photograph them in detail. Many others had tried but had failed. For three days Göring and Loerzer carried out flights over the Verdun area and came back with photographs so detailed that General Erich von Falkenhayn asked to see them personally. So delighted with the results were the High Command, that Crown Prince Wilhelm exercised his royal prerogative and invested both Göring and Loerzer with the Iron Cross 1st Class in the field.

In June 1915 Göring was posted to Freiburg for pilot training, graduating in October. He was posted to FA 25 and on 16 November 1915 opened his score by shooting down a Maurice Farman over Tahure.

In 1916 he was posted from one unit to another, first to Kek Stennay, flying Fokker E. IIIs, then in March to Kek Metz where on 30 July he shot down a Caudron whilst escorting bombers over Memang. He then went back to FA 25 on 9 July, then back again to Kek Metz on 7 September. From there he went to Jasta 7 and a few weeks later Jasta 5 on 20 October. It was whilst on patrol on 2 November 1916 that he first encountered the British Handley-Page bomber. He swooped in to look at it and came under fire. He returned fire, killing one of the gunners, but out of the clouds swooped a flight of Sopwith fighters who proceeded to rake his aircraft from stem to stern. Göring felt the bullets rip into the fuselage and into his thigh. He passed out, then came to as his aircraft plunged toward the ground. Managing to regain control, he flew toward what looked to him like a cemetery just over the German lines. As good fortune would have it, it turned out to be an emergency hospital and within a very short time of crash-landing, he was on the operating table being repaired.

After recuperating, Göring was posted to Jasta 26 at the beginning of February, now commanded by his friend Bruno Loerzer. By the end of that month he had raised his score to six and was attracting the attention of the High Command. He increased his score on 10 May when he shot down a D.H. 4 of 55 Squadron RFC. One week later he

Oberleutnant Hermann Wilhelm Göring as 27 Staffel Commander.

was given command of Jasta 27 and by the end of October had raised his score to fifteen. On 27 October Göring was awarded the Military Karl-Friedrich Merit Order, the Knight's Cross with Swords of the Hohenzollern House Order and the Knight's Cross 2nd Class with Swords of the Baden Order of the Zahringer Lion. By the end of the year his score had risen to sixteen.

In 1918 he increased his score steadily and by the end of June had taken his score to 22. At the beginning of June 1918 Göring was awarded Prussia's highest award, the Pour le Mérite. Then on 9 July he was given command of JG I – the Richthofen Squadron – and promotion to Oberleutnant. At this point Göring decided that his fighting days were over and did very little combat flying. At the end of the war, he was ordered to instruct his pilots to fly their aircraft to an Allied field. He knew that the Allies wanted the latest Fokkers, so he ordered his pilots to do so, but to set fire to the aircraft the moment they were on the ground. After the war Göring went to Denmark and Sweden in a flight-advisory capacity after fighting in the post-war revolution, but returned to Germany in the early 1920s.

Hermann Göring joined the Nazi Party and became Adolf Hitler's right-hand man. He progressed through the party as its strength grew and took over command of the newly formed Luftwaffe. Göring held a number of other posts throughout World War Two, but the Luftwaffe was his forte. During the war he received the Knight's Cross of the Iron Cross and the Grand Cross of the Iron Cross, the only person ever to receive it. He was promoted to Feldmarschall, then later to Reichsmarschall – heir apparent to Hitler.

Captured by the Americans at the end of the war, Göring stood trial for war crimes and was convicted. He was sentenced to death by hanging, despite his pleas to be executed by firing squad, but in the end he cheated the Allies by committing suicide on 15 October 1946, using poison he had been concealing on his person since his capture.

Oberleutnant Robert Ritter von Greim (1892–1945) 28 victories

The son of a police captain, Robert Greim was born on 22 June 1892 in Bayreuth, Bavaria. On 14 July 1911 he joined the regular army; he was put forward for officer training and on 29 October 1912 joined the Bavarian Field Artillery Regiment. He was commissioned leutnant on 25 October 1913.

When war started, Greim's regiment was one of the first in action and he led a battery in the Battle of Lorraine at Nancy-Epinal, on the assaults on St. Mihiel and Camp des Romains. For these actions he was awarded the Iron Cross 2nd Class and became 1st Battalion Adjutant on 15 March 1915. At the end of April 1915, Greim was awarded the Bavarian Military Merit Order 4th Class with Swords.

Greim applied for the German Army Air Service and was accepted. He began training as an observer on 10 August 1915 and was posted to FA 3b where he opened

Oberleutnant Robert Ritter von Greim wearing his Pour le Mérite.

his score by shooting down a Maurice Farman in October. He was posted to FA(A) 204 as an observer during the Battle of the Somme. Greim applied for pilot training toward the end of 1916 and after graduating, was awarded his pilot's certificate and badge. He was posted to FA 46b as a reconnaissance pilot on 22 February 1917 and one month later was sent to Jastaschule for single-seater training.

On completing his conversion training, he was posted to Jasta 34b on 3 April 1917, flying Albatros D Vs, Fokker Dr Is and Fokker D VIs. Greim had all his aircraft marked with his own markings of a red cowl, two red fuselage bands and a white-silvery tail.

Greim increased his score on 24 May by shooting down a SPAD over Mamey and the following day shot down a Caudron R4 over Rambaucourt. At the end of May, he was awarded the Iron Cross 1st Class and the Bavarian Military Merit Order 4th Class with Crown and Swords. By the end of 1917 he had raised his score to seven.

Greim continued to score steadily and on 21 March 1918 was given command of JG X and later JG IX. With his score standing at nine on 29 April 1918, he was awarded the Knight's Cross with Swords of the Royal Hohenzollern House Order. By the end of October 1918, Greim had raised his score to 28 and was awarded Prussia's highest honour, the Pour le Mérite. This was followed by the Bavarian Max

Joseph Medal which entitled him to put Ritter von in front of his name, making him a knight. He was also promoted to oberleutnant.

At the end of the war Greim was with the Bavarian Air Service and later he became an advisor to the Chinese Nationalist Air Force. In the early 1930s he became the Director of the Bavarian Sport Flyers' Association. In 1934 he joined the newly-formed Luftwaffe with the rank of major, taking over command of the Richthofen Geschwader.

In 1938 he was promoted to the rank of general and during World War Two commanded Fliegerkorps V, for which he received the Knight's Cross of the Iron Cross in 1940; on 2 April 1943 he was awarded the Oak Leaves and one year later the Swords to his Knight's Cross. He was promoted generaloberst, commanding the air fleets in Russia.

In 1945 he was captured by the Americans and ranked as head of the Luftwaffe, a post given to him personally by Adolf Hitler who also had promoted him to generalfeld-marschall. Greim committed suicide on 24 May 1945 at a hospital in Salzburg, Austria.

Leutnant der Reserve Wilhelm Griebsch (1887–1920)

Griebsch was born in Posen on 30 June 1887. During his school years he developed an interest in flying which gradually became a passion. At the age of 21 he entered the Technical College in Danzig and four years later, having gained his qualifications as an engineer, he went to Flying School at Berlin-Johannisthal.

Gaining his pilot's certificate on 29 December 1913, on an Etrich Taube, he set his sights on flying in the newly-formed German Army Air Service. When World War One broke out in 1914 Griebsch volunteered for the Army Air Service, and after initial army officer training left training school with the rank of leutnant der reserve in the territorial army.

Joining FA 250 as a reconnaissance pilot he was immediately in the thick of battle on the Western Front. He then began to fly as an observer with FA 250, and later with FA 213, where his technical knowledge proved invaluable. His particular speciality was long-range reconnaissance missions and he carried out the enormous total of 345 such missions. The outstanding information and technical details obtained by Griebsch whilst carrying out these missions proved of great value to the German High Command in their strategic battle plans and operations. Even though under enemy air attack he continued to observe and record the Allied positions beneath his wings, and fight back with his machine-gun.

His outstanding record of successful missions as an observer brought him Prussia's highest honour, the Pour le Mérite, on 30 September 1918. Griebsch was one of the very few observers to be awarded the decoration, most such decorations being awarded to fighter pilots.

Having spent almost four years in the midst of battle, he was taken off operational flying and sent back to Berlin to the Albatros Aircraft Company. He remained in Berlin till the end of the war.

Post-war he obtained work at the Junkers Aircraft Company in Dessau as a test pilot. On 20 July 1920 Griebsch took off to flight-test a new aircraft. With an injured left arm he was – apparently – unable to control the aircraft and when at 1,900ft over Mosigkau his aircraft fell out of the sky and crashed, killing him instantly.

Oberleutnant Jürgen von Grone (1887–?)

The youngest son of an army officer, Oberleutnant Otto von Grone, Jürgen von Grone was born at Schwerin on 14 November 1887. When World War One began he was a leutnant serving with the 11th Field Artillery Regiment on the Western Front. His unit was engaged in heavy fighting in the Namur sector of the Front and the battle experience gained was to be put to good use by von Grone later, when he became an observer. He was posted to the Eastern Front in 1915, and during heavy fighting was wounded and hospitalised. On returning to duty he became commander of one of the new mobile anti-aircraft trains the Germans had formed. He was awarded the Iron Cross 2nd Class, followed later by the Iron Cross 1st Class.

In December 1915 he applied for transfer to the Air Service as an observer and was accepted. After completing his training he was posted to FA 222. His specialist task as a reconnaissance observer was to photograph Allied troop movements and positions; by summer 1917 he had flown 130 combat reconnaissance missions and been promoted to command the Photography Troop of the German 7th Army. On 10 September 1917 he was the first observer to photograph Paris, from a height of 7,000m.

On 13 October 1918 Oberleutnant von Grone was awarded the Pour le Mérite for his outstanding contribution to the war effort. Part of his citation read:

> Oberleutnant von Grone performed outstanding deeds during the large battles of 7th Army. This long-range reconnaissance – up to 100km behind enemy lines – contributed substantially to our knowledge of enemy positions. Leutnant von Grone carried out numerous long-range flights, among them 12 over 100km behind the enemy front, despite enemy defences, up to 6,000m altitude under heavy air attack he prevailed. By reason of his above average performance I consider him worthy of the award of the Pour le Mérite.
> Signed: Hugo Sperrle,
Hauptmann, Commandant of Flyers, 7th Army.

(Sperrle later became a field marshal during World War Two.)

Von Grone survived World War One and was discharged from the Army in 1920, with the rank of hauptmann.

Leutnant der Reserve Walter Höhndorf. (1892–1917) 12 victories

Walter Höhndorf, the son of a school teacher, was born in Prutzke, Bavaria on 10 November 1892. Whilst in Paris in September 1913 he learned to fly and received his civilian pilot's certificate, No.582, on 3 November.

Höhndorf returned to Germany, taking part in many air displays, becoming one of the best aerobatic pilots in the country and carrying out aerobatic manoeuvres never seen before. He then turned his hand to designing, and helped with the production of aircraft with the Union Flugzeugwerke at Teltow.

At the outbreak of war in 1914, Höhndorf volunteered for the German Army Air Service, gaining a commission to leutnant on 15 March 1915. Because of his vast flying experience, albeit crammed into a relatively short time, he was assigned to Siemens-

Schuckert, the aircraft manufacturer, as a test pilot on their large aircraft. After nearly a year of test flying, Höhndorf applied for fighter pilot training and was sent to Jastaschule. On graduating he was sent to FA 12 and later to FA 67 as a reconnaissance pilot, where he was awarded the Iron Cross 2nd Class.

At the beginning of January 1917, he was posted to FA 12 where, on 17 January, he claimed his first victory when he shot down a French Voisin of Escadrille VB105 over the Alsace region. Two days later he shot down another Voisin, of Escadrille VB101, over Medevich.

Höhndorf was posted to Kek Vaux of FA 23 at the beginning of April 1916, and claimed his third victim, a Nieuport, on 10 April. The award of the Iron Cross 1st Class and the Knight's Cross with Swords of the Hohenzollern House Order came at the beginning of June, followed at the end of July by Prussia's highest award, the Pour le Mérite. His victory tally at this time stood at eleven. His last and twelfth victory was a Caudron G.4 on 17 September.

At the beginning of August he was posted to Jasta 1, then to Jasta 4, but it was decided that his experience in testing aircraft was just as valuable as his experience as a fighter pilot. He returned to test pilot duties and instructed at Valenciennes for a short period. On 15 August 1917 he was given command of Jasta 14 on the Western Front. The command was to be short lived: at the beginning of September 1917 he returned to Valenciennes to test an AEG D.I, No.4400/17, an aircraft he helped to design. During the test flight he experienced problems and crashed whilst attempting to land at Ire-le-Sec. He died from his injuries almost immediately.

Leutnant Walter Höhndorf.

Oberleutnant Erich Homburg (1886–?)

The son of a forester, Erich Homburg was born on 2 October 1886 in Rosenthal, Bavaria. After leaving school, he joined the Army as a cadet with Reserve Field Artillery Regiment No. 12. When war broke out in August 1914, Homburg had already been awarded a commission and was the regiment's ordnance officer, as well as the unit adjutant. The regiment moved to the Western Front and after many months of intense and heavy fighting, Homburg was awarded the Iron Cross 2nd Class.

During a lull in the fighting in the early part of 1915, Homburg was offered a flight in a reconnaissance aircraft. He was so taken with the flight and the relative freedom it afforded, that he applied for a transfer to the German Army Flying Service; in spring 1915 he was accepted and posted for flying training. On graduating in the autumn, Homburg was posted to FFA 34 as a reconnaissance pilot. He quickly developed an interest in communications and was assigned the post of communications officer. On 25 September 1915 he was awarded the Iron Cross 1st Class for his reconnaissance work.

During the next two years he created a reporting system that used ground-to-air radio, and became the first flyer to use it. During this time he also turned his attention and skills to aerial photography and carried out flight strip-photographic reconnaissance missions over the battles of the Somme, Verdun, Champagne and in Romania. During the German offensive in Italy Homburg was sent to carry out aerial photographic missions which helped the campaign tremendously. At the beginning of August 1918 he returned to the Western Front and was given command of Army Flight Unit 260. On 13 October Homburg was awarded Prussia's highest honour, the Pour le Mérite, one of the very few non-fighter pilots to receive the award. He was also promoted to oberleutnant in recognition of the 239 tactical reconnaissance and photographic missions he had flown over enemy territory.

When Germany finally capitulated in 1918, Homburg managed to get every single one of his aircraft, every piece of equipment and all his personnel back into Germany.

At the onset of World War Two, Homburg returned to active service with the Luftwaffe, attaining the rank of generalmajor on 1 November 1940.

Oberleutnant Hans-Georg Horn (1892–?)

Born on 28 April 1892, in the small town of Berbisdorf in Silesia, Hans-Georg Horn was the son of the local Lutheran pastor. After finishing his schooling, Horn attended the military school at Danzig as a cadet. At the outbreak of war in 1914 he was holding the rank of unteroffizier at the college, and was returned to the infantry regiment that was his parent unit. The regiment was moved to the Western Front, and within days of arriving they were in action. On 8 August 1914 Horn was involved in the storming of the Maas Heights during the battle of Longwy. One month later Horn was involved in the battle of Combres, his leadership during the battle earning him a promotion to leutnant and the Iron Cross 2nd Class.

In July 1915, whilst leading his troops from the front, Horn was wounded during a charge on the enemy positions. He returned to his unit after a week in hospital, but at the end of July was wounded again, this time badly. Whilst in hospital he was awarded the Iron Cross 1st Class, but a chance meeting with a pilot from the German Army Air Service was to change his whole attitude to the war. At the end of October, just after being released from hospital, Hans-Georg Horn applied for transfer to the German Army Air Service and was accepted.

Horn was posted to FEA 10 on 5 December 1915 for training as an observer, and on graduating in February 1916, he was posted to a defence squadron flying reconnaissance missions for the infantry – the rest of the year was spent flying missions. In January 1917 he was posted to Defence Squadron 11 for two months, then to Kagohl 221 in April.

The move to Kagohl 221 was to bring Horn into contact with some of the most intensive fighting of the war, including the battles at Verdun. He and his pilot, Otto Jahnke, flew almost daily and this was recognised by the German High Command on 15 July 1917, when he was awarded the Knight's Cross with Swords of the

Hohenzollern House Order. It was recognised that Horn was, without doubt, one of the best observers in the German Army Air Service.

This was borne out in November 1917 when, during the battles of 3rd Ypres (Passchendaele) near Gheluvelt, Horn and his pilot flew six flights in the most horrendous weather conditions. The information they brought back enabled the infantry on the ground to make important advances, whilst saving the lives of many of their troops. On 23 December 1917, Hans-Georg Horn was awarded Prussia's highest honour, the Pour le Mérite – one of only five observers to be so honoured. Jahnke received the Military Merit Cross.

In May 1918, Horn was posted to 7th Infantry Division as flying liaison officer for two months with the rank of oberleutnant. He returned to his unit in August and was wounded later the same month, which ostensibly ended his active flying career. At the end of the war, he had accumulated over 300 missions over enemy territory.

His flying days were not quite over, for with the signing of the Armistice he was assigned to Kagohl 401, flying reconnaissance missions for the border police. In November 1919 Hans-Georg Horn resigned from the army and returned to civilian life.

Oberleutnant Max Immelmann (1890–1916) 15 victories

Oberleutnant Max Immelmann.

The son of a wealthy factory owner in Dresden, Max Immelmann was born on 21 September 1890. He joined a railway regiment in Berlin-Schoeneberg with the rank of fahnrich. After obtaining a commission he entered the War Academy, but on the outbreak of war was returned to his regiment.

He applied for a transfer to the German Air Service and was posted for basic flying training at the school in Johannisthal, Berlin, in November 1914. On completion of training he was posted to Aldersdorf for advanced training before being qualified as a pilot. In February 1915 Immelmann passed his flying test and was posted to FFA 62 (later to become Kek Douai), flying LVG two-seaters on observation and escort patrols. With him on these patrols was another recently qualified pilot, Oswald Boelcke, and within a few months they had established themselves a reputation as top scouting pilots.

In May 1915 Immelmann was switched from the LVGs to the unit's single-seat fighter, the Fokker Eindecker.

1 August brought him his first victory, a B.E.2c of No.2 Squadron RFC. By the end of September his score had risen to three confirmed and two possibles: he was awarded the Iron Cross 2nd Class. October and November brought another four victories and promotion to oberleutnant. Further awards followed: the Iron Cross 1st Class and the Knight's Cross with Swords of the Hohenzollern House Order. On 12 January 1916 Max Immelmann, or the 'Eagle of Lille' as he had become known, was awarded the Pour le Mérite.

His score rose to 13 by the end of March and more awards were made to him: the Saxon Commander's Cross to the Military St. Henry Order 2nd Class; the Knight's Cross to the Military St. Henry Order; the Saxon Albert Order 2nd Class with Swords; the Saxon Friedrich-August Medal in Silver and the Bavarian Military Merit Order 4th Class with Swords.

On 18 June 1916 he was in a dogfight with F.E.2bs of 25 Squadron flying his Fokker, No. 246/16. Twisting and turning around in the packed skies, he came under fire from an F.E.2b flown by Captain G. R. McGubbin with his gunner, Corporal J. H. Waller. Their report states that they shot the Fokker's propeller away, causing the engine to tear loose from its mountings and sending the aircraft plunging to the ground. The German High Command announced that Immelmann had died because of a defective synchronising gear in the gun. This, they claimed, had caused Immelmann, when engaged by overwhelming enemy odds, to shoot off his own propeller, with the result that the torque of the engine caused it to be ripped from its mountings, plunging Max Immelmann to his death.

Leutnant Josef Carl Peter Jacobs (1894–1978) 48 victories

The son of a middle-class businessman, Josef Jacobs was born in Kreuzkapelle. Rhineland on 15 May 1894, and learned to fly at the age of 18. On the outbreak of World War One he enlisted in the German Army Air Service and was posted to FEA 9 to be trained as a military pilot. On graduating he was posted to FA 11, and for over a year was engaged in reconnaissance missions over the lines. Early in 1916, he was posted to Fokker Staffel West, flying Fokker E IIIs.

He opened his score – unofficially – on 1 February when he claimed a Caudron – but it was unconfirmed. The end of March brought a claim for a balloon, for which he was awarded the Iron Cross 2nd Class.

On 25 October 1916 Jacobs was posted to Jasta 22 at the request of its commander, Oberleutnant Erich Honemanns, a long-time friend. Within weeks of his arriving he was posted temporarily to Jastaschule 1 as an instructor, where he spent part of the winter. Returning to Jasta 22 at the end of January 1917, he was awarded the Iron Cross 1st Class. He shot down a Caudron R4 over Terny Sorny on 23 January, and by the end of August his score had risen to five and he was appointed commander of Jasta 7. With the appointment came the award of the Knight's Cross with Swords of the Royal Hohenzollern House Order.

By the end of 1917 Jacobs' score had risen to twelve and his Jasta was re-equipped with Fokker Dr Is. Jacobs had his aircraft painted all-black and it was soon to become instantly recognisable by Allied airmen.

The beginning of 1918 was quiet for Jasta 7. The lull didn't last long and in April Jacobs claimed his next victim, an R.E.8 of 7 Squadron RFC over Ostende. The fighting became intense and by the end of July, after surviving a mid-air collision with another DR I, Jacobs' score had risen to 24 and he was awarded Prussia's most prestigious award, the Pour le Mérite.

Jacobs became Germany's greatest exponent of the Fokker Triplane and by the end of 1918 had shot down 48 Allied aircraft.

Hauptmann Alfred Keller (1882–1974)

The son of a tax collector, Alfred Keller was born on 19 September 1882 in Bochum, Westphalia. On leaving school in 1897 Keller entered the army as a cadet, and on graduating in 1902 was assigned to Pioneer Battalion No.17. In autumn 1912 Keller applied for transfer to the newly formed German Army Air Service, and was accepted. He was posted to Metz for training as an observer and on completion of the course, re-applied for training as a pilot. He was posted to flying school at Niederneuendorf in spring 1913 and upon graduating, was posted to the flying station at Darmstadt.

On the outbreak of war in August 1914 Keller was posted to the Western Front in command of Kagohl 27 and promoted to hauptmann. He carried out a number of reconnaissance missions during the first year, among which was a reconnaissance flight in October of 1914 over Paris. This was the cause of great concern to the Parisians, as up to that point they thought that the hostilities were well away from them and offered no direct threat. This mission revealed the vulnerability of cities to their inhabitants and Keller was awarded the Iron Cross 2nd Class for this mission.

In 1915 Keller was given command of Army Flying Park 5 and saw extensive action in reconnaissance and scouting missions in the areas of the Somme and Verdun. In September 1915 he was given command of Kagohl 40 until autumn 1916, when he was asked to command Night Flying Unit 1, which brought a new concept to the war. Keller developed this unit until 1 April 1917, when he was given command of Bogohl 1 and awarded the Iron Cross 1st Class for his work in this field.

Bogohl 1 was the first official bombing squadron to carry out night bombing attacks. From then until the end of the war, Keller and his bomber crews carried out numerous missions, including one in September 1917 on Dunkirk that forced the British to retreat to the safety of Calais. Over 100,000kg of bombs were dropped on Dunkirk, causing a large number of casualties and considerable damage. For this, Keller was awarded the Knight's Cross with Swords of the Hohenzollern House Order. On 4 December, he was awarded Prussia's highest award, the Pour le Mérite.

Keller continued his night bombing attacks and on the night of 30–31 January 1918 led a surprise attack on Paris, causing great consternation and panic. Although the ground artillery put up a defence of sorts, his entire squadron returned without loss. Keller continued his aerial attacks on Paris with the result that more artillery pieces had to be taken from the front to help defend the capital, consequently creating a reduction in the artillery at the front.

At the end of the war Keller left the German Army Air Service and became the head of the German Luftreederi, which was involved in airship transport.

In the early 1930s Hermann Göring approached Keller and asked him for help in developing the new German Luftwaffe. Keller joined the Luftwaffe in 1935 with the rank of oberst, and was given command of Bogohl 154. He was promoted to the rank of generalmajor in April 1936, then to generalleutnant on 1 February 1938 and given the post of commanding general of the East Prussian Luftwaffe. Keller held the post for a year, after which he was given command of 4th Air Division HQ, Brunswick. On 24 June 1940 he was awarded the Knight's Cross of the Iron Cross (the award made him the recipient of Germany's highest awards for valour in both World Wars) and promoted to generloberst. This was followed by the appointment as commander-in-chief of Luftflotte I in Berlin and on the Russian Front.

At the end of the war Keller was commanding officer of the Luftwaffe Anti-Tank Service. He died in Berlin on 11 February 1974, at the age of 86.

Leutnant Hans Kirschstein (1896–1918) 27 victories

Leutnant Hans Kirschstein was born in Koblenz on 5 August 1896. At the outbreak of war he joined the 3rd Pioneer Battalion and was soon in action, first in Poland then in France. In spring 1915 his battalion was shipped to Galicia, Macedonia, and it was here that Kirschstein contracted malaria. He was shipped back to Germany for treatment and convalescence, returning to Galicia in December. While in hospital Kirschstein started to make enquiries about the newly formed German Army Air Service: in February 1916 he applied for transfer to the Aviation Service and was accepted.

At the beginning of May Kirschstein was posted to the flying school at Schliessheim, and after graduating was posted to bomber squadron FA 19. During the battles in Flanders he became respected amongst the Allies for his low-level strafing runs on tanks. He was also one of the first pilots to carry out a bombing run on Dover, for which he received the Iron Cross 2nd Class.

During 1917, Kirschstein flew with FA 256 and FA 3, building his reputation as he went along. At the beginning of February 1918 he asked to be posted to a fighter squadron and was sent to Jastaschule for conversion training.

On 13 March 1918 he was posted to Jasta 6 in the Richthofen 'Circus'. On 18 March he had opened his tally by shooting down a Sopwith Camel of 54 Squadron RFC. By the end of the month had raised it to three, and he received the Iron Cross 1st Class in May, followed by the Knight's Cross with Swords of the Hohenzollern House Order. On 10 June Kirschstein took over the command of Jasta 6 with his score at 24. By the end of June 1918 Kirschstein had raised it to 27, and on 24 June 1918 he received Germany's highest award the Pour le Mérite.

On 11 July Kirschstein took his personal Fokker to the Aircraft Park at Fismes for its annual complete overhaul. With him, flying a Hannover CL. II, was a new pilot, Leutnant Johannes Markgraf, who had joined Jasta 6 one week previously and who was to fly Kirschstein back to the squadron. Just after taking off the Hannover crashed, killing both men instantly. It was revealed later at a board of inquiry that Markgraf had never flown a Hannover before, and as nothing else appeared to contribute to the crash, it was deemed to be pilot error.

Oberleutnant Otto Kissenberth (1893–1919) 20 victories

Otto Kissenberth was born on 26 February 1893 in Landshut, Bavaria, the son of a local businessman. At the outbreak of war he volunteered for the newly formed German Army Air Service as a pilot.

He was posted to FEA 1 at Schliessheim for training; after graduating he was awarded his pilot's certificate and badge and posted to FA 8b as a reconnaissance pilot in October 1914.

Early in March 1915 he was promoted to vizefeldwebel, but on 21 March whilst on a reconnaissance patrol over the Vosges Mountains, his aircraft was attacked by Allied fighters. Although seriously wounded he managed to get the aircraft back to base.

When he recovered he was posted on 8 July to FA 9b, based at Toblach in the Dolomite Alps. His first mission with the squadron was a long-range bombing raid to Cortina on 31 July 1915. The raid was a complete success and Kissenberth's status amongst his fellow pilots rose dramatically.

Kissenberth applied for fighter pilot training and in the early part of 1916 he was accepted and posted to Jastaschule. After graduating he was posted to Kek Einsisheim, which had been created from FA 9b. On 12 October 1916, whilst on a bombing raid to Obendorf (a raid which was later to become famous), Kissenberth shot down three Allied aircraft: two Maurice Farmans of Escadrille F.123 and a Bréguet V of No.3 Naval Wing RNAS. This was even more remark-able, considering that Kissenberth wore glasses,

Otto Kissenberth.

something virtually unheard-of in fighter pilot circles. For his major part in the raid, Kissenberth was awarded the Iron Cross 2nd Class and commissioned to leutnant.

The German air force was expanding and Kek Einsisheim formed part of a new Jasta – Jasta 16. By July, Kissenberth's score had risen to six and on 4 August he was made commander of Jasta 23. He was awarded the Iron Cross 1st Class later the same month and continued to increase his score. His personal Albatros D V now wore his own insignia: a white and yellow Edelweiss on the fuselage. On 2 October 1917 Kissenberth scored his 18th victory. He was awarded the Bavarian Military Merit Order 4th Class with Crown and Swords on 5 December.

On 29 May 1918, with his score standing at twenty, Kissenberth was flying a captured Sopwith Camel, over which he had scored his last victory, when he crashed on landing and was severely injured. So bad were the injuries that he was told that he would not be fit enough to fight again. Whilst in hospital, he was awarded the Knight's Cross of the Royal Hohenzollern House Order and, on 24 July, Prussia's highest honour, the Pour le Mérite.

On 19 August, two days after being discharged from hospital, Kissenberth was promoted to oberleutnant and made commandant of the Schliessheim Flying School, where he stayed until the end of the war. Otto Kissenberth died whilst mountaineering in the Bavarian Alps in 1919.

Oberleutnant Erich Löwenhardt (1897–1918) 54 victories

The son of a doctor, Erich Löwenhardt was born in Breslau on 7 April 1897. He was educated at a military cadet school in Lichterfelde, and on the outset of war was posted to Infantry Regiment Nr.141. His regiment was moved almost immediately to the Eastern Front, where, on 2 October 1914, he was commissioned with the rank of leutnant. At the end of October he was badly wounded and was awarded the Iron Cross 2nd Class. After being discharged from hospital, he returned to his unit at the beginning of January 1915 and was assigned to duties in the Carpathian Mountains, where he saved the lives of five wounded soldiers. For this heroic feat, he was awarded the Iron

Erich Löwenhardt.

Cross 1st Class, and then transferred to the Alpine Corps. In October 1915 he requested a transfer to the German Army Air Service as an observer. Löwenhardt spent nearly a year training and working as an observer, then requested pilot training and was posted to FA(A) 265 early in 1916. Almost another full year was spent as a reconnaissance pilot, then he undertook fighter training early in 1917 and upon graduation was posted to Jasta 10 in March 1917.

A week after arriving at Jasta 10, Löwenhardt scored his first victory when he destroyed a French observation balloon, belonging to 58 Cie, over Recicourt. By September he had raised his tally to five and almost got himself killed in a dogfight with a British fighter, which left him, in the end, with only a slight wound. He managed to force land his aircraft near Roulers (Roeselare). Then on 6 November, with his tally raised to eight, his lower wing broke whilst in combat and again he had to make a forced landing near St. Eloois-Winkel.

The new year started well for Löwenhardt, when on 5 January he destroyed another observation balloon, bringing the number of balloons he had destroyed to five. Another two balloons followed on 12 and 15 March, together with a Bristol F2.b on 18 January. By the end of March he had raised his tally to fifteen. One week short of his 21st birthday, he was appointed commander of Jasta 10, one of the youngest commanders in the German Army Air Service. On 11 May, with his tally at twenty, he was awarded the Knight's Cross with Swords of the Royal Hohenzollern House Order. This was followed on 31 May by the award of Germany's most prestigious honour, the Pour le Mérite (Blue Max).

Löwenhardt continued his unerring destruction of Allied aircraft and by the end of July 1918 his tally had risen to 48. During the months of June and July, he had been acting commander of the Jagdgeschwader, an incredible responsibility for a man who was still only 21.

On 8 August 1918, a patrol led by Löwenhardt encountered a patrol of Sopwith Camels. Löwenhardt himself accounted for three whilst the rest of the Sopwith Camels scattered. This brought his tally to 51, Löwenhardt becoming the second of only three German pilots to reach this figure. Next day, two more victories.

Then tragedy struck. On 10 August, while engaged in a dogfight with some S.E.5as from 56 Squadron RAF. Löwenhardt had just shot down one S.E.5a, when he collided in mid-air with Leutnant Alfred Wenz, a member of Jasta 11, whose patrol had joined up with that of Jasta 10. Both pilots took to their parachutes; Löwenhardt's failed to open and he was killed.

Leutnant Karl Menckhoff (1883–1948) 39 victories

Born on 4 April 1883 at Herford, Westphalia, Karl Menckhoff joined the German Army at the age of twenty. His time in the army was short lived: within six weeks he was taken ill with acute appendicitis and invalided out. He returned to Herford, where he stayed for the next eleven years. When war broke out in 1914 he immediately volunteered and joined Infantry Regiment No.106 at Leipzig. Such was the demand for men at the time, that his training was a matter of collecting his uniform, cleaning his rifle and heading for the front line in Alsace-Lorraine. Menckhoff took part in the Battle of the Marne, and proved to be an aggressive soldier. He rapidly made his mark. Towards the end of his first year as a soldier, he was selected for a mission behind the lines dressed in a French uniform, for which he was awarded the Iron Cross 1st Class. A few months later he was seriously wounded during a battle and returned to Herford to recuperate.

His recovery was extremely slow and, when finally recovered, he was deemed unfit for infantry duties. Menckhoff immediately applied for flying duties and was accepted. During his training it was discovered that his aggression on the ground was matched by his aggression in the air. He took to flying

Leutnant Karl Menckhoff wearing his Pour le Mérite.

naturally, and was a good pilot, but on the ground his maverick and cavalier attitude toward army discipline and etiquette caused problems. He may have been a good fighter, but he was not a good soldier, and he was very nearly discharged from the German Air Service. He only stayed in the service because his instructors maintained that his exceptional flying ability outweighed his indifference toward the drillbook and army etiquette. Germany's desperate need for pilots probably also influenced their decision.

Menckhoff's first posting was to the Eastern Front, where he gained a great deal of flying knowledge but very little combat experience. Early in 1916, he was recalled for duty as an instructor, but his aggressive nature soon made it clear that he would be far better employed with a fighting squadron. He was posted to Flamars for a special short course in air combat, then early in 1917 posted to Jasta 3 in Flanders, with promotion to vizefeldwebel. Within days he scored his first victory, a Nieuport 23 of 29 Squadron, RFC. Two more followed by the end of the month, and by September he had raised his tally to twelve. On 28 September he was shot down and wounded by aircraft from 56 Squadron, RFC. After recovering from his wounds, he returned to Jasta 3, threw himself back into the war and, by the end of 1917, had raised his tally to eighteen.

In February 1918 Menckhoff was awarded a commission and given command of Jasta 72. He was also awarded the Knight's Cross with Swords of the Royal Hohenzollern House Order. This was followed on 23 April 1918, by the award of the Pour le Mérite.

The following four months saw Karl Menckhoff's tally rise to 39. Then he met his equal when he encountered Lieutenant William Avery of 95th Aero Squadron, USAS. After a short fight, Menckhoff was forced down behind Allied lines and taken prisoner. After interrogation, he was transferred to Camp Montoire near Orléans where he joined an ever-growing number of pilots from the German Air Service. His impatience was fuelled by his aggression and, tired of waiting for repatriation, he escaped on 23 August, heading for Switzerland. One week later he crossed the border, and remained in Switzerland until the end of the war. Seeing the state of Germany after the war, Karl Menckhoff decided to set up in business in Switzerland. There he remained until his death in 1948.

Oberleutnant Lothar Freiherr von Richthofen (1894–1922)

40 victories

Younger brother of the famous Red Baron, Manfred von Richthofen, Lothar was born on the Richthofen family estate at Breslau on 27 September 1894. He was in the cavalry when World War One broke out, serving with the 4th Dragoon Regiment, but spurred on by the example of his older brother, he transferred to the German Air Service in the autumn of 1915. He served as an observer with KG4, but was determined to be a fighter pilot, and after training, gained his pilot's certificate in 1916.

On 6 March 1917 he had his first operational posting as a pilot to Jasta 11, commanded by his brother Manfred. He scored his first victory on 28 March, when he shot down F.E.2b No.77.15 of 25 Squadron RFC. Remarkably, his victory total began to increase almost daily: he shot down two aircraft a day on 11, 13 and 14 April. By the end of the month he had downed another nine aircraft, making his tally for April 1917 fifteen confirmed kills. He was awarded the Iron Cross 1st Class to add to his Iron Cross 2nd Class.

The first of May dawned and Lothar continued his relentless pursuit of Germany's opponents. On 10 May he was awarded the Knight's Cross with Swords of the Hohenzollern House Order. By 13 May he claimed several more kills, bringing his score to 24. But 13 May proved unlucky for him, as he was badly wounded in combat and hospitalised. The next day proved better. Lying in hospital, he was awarded Prussia's highest honour for bravery in combat – the Pour le Mérite – a short five months after the same award was given to his brother Manfred.

Lothar returned to flying duty on 24 September 1917, and took command of Jasta 11. Six weeks later, on 9 November, he was back in combat and shot down a B.F2b of 8 Squadron near Zonnebeke. On 23 November he added his 26th kill to his score by bringing down another B.F2b. It was three months into 1918 before he scored again, shooting down a B.F2b of 62 Squadron on 11 March, followed the next day by two more B.F2bs.

Once again the 13th of a month proved unlucky for Lothar when he was severely wounded on 13 March. He had

Oberleutnant Lothar Freiherr von Richthofen (brother of Manfred von Richthofen).

some consolation: while in hospital he was promoted to oberleutnant and also awarded the Bavarian Military Merit Order 4th Class with Swords. Returning to Jasta 11 on 19 July, he shot down his 30th aircraft, a Camel of 73 Squadron, on 25 July. Ten more enemy aircraft went to his credit during August – three of them in one day – on the 8th. His final victories came on 12 August, when he brought down two Camels of 98 and 209 Squadrons: making a total of 40 confirmed victories. Again, he was badly wounded and did not return to combat. Lothar survived the war and returned to flying after the Armistice. He died in a flying accident on 4 July 1922.

Rittmeister Manfred Freiherr von Richthofen (1892–1918) 80 victories

The legendary 'Red Baron' was born at Breslau on 2 May 1892, into the aristocratic Prussian family of Albrecht Freiherr von Richthofen, a major in the 1st Regiment of Cuirassiers, and the Baroness Kunigunde von Richthofen.

At the age of eleven he entered the military school at Wahlstatt, followed by admission to the Royal Prussian Military Academy. Easter 1911 saw him join a famous regiment of lancers, Uhlan Regiment No.1 'Kaiser Alexander III'. In the autumn 1912 he was commissioned as a leutnant in the 1st Uhlans. On the outbreak of World War One 1st Uhlans went to Russian Poland, but within two weeks were transferred to the Meuse in France, where they were allocated to the Crown Prince's German 5th Army.

Trench warfare ended Richthofen's cavalry unit. He was attached to 6th Army Corps and awarded the Iron Cross 2nd Class for his service with the Uhlans, and transferred to the Air Service in May 1915. After four weeks' training as an observer at FEA 7 Cologne and FEA 6 Grossenheim, he was posted to FA 69 on the Eastern Front as an observer in an Albatros B II: his pilot, Leutnant Zeumer, was dying from tuberculosis and had a death wish to die in action. In August 1915 they were posted to the 'Mail Carrier Pigeon Unit' at Ostende, the innocuous title being a cover name for a long-range bomber unit training to bomb England.

On 1 September 1915 Richthofen had his first taste of aerial combat. Flying as an observer in an AEG with Zeumer, he spotted an RFC Farman flying nearby and ordered Zeumer to close to combat. Richthofen opened rifle fire on the Farman but missed with his four shots; the observer in the Farman returned fire and scored several hits on the AEG. A week later Richthofen was flying as an observer in an Albatros piloted by Leutnant Osteroth when he sighted a solitary Farman flying over French lines. Richthofen opened fire with his machine-gun and poured 100 rounds at the Farman, which crashed behind French lines. However, the victory was unconfirmed and Richthofen was not credited with this, his first aircraft downed.

On 1 October 1915 Richthofen was posted to Metz to join another bomber unit. En route by train he met the already legendary Oswald Boelcke, whom he engaged in conversation. Fired by Boelcke's example, Richthofen decided to become a pilot and asked Zeumer to teach him to fly. His first attempt ended in disaster when he crashed on landing. He persisted in training and on Christmas Day 1915 qualified as a pilot.

Initially posted to Russia, it was not until March 1916 that he returned to the Western Front; but he was ordered to fly a two-seater Albatros, not single-seater fighters. He adapted the Albatros by fitting a machine-gun on the upper wing which he could fire from the pilot's seat. On 26 April 1916, he used it against a French Nieuport. The Nieuport, riddled with bullets, crashed at Douaumont, behind French lines: again his victory was unconfirmed.

Richthofen joined Oswald Boelcke's Jasta 2 on 1 September 1916, flying new Albatros D IIIs. On 17 September Boelcke led his eight-strong Jasta against eight B.E.2cs of 12 Squadron RFC and six F.E.2bs of 11 Squadron bombing Marcoing railway station. Richthofen – flying Albatros D III 491/16 – exchanged fire with an F.E.2b. Richthofen banked out of range, then came back under and behind the F.E.2b. Closing to point-blank range, and unseen by the enemy aircraft's crew, he fired a burst into the F.E.2b's engine and cockpit, which hit both the pilot, 2nd Lieutenant L. B. F. Morris, and his observer, Lieutenant T. Rees. The doomed F.E.2b plunged downwards with the dying Morris managing to land the crippled aircraft behind German lines. Richthofen followed it down and landed nearby where he found the pilot mortally wounded and the observer dead.

Richthofen had scored his first officially confirmed victory and to mark the event had a silver cup made by a Berlin silversmith to commemorate the victory: it was to be the first of many such cups.

By the end of October 1916 Richthofen had six confirmed victories to his credit. On 28 October Boelcke was killed in an aerial collision with Erwin Boehme and Jasta 2 was renamed Jasta Boelcke (Royal Prussian), with Oberleutnant Stephen Kirmaier in command.

Richthofen's score continued to increase – by 20 November he had ten confirmed kills. Two days later he shot down the RFC's leading ace – Major Lanoe Hawker, VC, DSO, flying a D.H.2 of 24 Squadron – in a dogfight. When Richthofen learned who his opponent had been he flew over British lines and dropped a message to inform 24 Squadron of Major Hawker's death. Jasta Boelcke pilots arranged a military funeral for Major Hawker, but Richthofen did not attend: it was not the 'done thing' so to do.

Richthofen was promoted to flight commander with Jasta Boelcke and had his Albatros painted bright red. This was to let his aerial opponents know with whom they fought and led to his most famous title, 'Red Baron'.

When he scored his sixteenth victory, on 4 January 1917, the Kaiser awarded him – by special citation – the Pour le Mérite. He was but 24 years old, and now Germany's national hero.

From left: Festner, Schafer, Manfred von Richthofen, Lothar von Richthofen and Wolff.

Rittmeister Manfred Frhr. von Richthofen

Rittmeister Manfred Freiherr von Richthofen, Germany's top ace with 80 victories.

With the decoration came promotion to rittmeister (cavalry captain) and command of Jasta 11. On 11 April 1917 Richthofen had taken his score to 40 kills, and by the end of April it had risen to 52 confirmed. On 30 April he crossed swords with the Canadian ace Billy Bishop (who ended the war with 72 kills) over Drocourt.

Try as he might Richthofen could not best Bishop, who outflew him and riddled his Albatros with bullets. Richthofen broke off the duel and retreated eastward, towards safe territory.

On 26 June the German High Command grouped Jastas into Jagdgeschwaders and Richthofen took command of JG 1, which comprised Jastas 4, 6, 10 and 11. These JGs were highly mobile, and with their aircraft being brightly painted they were soon nicknamed 'Flying Circuses'. Richthofen continued to increase his score, but was wounded in the head in combat with six F.E.2ds of 20 Squadron RFC, causing him to break off combat and make a heavy landing near Wericq. After being hospitalised Richthofen returned to duty, but was plagued by headaches and dizziness. Nevertheless, he managed to fly and score victory after victory, and by 30 November 1917 he had shot down 63 enemy aircraft.

Richthofen did not then score until March 1918, during which month he shot down eleven aircraft. On 2 April he was awarded the last of his 26 decorations, the Order of The Red Eagle with Crowns and Swords, by the Kaiser. On 20 April he reached what was to be his final score: 80 confirmed victories.

On Sunday 21 April 1918 Rittmeister Manfred Freiherr von Richthofen, the Red Baron, took off from his base at Cappy with Jasta 11 on what was to be his final flight, in his red Fokker Dr I triplane. A huge dogfight over Le Hamel ensued, with the Red Baron in the thick of it. Richthofen swung onto the tail of a Camel of 209 Squadron RAF flown by a young pilot, Lieutenant Wilfred May, and gave chase. Captain A. Roy Brown, DSC, flying above, saw May's perilous position and dived to the rescue. Coming up on Richthofen's aircraft from behind, Brown opened fire and a long burst hit the all-red Dr 1. Apparently unharmed, Richthofen continued to chase and machine-gun May's Camel.

As Richthofen flew low over Morlancourt Ridge he came under a hail of fire from Australian gunners on the ground. Machine-gun fire raked the red triplane and the gunners saw the Red Baron's head snap backwards in his cockpit. His aircraft side-slipped, then glided into the ground nose-first. The Red Baron was dead.

The following message was dropped by a British aircraft, addressed to the German Flying Corps:

> To – The German Flying Corps.
> Rittmeister Baron Manfred von Richthofen was killed in aerial combat on April 21st, 1918.
> He was buried with full military honours.
> From British Royal Air Force.

Baron Manfred von Richthofen was buried with full military honours at Bertangles, with his coffin draped with the Imperial German Flag. Pilots of the German Air Service flew over his grave and dropped wreaths unhindered. His remains were returned to Berlin in 1925 and reburied at the Invaliden.

Hauptmann Eduard Ritter von Schleich (1888–1947) 35 victories

'The Black Knight', Eduard Schleich was born in Munich, Bavaria, on 9 August 1888. Little is known of his early life until his military career began in 1908, when he joined 11 Bavarian Infantry Regiment as fahnrich (cadet). Two years later he received his commission and was placed on the reserve list. In 1914 he was called up to join his old regiment, and within months was in the thick of the action. On 25 August 1914 he was severely wounded, and it was while he was convalescing in Munich that he decided upon a career change, and applied to be transferred to the German Air Service. He was accepted, and in May 1915 was posted to FEA 1 at Schleissheim for training. He received his pilot's badge on 11 September, but the fact that it was only the Bavarian pilot's badge was to cause problems later.

Schleich's first posting was to FA 2b in October 1915. After a number of reconnaissance flights, he was wounded during an encounter with Allied fighters in February 1916. After recuperating, in September 1916, he was suddenly and unexpectedly put in command of Fliegerschule I, where he became a flying instructor. Early in February 1917 he was transferred to a Bavarian escort unit, Schutzstaffel 28, as its commanding officer, but was dismayed to find that due to the shortage of aircraft, he was unable to lead his unit, but had to 'fly' a desk. Within weeks he had written furious letters to KOFL (Fifth Army) headquarters requesting that he be transferred to a fighter unit. Although he had been an instructor, he was posted to fighter training school at Famars, near Valenciennes. There, after two weeks, his instructor, Leutnant Boehme, announced that there was nothing further to teach Schleich, and suggested that Schleich be posted to a fighter unit.

Schleich was posted to Jasta 21 on 21 May 1917 with the rank of oberleutnant, and again given command, albeit only temporary, of the squadron – without having scored a single victory. He achieved his first kill on 25 May, when on patrol over Moronvillers, shooting down a SPAD VII. For a first victory this was a notable one: his opponent was none other than the French Sous Lieutenant René Pierre Marie Dorme, who at the time had 43 victories to his credit. Dorme's gold watch was later dropped over a French

Ritter von Schleich wearing his Pour le Mérite.

airfield, together with a note from Jasta 21 stating that Dorme had died bravely for France.

After his second victory – a Sopwith 1½ Strutter – on 17 June, he was given permanent command of the squadron. It was then that problems started. The feudal system still existed in Germany, and the fact that Jasta 21, originally a Prussian unit, had been re-designated a Saxon unit and was now being commanded by a Bavarian, was a source of embarrassment to the senior members of the old military guard, who still held positions of high authority in the German military machine. Schleich's command was put under the microscope, and any infringement, no matter how minor, was jumped upon by the powers that be.

In the following four months Schleich raised his victory tally to 25, but his command came under attack for the lack of results from his other pilots. After one incident concerning three of his flyers, which earned him a severe reprimand, he assembled all his pilots and warned them that, unless they showed more attacking spirit, they would be dismissed from the squadron in disgrace. Within days, the pilots started scoring victories and the pressure from above eased. But success was not without its losses. In July, the squadron had moved to Chassogne-Ferme, near Verdun, and during one skirmish with the enemy, Schleich's friend Leutnant Limpert was killed. Out of respect for Limpert, Schleich had his Albatros D Va painted jet black. The black fighter, with its white band round the fuselage, became well known to Allied fighter pilots and soon earned him the nickname 'The Black Knight'.

Although a commanding officer, Schleich had his own foolish moments. One incident happened after a SPAD had been forced down intact. Schleich had the aircraft painted in German markings and took off in it for the front, where he actually joined up with a French squadron on patrol. The French pilots did not realise what was happening for several minutes, but before they could react, Schleich had headed back for his own lines – only to be fired on by German anti-aircraft gunners. Fortunately, their aim was bad, and he returned safely to his own airfield. KOFL was not amused, and severely reprimanded him for the escapade.

The rest of the squadron was now performing well. Its members included Leutnant Emil Thuy and Leutnant Karl Thom, who were both later awarded the Pour le Mérite. Just after achieving his 25th victory, Schleich fell ill with dysentery and was rushed to hospital in a serious condition. Some months later, he was told that the Prussian bureaucracy had taken advantage of his enforced absence, and had removed him from command. They decreed that no Bavarian should serve in a Prussian unit, let alone command one. On 23 October 1917, with his tally at 35, Schleich was given command of Jasta 32 – an all-Bavarian squadron. He was awarded the Pour le Mérite on 4 December 1917, but did not receive the customary Royal Hohenzollern House Order that usually went with it.

The following month he was given command of Jastaschule I and in March 1918 he took command of Jagdgruppe Nr.8 which consisted of Bavarian Jastas 23, 34 and 35. At the end of the year he learned that he had been awarded the Knight's Cross of the Military Order of Maximilian-Joseph, the Saxon Knights Cross, the Albrecht Order 2nd Class and the Bavarian Military Merit Order 4th Class with Crown and Swords. With these awards came promotion to hauptmann and a noble title: Eduard, Ritter von Schleich. He remained in control of Jagdgruppe Nr.8 until the end of the war, and became a member of the Armistice Committee.

In the 1920s Schleich joined Lufthansa, staying with that organisation until the rise of Nazism, when, in 1933, he joined the Luftwaffe. He even visited Britain in the black uniform of the Waffen SS. During World War Two he rose to the rank of generaloberst, commanding combat units. He later took up a post in occupied Denmark, before becoming general der flieger in Norway. He was taken prisoner at the end of the war and, following a short illness, died in a prisoner-of-war camp for high-ranking officers.

Oberleutnant Ernst Udet (1896–1941) 62 victories

One of the most charismatic German pilots of World War One, Ernst Udet was born in Frankfurt-am-Main on 26 April 1896, the son of a wealthy landowner. Udet had a natural flair for anything mechanical and had his own motor cycle, which he used as a messenger for the German Automobile Club after the German occupation of Liège on 7 August 1914. He applied to join the Army at the age of seventeen, but was rejected several times before he was finally able to persuade the authorities to accept him on 21 August 1914. He was assigned to the 26 Württemburg Reserve Division as a motor cycle messenger.

For the next few months, Udet rode his motor cycle backwards and forwards behind the lines delivering messages. Then one night, when the sound of guns appeared to be encircling him, he swerved to miss a shell-hole in the road and crashed. After ten days in hospital, he was sent to Belgium to catch up with his division, but could not find them. In Liège he was given another messenger job, and it was there that he met Leutnant von Waxheim, a pilot, who was to have a huge influence on Udet's life.

Orders came for Udet to be sent home where he immediately volunteered for the Pilot's Reserve Detachment in Schleissheim. His meeting with von Waxheim had convinced him that this was where his future lay. Whilst waiting for a response to his request, he trained as a pilot at his own expense, sending further applications to the air service. After a few weeks, orders came through for him to go to Darmstadt for pilot training. On completion of this, he was posted to FA(A) 206 as a gefreiter, becoming observer for Leutnant Bruno Justinus. After a three-week spell of patrols in which they never saw an Allied aircraft, they spotted a French monoplane attacking a railway station. As they approached, they realised that the Frenchman was in trouble and was gliding toward the ground. Udet, tucking in behind, noticed that the aircraft had a gun mounted behind the propeller. The French aircraft, encouraged by Udet, made a forced landing and before the pilot could set fire to his aircraft, it was captured by German soldiers. The pilot, it was discovered later, was Roland Garros and the capture of his aircraft, together with the gun and its interruptor gear intact, was to alter the course of air-to-air fighting dramatically. Udet received the Iron Cross 2nd Class for the incident.

On 18 March 1916, Udet was posted to FA 68, which later became Kek Habsheim, and scored his first victory when he shot down a Farman F.40 while defending Mulhausen during a raid by French aircraft. On 28 September he was posted to Jasta 15, where, by the end of the year he had raised his tally to two. In January 1917 he received the Iron Cross 1st Class and his commission to leutnant.

Udet recorded his sixth victory in May 1917, and requested a transfer to Jasta 37, which took place on 19 June. He took command of the Jasta five months later. Two weeks after this, by which time he had raised his tally to fifteen confirmed victories, Udet was awarded the Knight's Cross with Swords of the Royal Hohenzollern Order. On 23 March 1918, he was posted to Jasta 11 as commanding officer, remaining there only until 8 April. Three days before his 22nd birthday a telegram arrived, reading:
'His Majesty the Emperor has been gracious enough to bestow upon you the Pour le Mérite in recognition of the twenty planes shot down by you.'

The very next day Udet was given command of Jasta 4. His aircraft was distinctive: a Fokker D VII with a red fuselage and red and white stripes on the upper surfaces of the top wing. Written on the upper tail surface, for any attacker from the rear to read, was the inscription 'Du noch nicht!' ('Not you yet'). His aircraft also carried the initials of his fiancée: 'LO'.

With his tally of victories standing at 40, he was shot down during a dogfight with Bréguet aircraft. As his aeroplane spun earthwards, Udet scrambled out of the cockpit only to find that his parachute harness had caught on the control column. He eventually struggled free, his parachute opening some 300 feet from the ground. He landed heavily in a shell hole and was rescued by German infantry.

In the following two months he raised his tally to 60 confirmed victories, and was awarded the Lübeck Hanseatic Cross and the Hamburg Hanseatic Cross. On 26 September 1918, with his tally standing at 62, he was badly wounded in the thigh, putting an end to his combat flying days.

After the war Udet became a test pilot and a movie stunt pilot, flying all over the world. At the onset of World War Two, he was persuaded to join the Luftwaffe and attained the rank of generaloberst. He was later given the post of G.O.C. Aircraft Production, and immediately set about developing a new fighter/bomber. But in his rapid rise up the ladder of promotion, he had made enemies, none so deadly as Generaloberst Erhard Milch. Milch started to undermine Udet's authority and cause him many problems.

On 17 September 1941 Ernst Udet died. The German propaganda machine stated that he had died whilst testing a new aeroplane, and Hitler announced that Udet would be given a state funeral. In reality, Udet had committed suicide by shooting himself with a Colt revolver that he had brought back from America during his stunt pilot days. The political infighting within the Luftwaffe and the fact that his position was being completely undermined caused him to take his own life.

His coffin was placed on the catafalque in the Air Ministry's Hall of Honour in Berlin, and then taken by gun carriage to the Invaliden Cemetery. He was buried with full military honours.

Leutnant Werner Voss (1897–1917) 48 victories

The eldest son of an industrial dyer, Werner Voss was born in Krefeld on 13 April 1897. He was expected to follow in his father's footsteps and enter the dyeing trade, which had been the tradition of the Voss family for generations. But, Werner Voss had other ideas. He was to enter another trade, concerned with dying, not dyeing; one that would see him meet his demise at the early age of twenty.

Leutnant Werner Voss.

Voss was a member of the Krefeld Militia, and liked nothing better than to wear the uniform of the Krefeld Hussars two evenings a week and for two months during the summer. When war broke out, he was assigned to the 11th Westphalian Hussar Regiment and sent to the French border. Within days of arriving there, France declared war on Germany, and Voss found himself in the last battle in which cavalry were to play a vital role. Elsewhere in Germany cavalry units were being disbanded: it was decided they were of no more use, and the Hussars were turned into infantrymen. Voss had no liking for this, and instead applied for pilot training in the German Imperial Air Service. In August 1915 he was accepted and, by this time considered a veteran, he was promoted to unteroffizier and was awarded the Iron Cross 2nd Class. He was just eighteen years old.

Voss was sent to pilot school, where it was soon discovered that he was a natural pilot. His first posting after completing his training was to FEA 7 as an instructor. One month later, he was promoted to vizefeldwebel and posted to Kampfgeschwader 4, initially as an observer, but, on being awarded his pilot's badge, taking over the controls of an Aviatak two-seater fighter/bomber. In September he was promoted to a commissioned rank and posted to Jasta 2 in November, where he was to fly with the legendary Baron Manfred von Richthofen. One month later, after scoring two victories (Nieuport scout and a D.H.2), he was awarded the Iron Cross 1st Class. By the end of February 1917 his tally of victims had risen to twelve, and in March he was awarded the Knight's Cross with Swords of the Royal Hohenzollern House Order.

Voss was becoming a household word in Germany, and on 8 April 1917, with his tally now at 24, he was awarded the Pour le Mérite, Prussia's highest award.

May 1917 saw Werner Voss posted to Jasta 5, where, by the end of June, he had taken his tally to 34. He was promoted to commander of Jasta 29 for the month of July and then to Jasta 14 as acting commander. He was still only twenty years old. At the end of July he was appointed staffelführer of Jasta 10, with his tally now standing at 34. He now flew a Fokker DR I marked with the distinctive chrome yellow cowling of Jasta 10 and with a face painted on the aircraft cowling.

During August and September 1917, Voss increased his tally to 48, but then on 23 September, he became engaged in what was to later become known as one of the most famous dog-fights of the war.

On patrol he came on a flight of British S.E.5s of 56 Squadron, but unfortunately for him, the flight consisted of a number of top 'aces', including McCudden, Rhys-Davids, Barlow, Muspratt, Cronyn, Childlaw-Roberts and Bowman. For over ten minutes Voss almost single-handedly fought the British flight, inflicting damage, some serious, on all of the opposing aircraft. It was Lieutenant Arthur Rhys-Davids who finally managed to get his sights on the tailplane of the elusive Voss, and a burst from his machine-guns sent Voss's Fokker triplane 103/17 plunging earthwards.

Voss was buried by British soldiers on the spot where he crashed and died. Major James McCudden said of Voss afterwards: 'His flying was wonderful, his courage magnificent and in my opinion he is the bravest German airman whom it has been my privilege to see fight.' Leutnant Werner Voss was just twenty years old.

GERMAN ACES 1914–18

80 Rittmeister Manfred von Richthofen	Menckhoff	*30 kills*	Ritter von Tutschek
62 Oberleutnant Ernst Udet★★	39 Leutnant Reinrich Gontermann	Leutnant Karl Allmenroder	Leutnant Kurt Wusthoff
54 Oberleutnant Lowenhardt	36 Leutnant Max Muller	Leutnant Karl Degelow	*26 kills*
48 Leutnant Werner Voss	35 Leutnant Julius Buckler	Leutnant Heinrich Kroll	Oberleutnant Harald Auffahrt
45 Leutnant Fritz Rumey	35 Leutnant Gustav Dorr	Leutnant Josef Mai	Oberleutnant Oscar Frhr von Boenigk
44 Hauptmann Rudolph Berthold	35 Hauptmann Eduard Ritter von Schleich	Leutnant Ulrich Neckel	Oberleutnant Eduard Dostler
43 Leutnant Paul Baumer	34 Leutnant Josef Veltjens	Leutnant Karl Schaefer	Leutnant Arthur Laumann
41 Leutnant Josef Jacobs	33 Leutnant Otto Koennecke	*29 kills*	*25 kills*
41 Hauptmann Bruno Loerzer	33 Kurt Wolff	Hermann Frommerz	Leutnant O. Frhr Beaulieu-Marconnay
40 Hauptmann Oswald Boelcke	33 Leutnant Heinrich Bongartz	*28 kills*	Leutnant Max Nather
40 Leutnant Franc Buchner	32 Leutnant Theo Osterkamp★★	Leutnant Walter von Bülow	Leutnant Fritz Putter
40 Oberleutnant Lothar Frhr von Richthofen	32 Leutnant Emil Thuy	Leutnant Walter Blume	*24 kills*
39 Leutnant Karl	31 Leutnant Paul Billik	Oberleutnant Fritz Ritter von Roth	Leutnant Erwin Böhme
	31 Rittmeister Karl Bolle	*27 kills*	*23 kills*
	31 Oberleutnant Gothard Sachsenberg	Oberleutnant Fritz Bernert	Leutnant Hermann Becker
		Vizefeldwebel Otto Fruhner	Leutnant Georg Meyer
		Leutnant Hans Kirschstein	*22 kills*
		Leutnant Karl Thom	Oberleutnant Hermann Göring★★
		Hauptmann Adolf	

Boelcke, Immelmann and other pilots.

Hauptmann Boelcke und Oberleutnant Immelmann
Im Kreise ihrer Kameraden

Leutnant Hans Klein	*21 kills*	*20 kills*	Leutnant Walter
Leutnant Pippart	Leutenant Hans Adam	Vizefeldwebel Frederich	Goetsch
Leutnant Werner Preuss	Oberleutnant Friedrich	Altemeir	Leutnant Friedrich
Vizefeldwebel Karl	Christiansen	Oherleutnant Hans	Noltenius
Schlegel	Leutnant Fritz	Bethge	Hauptmann Wilhelm
Leutnant Rudolph	Friedrichs	Leutnant Rudolph von	Reinhard
Windsch	Leutnant Fritz Hohn	Eschwege	

Far left: Leutnant Hans Adam.
Left: Leutnant Hartmuth Baldanus.

157

Right: Leutnant Joachim von Bertrab. Far right: Hauptmann Brandenburg, a KG 4 bomber pilot.

19 kills
Vizefeldwebel Gerhard Fiesler
Leutnant Wilhelm Frankl
Leutnant Otto Kissenberth
Oberleutnant Otto Schmidt

18 kills
Leutnant Hartmuth Baldamus
Leutnant Franz Hemer
Vizefeldwebel Oskar Hennrich
Leutnant Kurt Wintgens

17 kills
Leutnant Walter Boning
Leutnant Ernest Hess
Leutnant Franz Ray
Leutnant Hans Rolfes
Vizefeldwebel Josef Schwendmann

16 kills
Leutnant Hans Boehning
Leutnant Hans von Freden
Leutnant Ludwig Hanstein
Leutnant Rudolf Klimke

Leutnant Karl Odebrett
Leutnant Hans Weiss

15 kills
Leutnant Albert Dossenbach
Vizefeldwebel Christian Donhauser
Vizefeldwebel Albert Haussmann
Leutnant Alois Heldmann
Oberleutnant Max Immelmann
Leutnant Johannes Klein
Leutnant Otto Loffler
Leutnant Victor von Pressentin
Leutnant Theodor Quant
Leutnant Julius Schmidt
Leutnant Kurt Schneider

14 kills
Leutnant Ernst Bormann
Vizefeldwebel Rudolf Franke
Offizierstellvertreter Edmund Nathanel
Leutnant Franz

Piechurek
Leutnant Karl Plauth
Vizefeldwebel Wilhelm Seitz
Vizefeldwebel Emil Schape
Leutnant Georg Schlenker
Leutnant Paul Straele
Leutnant Rudolf Wendelmuth

13 kills
Vizefeldwebel Karl Bohnenkamp
Hans Joachim Buddecke
Leutnant Siegfried Buttner
Leutnant Heinrich Geigl
Vizefeldwebel Robert Heibert
Vizefeldwebel Reinhold Jorke
Leutnant Johann Janzen
Vizefeldwebel Christel Mesch
Vizefeldwebel Otto Rosenfeld
Oberleutnant Kurt Schoenfelder
Oberleutnant Erich Ruduger von Wedel

12 kills
Vizefeldwebel Erich Buder
Leutnant Diether Collin
Oberleutnant Theodor Cammann
Vizefeldwebel Gottfried Ehmann
Offizierstellvertreter Otto Esswein
Vizefeldwebel Sebastian Festner
Leutnant Walter Hohndorf
Vizefeldwebel Max Kuhn
Vizefeldwebel Friedrich Manschott
Leutnant Hans Mueller
Oherleutnant Franz Schleiff
Leutnant Richard Wenzl

11 kills
Leutnant Heinrich Arntzen
Leutnant Joachim von Busse
Leutnant Frhr. Raven von Barnekow
Oberleutnant Kurt von Doering
Leutnant Xaver Dannhuber

Far left: Leutnant Otto Brauneck.
Left: Vizefeldwebel Sebastian Festner.

Far left: Hauptmann Otto Hartmann.
Left: Leutnant Ernest Hess.

*Right: Oberleutnant
Stefan Kirmaier.
Far right: Oberleutnant
Hans Klein.*

*Right: Leutnant
Heinrich Kroll.
Far right: Leutnant
Gustave Leffers.*

Leutnant Heinz
Dreckmann
Vizefeldwebel Willi
Gabriel
Oberleutnant Stephan
Kirmaier
Leutnant Hans von
Keudell
Leutnant Alfred
Lindenberger
Leutnant Fritz Loerzer
Leutnant Hermann
Pfeiffer
Leutnant Hugo
Schaefer
Leutnant Renatus
Theiller
10 kills
Offizierstellvertreter
Paul Aue
Vizefeldwebel Dietrich
Averes
Oberleutnant Hans Berr
Leutnant Franz Brandt
Vizefeldwebel Fritz
Classen
Leutnant Martin
Dehmisch
Leutnant Wilhelm
Frickart
Leutnant Justus
Grassman

Leutnant Max Mulzer
Leutnant Rudolf
Mattaei
Vizefeldwebel Alfons
Nagler
Leutnant Wilhelm
Neuenhofen
Oberleutnant Hans
Schuez
Leutnant Werner
Steinhauser
Leutnant Paul Turck
Leutnant Erich Thomas
Offizierstellvertreter
Bernhard Ultsch
Leutnant Paul Wenzel
Leutnant Joachim Wolff
9 kills
Oberleutnant Ernst von
Althaus
Leutnant Arno Benzler
Leutnant Otto Brauneck
Leutnant Albert Dietlen
Leutnant Otto Fitzner
Leutnant Karl Gallwitz
Vizefeldwebel Friedrich
Huffzky
Leutnant Herbert
Knappe
Leutnant Egon Koepsch
Vizefeldwebel Fritz
Kosmahl

Leutnant Walter Kypke
Leutnant Paul Lotz
Leutnant Gustav
Leffers
Leutnant Herbert Mahn
Leutnant Hans von der
Marwitz
Leutnant Eberhardt
Mohicke
Leutnant Hans Muller
Unteroffizier Hans
Nulle
Vizefeldwebel Karl Pech
Vizefeldwebel Karl
Schattauer
Leutnant Adolf Schulte
8 kills
Leutnant Leopold
Anslinger
Leutnant Alois
Brandenstein
Leutnant Konrad
Brendle
Leutnant Gunther
Dobberke
Vizefeldwebel Friedrich
Ehmann
Oberleutnant Walter
Evers
Leutnant Max Gossner
Leutnant Wolfgang
Guttler

Vizefeldwebel Willi
Hippert
Leutnant Hans Hoyer
Unteroffizier Paul
Huttenrauch
Vizefeldwebel Willi
Kampe
Leutnant Fritz
Kieckhaefer
Leutnant Artur Korff
Leutnant Otto Parschau
Vizefeldwebel Friedrich
Puschke
Leutnant Wolfram Frhr.
von Richthofen
Leutnant Karl
Ritscherle
Leutnant Richard
Runge
Oberleutnant Hans
Schilling
Leutnant Karl von
Schonebeck
Leutnant Viktor
Schobinger
Leutnant Wilhelm
Schwartz
Leutnant Fritz Thiede
Leutnant Georg Weiner
7 kills
Leutnant Gerhard
Anders

*Far left: Oberleutnant
Bruno Loerzer.
Left: Leutnant Max
Ritter Muller.*

*Above: Leutnants
Parschau and Keudell.
Above right:
Offizierstellvertreter
Edmund Nathanael.
Right: Leutnant Hans
Martin Pippart.
Far right: Prince
Friedrich Sigismund
von Preussen.*

Leutnant Gerhard
  Bassenge
Leutnant Ludwig
  Beckmann
Leutnant Karl Bohng
Leutnant Helmut
  Brunig
Leutnant Otto Creutz-
  mann
Leutnant Helmut
  Diltheg
Oberleutnant Hans
  Gandert
Leutnant Herman
  Habich
Leutnant Hans von
  Haebler
Hauptmann Otto
  Hartmann
Leutnant Kurt Jacob
Leutnant Martin Johns
Vizefeldwebel Max
  Kahlow
Leutnant Franz
  Kirchfeld
Leutnant Emil Koch
Offizierstellvertreter
  Wilhelm Kuhne
Oberleutnant Hans
  Kummetz
Leutnant Helmut Lange
Leutnant Hermann
  Leptien
Vizefeldwebel Albert
  Lux
Leutnant Heinrich
  Maushake
Leutnant Albert Mendel
Leutnant Kurt
  Monnington
Leutnant Alfred Neider-
  hoff
Hauptmann Hennig von
  Osteroth
Leutnant Richard
  Plange
Vizefeldwebel Johann
  Putz
Leutnant Fritz Riemer
Leutnant Willi
  Rosenstein
Vizefeldwebel Gustav
  Schneidewind
Vizefeldwebel Edgar
  Scholz
Vizefeldwebel Georg
  Strasser
Hauptmann Franz Walz
Leutnant Hans Werner
Unteroffizier Wilhelm
  Zorn
6 kills
Vizefeldwebel Karl
  Arnold
Unteroffizier Johann

Baur
Leutnant M. W.
  Bretschneider
  Bodener
Vizefeldwebel Paul
  Bona
Vizefeldwebel Adolf
  Borchers
Leutnant Harry von
  Bulow
Oberleutnant Hermann
  Dahlmann
Leutnant Karl
  Deilmann
Leutnant Julius Fichter
Leutnant Gustav
  Fradich
Unteroffizier Friedrich
  Gille
Leutnant Hermann
  Gilly
Leutnant Gisbert
  Wilhelm Groos
Oberleutnant Fritz
  Grosch
Oberleutnant Adolf
  Gutknecht
Unteroffizier Heinrich
  Haase
Oberleutnant Erich
  Hahn
Leutnant Georg Hengl
Leutnant Heinrich
  Henkel
Leutnant Albert Hets
Leutnant Robert
  Hildebrandt
Vizefeldwebel Josef
  Hohlg
Leutnant Otto Hohne
Unteroffizier Michael
  Hutterer
Leutnant Johnnes
  Jensen
Leutnant Erich Just
Leutnant Hans
  Imelmann
Vizefeldwebel Gustav
  Kludat
Leutnant Erich Koenig
Vizefeldwebel Hans
  Korner
Vizefeldwebel Fritz
  Krebs
Leutnant Hermann
  Kunz
Leutnant Alfred Lenz
Leutnant Ludwig Luer
Leutnant Friedrich
  Mallinckrodt
Oberleutnant Hans
  Mettlich
Leutnant Alfred Mohr
Leutnant Hans
  Oberlander

Leutnant Fritz Putter.

*Leutnant Julius
Schmidt.*

Leutnant Arthur Rahn
Leutnant Rudolf Rienau
Feldwebel Karl
  Schmuckle
Leutnant Willi Schultz
Leutnant Gunther
  Schuster
Leutnant Heinrich
  Seywald
Unteroffizier Erich
  Sonneck
Leutnant Otto
  Splitgerber
Leutnant Rudolf Stark
Vizefeldwebel Georg
  Staudacher
Unteroffizier Karl
  Treiber
Offizierstellvertreter
  Reinhard Treptow
Vizefeldwebel Kurt
  Ungewitter
Oberleutnant Hans
  Waldhausen
5 kills
Leutnant Hans Auer
Leutnant Joachin von
  Bertrab
Unteroffizier Rudolf
  Besel
Lieutenant von Breiten
  Landenberg
Oberleutnant H. H. von
  Boddien

Unteroffizier Gustav
  Borm
Leutnant Herbert Bog
Vizefeldwebel Hans
  Bowski
Hauptmann F. K.
  Burchardt
Leutnant August
  Burkard
Leutnant Karl Christ
Oberleutnant Theodor
  Croneiss
Leutnant August
  Delling
Leutnant Willi
  Fahlbusch
Vizefeldwebel Gaim
Leutnant Sylvester
  Garsztka
Leutnant Johannes
  Gildmeister
Leutnant Siegfried
  Gussmann
Leutnant Kurt Haber
Leutnant August Hanko
Leutnant Kurt Hetze
Vizefeldwebel Fritz
  Jakobsen
Vizefeldwebel Hermann
  Juhnke
Leutnant Werner Junck
Vizefeldwebel Otto
  Klaiber
Leutnant Wilhelm

Kohlbach
Offizierstellvertreter
  Johann Kopka
Leutnant Kurt Kuppers
Leutnant Wilhelm
  Leusch
Oberleutnant Heinrich
  Lorenz
Unteroffizier Hans
  Marwede
Unteroffizier Erich
  Meyer
Leutnant Werner
  Niehammer
Leutnant Rudolph Otto
Leutnant Hans von der
  Osten
Offizierstellvertreter
  Leopold Reimann
Leutnant Hans
  Rosencratz
Vizefeldwebel Paul
  Rothe
Vizefeldwebel Richard
  Rube
Leutnant Theodor
  Rumpel
Leutnant Alfons
  Scheicher
Grefreiter Johann
  Schlimpen
Leutnant Roman
  Schneider
Leutnant Herbert

Schroder
Vizefeldwebel Friedrich
  Schumacher
Vizefeldwebel Erich
  Schutz
Leutnant Konrad
  Schwartz
Leutnant Eugen
  Simpelkamp
Leutnant Wilhelm
  Sommer
Vizefeldwebel Wilhelm
  Stohr
Vizefeldwebel Karl
  Strunkelberg
Oberleutnant Kurt
  Student
Leutnant Alwin Thurm
Vizefeldwebel Oswald
  Tranker
Leutnant Gerold
  Tschentschel
Leutnant Alfred Ulmer
Leutnant Hermann
  Vallendor
Leutnant Hans Viebeg
Vizefeldwebel Ernst
  Wiehle
Leutnant Ernst
  Wiessner
Leutnant Kurt
  Wisseman
Hauptmann Martin
  Zander

Right: Oberleutnant
Adolf Ritter von
Tutschek.
Far right: Oberleutnant
Kurt Wolff.

AUSTRIA-HUNGARY

8

A s early as 1912 Austrians foresaw the flying machine as a weapon of war: an Army engineer, Emil Uzelac, was requested to form an air arm for the Austro-Hungarian armed forces. Oberst Uzelac was a non-flying officer but quickly gained pilot skills within a short four months.

In 1913 a Fliegerkompaigne (flying company) was established with six aircraft, but by the outbreak of World War One the strength of the air arm was 36 aircraft – Etrich Taubes of A1 and A11 types and Lohner *Pfeil* (arrow) biplanes – plus an airship and about ten balloons.

As they were fighting Russia on the German side, the Austro-Hungarians asked the Germans for aircraft. A few obsolete Rumpler and Aviatik aircraft were supplied, but it became clear to the Austro-Hungarians that they would have to build their own aircraft, some, like the Albatros Phonix, under licence.

No real air warfare occurred during the initial stages of war – the Russians and their Serbian allies had no substantial air warfare capability. On 24 May 1915 Italy joined the Allies and declared war on Austria-Hungary. At first the Italians – like the Russians – posed no real threat. The Austro-Hungarians – flying a variety of Fokker E Is, Lohner B-types, Albatros B Is (Phonix-built), Lloyd C IIs and Aviatik B-types, flew a somewhat 'phoney' war with desultory bombing, reconnaissance and observation sorties.

Fokker V12 with Leutnant Stefan Laslo third from right and Linke Crawford (wearing scarf) in centre.

Early in 1916 the situation began to take on a new dimension – the Italians were now equipped with French Nieuport 10s and 11s as well as Caproni bombers, and began to be more dashing and aggressive. The three-engined Capronis began to cause severe damage and disruption. And the Italian ace Baracca came to the fore in a Nieuport 11 when he began to shoot down Austro-Hungarian aircraft on 7 April.

As the air war hotted up, the Germans sold 50 Fokker B IIs to the Austro-Hungarians and two home companies – Phonix Aeroplane Works and Ufag (Hungarian Aeroplane Factory) – built the outstanding Brandenburg D.T (KD) Star Strutter under licence. Oeffag (Austrian Aeroplane Factory) built the German D.II. The opposing Italians flew the French Hanriot HD. I, the French Nieuport 17 and the formidable SPAD S.7. Italian SAML, SIA 7B and Pomilio types were brought into action to replace obsolete pusher-type aircraft.

German-crewed aircraft combined with the Austro-Hungarian air arm in October 1917 and their ground troops broke through the Italian front at Caporetto. The German Jasta 39 decimated the Caproni bombers, and the Italians lost their front-line airfields. French and British squadrons came to the Italians' aid just in time, stemmed the onslaught and regained air superiority. All the lost ground was retaken. German forces were withdrawn in March 1918, leaving the Austro-Hungarians to fight on their own with but thirteen squadrons to carry on the air battle.

The Italians began to increase the pressure on their enemy with long-range probing raids on Vienna and aggressive fighter patrols. The Italians also used their Macchi fighter flying boats (some copied from the Lohner flying boat) to great effect. On 4 November 1918 an Armistice was declared and the war was over for Austria-Hungary.

Ofz. Julius Arigi, 32 victories, most decorated NCO pilot.

Offizierstellvertreter Julius Arigi (1895–?) 32 victories

Offizierstellvertreter Arigi was born on 3 October 1895 of Czech descent at Tetschen. He graduated as an NCO pilot on 23 November 1914. At this stage of the war rank and class prevailed: officers were in charge as observers and NCOs flew the aircraft.

Arigi saw action in that his aircraft came under ground fire, but he did not participate in aerial combat until 4 September 1916, when he and his observer shot down a Farman of the Italian 34 Squadron over Fier, Albania.

With spring 1917 came a transfer to single-seaters and duty with Flik 60, commanded by Oberleutnant Frank Linke Crawford. Arigi now began to shoot down enemy aircraft at a steady rate. He was decorated with four gold, eight silver, and three bronze medals, becoming the most decorated NCO in the Air Arm. Inexplicably, he remained an NCO throughout the war.

Post-war Arigi flew as a test pilot, then after Hitler annexed Austria in 1938 he joined the Luftwaffe as an instructor. He survived World War Two.

Leutnant Kommander (Navy) Gottfried von Banfield (1890–?)

9 victories

Gottfried von Banfield was born at Pola on 6 February 1890, into a naval family. After education at St. Polten Military Academy and Fiume Naval Academy, he joined the embryo Imperial and Royal Navy of Austria-Hungary in 1912 and learned to fly fighter flying boats.

When war broke out Banfield was stationed at Pola Naval Base on the Istrian coast. Pola's aircraft strength at the time stood at 22 aircraft. On 12 August 1914 the Imperial and Royal Navy went into action for the first time at Mount Lovcen in Montenegro. With Italy a short 25 miles across the Adriatic it was easy for the Austrians to raid military targets by night and day. Banfield's first four victories were against balloons on the Isonzo Front.

The Italian and French air arms were raiding Trieste and Banfield went up to intercept the intruders, shooting down a Caproni bomber and three FBA flying boats by September 1916. Banfield, flying the prototype Hansa Brandenburg CC (Camilo Castiglioni) fighter flying boat No.A13, then shot down an Italian Farman in October 1916. He was also put in command of the naval air station at Trieste.

In January 1917 Banfield clashed with the Italian ace Baracca over the Isonzo river. Banfield was in a Brandenburg KDW fighter flying boat, No.A24, and Baracca in a Nieuport 11 fighter. This unusual duel, fought in appalling weather, did not bring victory to either pilot and the fight was broken off.

Banfield became von Banfield when, in March 1918, he was admitted to the Maria Theresa Order as a military knight.

Austrian Navy ace Leutnant Kommander Gottfried von Banfield.

Hauptmann Godwin Brumowski (1889–1937) 40 victories

Of Polish descent, Brumowski was born on 26 July 1889 at Wadowice, Galicia. He became a career soldier with Field Artillery Regiment No.6 during 1914–15 on the Eastern Front. During 1915 he transferred to the Air Service as an observer, learning to fly by instruction from his sergeant pilots.

Austria's top-scoring ace, 40 victories, Oberleutnant Godwin Brumowski.

He became commanding officer of Flik (*Fliegerkompagnie*) 12 after he had self-qualified as a pilot. A year later, in 1917, he was posted as commanding officer to Flik 41 which was equipped with Brandenburg D.Is. He had a white skull on a black background painted on Flik 41 aircraft as an identifying badge. In summer 1917 Flik 41 received the outstanding Oeffag Albatros D III and Brumowski had the new scouts painted red – again with a white skull on the fuselages.

Brumowski's victory score now stood at six enemy aircraft and on 17 July 1917 he made it seven when he shot down a Voisin. On 11 August 1917 he shot down a Caudron and a Nieuport, and by 31 August his score had totalled nineteen.

Another Flik 41 ace – Frank Linke Crawford – was flying as Brumowski's wingman and the combination began to play havoc with the Italians. An Italian balloon was downed on 4 October followed by two seaplanes on 6 October then two Nieuports on 23 October. By the end of 1917 Brumowski had taken his score to 27.

During 1918 Brumowski increased his score to 40, becoming the top Austro-Hungarian ace. He survived the war but died in an air crash in Holland in 1937.

Oberleutnant Benno Fiala, Ritter von Fernbrugg (1890–1964)
29 victories

Oberleutnant Benno Fiala was born in Vienna on 16 June 1890. When war was declared he applied for flying duty but this was refused and he was gazetted as an engineer officer with Flik 1. Fiala wanted to fly and again applied for flying training – this time he was given training as an observer and sent to the Russian Front. He was then posted to Flik 10 on the Italian Front, flying as observer in Brandenburg C.Is.

On 4 May 1916 he scored an impressive and unusual victory when he shot down the Italian airship M.4 over Gorizia on the River Isonzo Front. Flying as observer in a Brandenburg C.I with Hauptmann Heyrowsky as pilot, Fiala poured incendiary bullets into the drifting airship (it was believed to have run out of fuel) and M.4 flamed into the ground. By this time Fiala had scored five victories.

Fiala then qualified as a pilot and continued to fly Brandenburg C.Is, this time as pilot. Early in 1917 he moved onto Brandenburg D.Is, flying from Aidussina airstrip and scoring several more victories. Honours followed: the Order of Leopold, the Gold Medal of Merit, the Order of the Crown and the German Iron Cross 1st Class. He was also given command of Flik 51J.

A notable 14th victory occurred on 30 March 1918 when Fiala, flying an Albatros D-type, shot down Camel B5645 of 66 Squadron RFC flown by Lieutenant Alan

Jerrard. In a superb display of flying and marksmanship, Fiala poured 163 rounds into Jerrard's Camel during a large dogfight, which caused the Camel to crash at Gorgo al Montico. Prior to being shot down by Fiala, Jerrard was believed to have shot down six Austrian aircraft in the dogfight and was invested with the Victoria Cross on 5 April 1919. The gentlemanly Fiala landed his Albatros nearby, went to the scene of Jerrard's crash and chivalrously took charge of Lieutenant Jerrard.

Fiala ended the war with 29 victories and died on 29 October 1964.

Above left: Oberleutnant Benno Fiala Ritter von Fernbrugg.

Above: Studio portrait of Sergeant Josef Kiss, (posthumous Leutnant), much decorated NCO pilot.

Leutnant Josef Kiss (1896–1918) 19 victories

Leutnant Josef Kiss was born in Hungary on 26 January 1896. When the war broke out in 1914 he enlisted in the Army and volunteered for the air arm. Accepted for training as a pilot, he graduated as a sergeant pilot in April 1916.

He began his operational flying career on the River Isonzo Front, flying alongside the top ace Hauptmann Godwin Brumowski. Kiss was a courageous and skilful pilot, regardless of danger and eager for battle. He was wounded twice in air action. In 1917 his tally of victories rose sharply when he was posted to the Trentino area. He had his Albatros D III painted with a black nose and wheels; later he had the Albatros (a 200hp Oeffag-built Series 153) painted black all over with the letter 'K' (for Kiss) on both side of the fuselage. Kiss was decorated with three gold and four silver medals for bravery in the air.

On 25 May 1918 the 22-year-old Josef Kiss took off for his final flight in his black Albatros and flew into action over Valsugana. He was killed in action and posthumously commissioned to leutnant to mark his courage and bravery.

Oberleutnant Frank Linke Crawford (1893–1918) 30 victories

Oberleutnant Frank Linke Crawford was born at Cracow of Polish descent on 18 August 1893. Between 1914 and 1916 he was in action with a Dragoon cavalry regiment on the Russian Front.

In April 1916 he applied for transfer to the air arm, being posted to Flik 12 after completing his flying training. Three months later he transferred to Brumowski's Flik 41, flying Brandenburg D.Is. Linke Crawford began to wear a glaring red flying helmet and acquired the nickname 'The Red Head'.

Midsummer 1917 saw Flik 41 acquiring the formidable Albatros D III aircraft. Linke Crawford's aircraft had a 'displayed' (outspread) eagle blazoned on the fuselage as an escutcheon (shield). This shield became well known to the Italian air arm, with Linke Crawford shooting down several Italian Sp 2 aircraft.

In November 1917 he was given command of Flik 60 at the age of 24 years, and continued to increase his victory score during the remaining few months of his life.

On 31 July 1918 Oberleutnant Frank Linke Crawford died in aerial combat over Montelle. His aircraft went down in flames and he was burned beyond recognition. As was the custom, he was buried locally but, post-war, his remains were exhumed and re-interred at Salzburg.

AUSTRO-HUNGARIAN ACES 1914–19

Austria-Hungary only classed airmen as aces if they scored more than ten confirmed victories. Some records show the following scores, others differ:

40 kills Hauptmann Godwin Brumowski
32 kills Offizierstellvertreter Julius Arigi
30 kills Oberleutnant Frank Linke Crawford
29 kills Oberleutnant Benno Fiala
19 kills Leutnant Josef Kiss

Leutnant Franz Graser
15 kills Feldwebel Stefan Fejes
Feldwebel Eugen Bonsch
14 kills Offizierstellvertreter Kurt Gruber
Oberleutnant Ernst Strohschneider

12 kills Hauptmann Raoul Stojsavljevic
10 kills Leutnant Franz Rudorfer
Hauptmann Adolf Heyrowski
Oberleutnant Friedrich Navratil

Hauptmann Josef Meier
9 kills Leutnant Kommander Gottfried Banfield

Another fourteen airmen were believed to have shot down between five and ten enemy aircraft.

Good shot of a Hansa Brandenburg C.1 with 7 airmen, plus two high-ranking officers with their ladies in front.

INDEX